Focus on Literature:
A Context for Literacy Learning

Focus on Literature:
A Context for Literacy Learning

Joy F. Moss

RICHARD C. OWEN PUBLISHERS, INC., KATONAH, NEW YORK

Library of Congress Cataloging-in-Publication Data
Moss, Joy F., 1937–
    Focus on literature : a context for literacy learning / by Joy F.
Moss.
        p.   cm.
    Includes bibliographical references.
    ISBN 0–913461–17–2
    1. Children—Books and reading.   2. Language arts (Elementary)
3. Children's literature—Study and teaching (Elementary)
I. Title.
Z1037.A1M8827   1990
372.6—dc20   89–22804
                                                           CIP

RICHARD C. OWEN PUBLISHERS, INC.
135 Katonah Avenue
Katonah, New York 10536

Printed in the United States of America

Book design by Ken Venezio

Dedicated to Arthur; Kathy and Jeff; Debbie and Keith; and David.

Contents

Preface

The purpose of this book is to demonstrate that the study of literature can become an integral part of the elementary-school curriculum and that children can become thoughtful students of literature. The reader is invited to observe a working literary curriculum made up of a series of units designed to introduce children to literature and in which literature serves as a rich natural resource for developing literary, language, and thinking skills. These literature units are called "Focus Units" because each is structured around a central theme, topic, or focus. Each represents a translation of theory into practice and a collaboration between teachers and students in the classroom.

The first two chapters provide a synthesis of relevant research and theory and serve as the framework for Focus Units described in Chapters 3–12.

Designed as a practical text to help teachers translate theory into practice and build a literature program which will provide a context for literacy learning across the curriculum, the book provides theoretical rationales for the ideas and strategies featured in each Focus Unit; extensive bibliographies to assist teachers in developing their own units; excerpts from children's oral and written responses to literature; and examples of instructional plans and learning experiences developed to foster literary and literacy growth in the social context of the classroom.

Focus on Literature is addressed to all those who want to bring quality literature into the lives of children and who want to build a literary context for literacy learning. It is intended for those who are or plan to be classroom teachers; specialists in reading, learning disabilities, or English as a Second Language (ESL); librarians; administrators; and parents.

The book is about children who have learned to enjoy and appreciate literature and whose responses to literature reflect a level of critical and creative thinking which might surprise many educators. It is about teachers who have created literary environments in which children are challenged to stretch their minds and imaginations and are given opportunities to build and use literary and literacy skills.

Language development begins in the home. Parents who share literature with their children contribute significantly to their growth as readers and their capacity to enjoy the world of books. *Focus on Literature* is also intended to assist parents interested in providing rich literary experiences for their children.

Although the Focus Units in this book were originally designed for elementary-school children whose native language is English, many units have been adapted for use with older students and those who are learning English as a Second Language. For example, Chapter 11 describes a cross-cultural study of "Cinderella" variants which was adapted by several teachers for use with high-school students. The reader is similarly encouraged to use the book as a starting point for creating new ideas for bringing children and books together.

I would like to express appreciation to the children, teachers, librarians, administrators, and parents who have contributed to my ongoing learning about literature and literacy, and to those whose voices have enriched the descriptions of Focus Units in this book. I am indebted to my parents who taught me to love literature. I would like to thank Richard Owen for his support and encouragement; Louise Waller for her thoughtful review of the manuscript and her warmth and sensitivity; Bonnie DeConinck for her secretarial proficiency; and Arthur, especially, for being there from the beginning.

—J.F.M.

Focus on Literature:
A Context for Literacy Learning

Introduction

Focus on Literature: A Context for Literacy Learning is an invitation to preservice and inservice teachers to discover and rediscover the world of literature, and to view it as a rich resource and context for literacy learning and a source of aesthetic experience, a subject of study in itself. It is written for those who want to bring literature into the classroom and into the lives of children.

In this book the primary thesis is that the enjoyment and study of literature in its own right should be an integral and significant part of the elementary-school curriculum. Investigators from various fields and disciplines, many of whom conducted their research in naturalistic settings, have contributed significantly to our understanding of literacy and have confirmed the central role of literature in literacy learning and in the general curriculum. There has been a growing accumulation of evidence to support the thesis which is the foundation for this book. To translate this thesis into classroom practice it is necessary for teachers to become familiar with a wide range of literature appropriate for elementary-school children. Therefore, this book provides exposure to various kinds of literature and suggests ways literature can be studied in the elementary-school classroom.

An instructional model called a "Focus Unit," which I developed for and with my students and which I have used as a framework for building a literary curriculum, is detailed in my 1984 book, *Focus Units in Literature: A Handbook for Elementary School Teachers*. The term Focus Unit is used because each unit is structured around a central theme or focus. Each unit consists of an instructional sequence designed to introduce children to literature; and to use literature as a rich natural resource for developing literary, language, and thinking skills and for generating diverse reading and writing experiences for children. The Units are intended to help children become motivated and thoughtful readers and writers who view literacy as a significant dimension of their total life experiences. The ultimate goal is to contribute to children's literary awareness and appreciation and to their capacity to enjoy literary experiences.

It is difficult, if not impossible, to separate literary experiences from literacy learning. The more literary experiences one has, the more opportunities there are to build literacy skills. In recent years an educational movement grounded in "whole language" philosophy has generated some rethinking about current practices in literacy education. The research and theory of the past two decades have raised significant questions about the nature of literacy and the optimal conditions for becoming literate. Such questions are being addressed in an ongoing dialogue about whole language philosophy among classroom teachers, school administrators, and university professors. In recent years this dialogue has linked educators into an international network. Those engaged in this dialogue have raised questions about the extensive use of basal reader programs to teach reading and at the same time about the role of literature as a rich natural resource for literacy learning.

Chapter 1 of this book is devoted to a discussion of "whole language" and some of the research and theory out of which this philosophy emerged.

ABOUT THE FOCUS UNITS IN THIS BOOK

Focus Units suggest ways that children can learn about literature and, in the process, expand their literacy skills. In each unit literary and literacy experiences complement and build on each other. The research and theoretical models, the whole language philosophy, and the role of dialogue discussed in the first two chapters provide the larger context in which these literature units were developed. Each of the Focus Units featured in Chapters 3–12 highlight selected theoretical insights about literacy learning, as well as ideas for translating theory into classroom practice.

Professional references cited in the discussion of each Focus Unit can be found in the Reference sections at the end of chapters. Children's books mentioned in the Unit are listed in the Bibliographies.

As a teacher working daily with elementary-school children since 1970 I have developed each of the Focus Units described in this book for and with at least three different groups of children. Over the years I have introduced the Focus Unit model and its theoretical rationale to hundreds of preservice and inservice teachers in university courses, in professional development workshops, and at regional conferences. Many of the teachers who chose to adopt this model for use in their classrooms have shared their experiences with me. Some invited me to observe in their classrooms, to record their students' oral responses to these literary experiences, and to read their students' written work. Some shared their journal notes about planning and implementing Focus Units. This feedback provided important information about the development of Focus Units in a wide range of classroom settings. I learned a great deal about the way these Units evolved in settings significantly different from the one in which I am a practitioner. This feedback also provided evidence that the Focus Unit model can be adapted and used successfully by teachers working with diverse populations and in diverse settings.

In many of the chapters in this book I have included data gathered from these teachers although, in most cases, I have described personal experiences with my students. To provide continuity in the text I have chosen to use the third person to refer to the teacher featured in each chapter. The word "teacher" is intended to represent a composite of the many different teachers who have used these Focus Units. The oral dialogues and comments and the written work quoted in the text are the actual words of specific teachers and children (including my students and myself) which have been carefully recorded to illustrate children's responses to literature and the nature of the dialogue that is the core of the Focus Unit.

I invite the reader to think of the teacher who guides and supports literary and literacy learning in these chapters as a representative of practitioners who make up the teaching profession. I also invite the reader to consider each Focus Unit in light of his or her own students, classroom setting, teaching style, special interests, and educational philosophy; and to view each Unit as a *possibility* for adaptation in that classroom in collaboration with those students. Each of the Units is intended to suggest ways of bringing literature into the curriculum and of fostering literary learning and enjoyment among children of all ages; from diverse backgrounds; and with a wide range of abilities, learning needs, and interests. These Focus Units are for all children, to give them a chance to learn to love books and to become perceptive readers.

These Focus Units are also intended as invitations to teachers to become students of children's literature and to discover its joy and power for themselves. Each of the Units evolved out of my own study of the particular topic selected as its focus. Because of space limitations only two of the chapters reflect the depth of my literary explorations prior to introducing the Unit in the classroom and, subsequently, as I engaged in collaborative study with my students. In Chapters 8 and 11 I have included some of the rich literary background which resulted from these shared experiences of inquiry and discovery.

ABOUT THE LITERATURE FEATURED IN THE FOCUS UNITS

A literature program in the elementary school should provide children with opportunities to experience a wide variety of literature: traditional and modern, prose and poetry, realism and fantasy, contemporary and historical fiction, and nonfiction. A series of Focus Units, each built around conceptually related texts, could be developed as a framework for exposing children to different types of literature or literary genres and for developing literary experiences which lead children to discover the joys of literary involvement and the many different ways of becoming involved with literature. Children's experiences with a wide range of literary genres can stretch their minds and imaginations and touch their hearts. In addition to enriching their personal lives these many literary experiences can provide a rich context for learning to read and write.

Although the Focus Units feature a wide variety of genres for oral presentation in group sessions and for independent reading by individuals, the reader will notice that I have given traditional literature special attention. My rationale for this emphasis is outlined below.

The Value of Traditional Literature

According to Stith Thompson, a pioneer in the classification and analysis of folk literature, the work of folktale collectors and scholars since the turn of the century has enabled us "to see the oral-tale as the most universal of all narrative forms, and to understand its relation to the literary stories of our own civilization. We are learning of the function of the tale in the lives of those who tell and those who listen, and of the nature of this art in different lands and different times."[1] Charlotte Huck, emeritus professor of education and authority in children's literature, discusses the value of folk literature for children in this way:

Traditional literature is a rightful part of a child's literary heritage and lays the groundwork for understanding all literature. . . . Northrop Frye maintains that "all theme and characters and stories that you encounter in literature belong to one big interlocking family."[2] As you meet recurring patterns or symbols in mythlike floods, savior heroes, cruel stepmothers, the seasonal cycle of the year, the cycle of human life, you begin to build a framework for literature. Poetry, prose, and drama become more emotionally significant as you respond to these recurring archetypes.[3]

In addition to providing the context for learning about literature folklore introduces children to other cultures and other times and provides insights about the human condition and the universal nature of human qualities. The oral tradition plays a critical role in the education of the imagination and the development of fantasy. In his eloquent defense of the fairytale as a valuable element in the life of all children Kornei Chukovsky, a student of language and literature, writes:

Fantasy is the most valuable attribute of the human mind and it should be diligently nurtured from earliest childhood. . . .[4]

Another reason for emphasizing traditional literature relates to children's interest in fairytales. F. André Favat, student of literature, drew these conclusions from a survey of empirical investigations of children's reading interests:

1. Children between the ages of 5 and 10 . . . , whether they select books voluntarily, or are presented with books and asked for their opinion, express interest in the fairytale.
2. This interest follows what might be called a *curve of reading preference*; that is, children's interest in fairytales emerges at a prereading age and gradually rises to a peak of interest between the approximate ages of 6 and 8, and then gradually declines to a point of noninterest by the ages of 10 or 11.
3. Concurrent with this decline in interest in the fairytale, there is an emergence of interest in stories of reality.[5]

Favat designed an analytic study in an attempt to explain this interest in the fairytale and its varying intensity at different ages. He found a significant correspondence between the characteristics of the child's mind and the characteristics of the fairytale. "In a very real sense the tale embodies an accurate representation of the child's conception of the world."[6] Favat also concluded that children are attracted to fairytales because of their predictability and because

[1]Stith Thompson. *The Folktale*. Berkeley: University of California Press, 1977, p. vii.

[2]Northrop Frye. *The Educated Imagination*. Bloomington: Indiana University Press, 1964, p. 48.

[3]Charlotte Huck, Susan Hepler, Janet Hickman. *Children's Literature in the Elementary School*, 4th ed. N.Y.: Holt Rinehart and Winston, 1987, p. 253.

[4]Kornei Chukovsky. *From Two to Five*, Miriam Morton, trans. and ed. Berkeley: University of California Press, 1963, p. 117.

[5]F. André Favat. *Child and Tale: The Origins of Interest*. Urbana: NCTE, 1977, pp. 4–5.

[6]Favat, p. 38.

these tales reaffirm the child's conception of the world as a stable and gratifying universe. In a discussion of the implications his investigation makes for teachers and parents, Favat comments: "The power of the tales to provide the comfort and reassurance that children seek in the first place is doubled when adults read the stories aloud."[7] He adds that older children enjoy being read to, and that adults can contribute significantly to older children's emotional well-being by setting aside regular times for reading aloud to them. "In a sense [older children], require an occasional rest from the struggle of learning about the real world."[8]

From my own experiences as a teacher I found that as children moved from primary to intermediate levels, they began to show a preference for realistic stories and informational books for their independent reading. They also seemed to enjoy the intellectual challenge involved in studying traditional literature as an art form, as a cultural mirror, and as a basis for understanding all literature. They enjoyed discovering recurring patterns and motifs, similarities between diverse tales, differences between variants of the same tale, and connections between traditional and modern tales. Their study of folklore led them to focus on universal themes and structures, rich language patterns, the art of storytelling, and the nature of the oral tradition. They learned to read like writers and to think like folklorists.

I found only a few children who rediscovered the joys of folklore after ages nine or ten without an adult guide. My observations of children's reading choices, independent of adult input, seemed to confirm Favat's conclusions about the reading interests of older children. After being introduced to beautifully illustrated single editions or the superb collections of tales appropriate for older readers, many of these students developed a new interest in traditional literature and returned again and again to the Dewey Decimal 398 section of the library to select books for independent reading.

Children should be given the freedom to choose their own reading material. However, parents and teachers have a responsibility to introduce them to the wide range of books available to them for enjoyment as listeners and readers. The adult serves as a guide, inviting children to explore the world of books and then to develop their own interests and preferences as independent readers. As one of these adult guides in the world of books I have found that some parts of this world are less likely to be discovered by children on their own than others. For example, children have little trouble finding *Curious George* or *Ramona* or Judy Blume's books, but seem to need assistance finding traditional literature. My decision to emphasize folklore in the Focus Units grew out of my own feeling of responsibility to children and my desire to ensure that they do not miss the opportunity to discover their literary heritage.

Because stories from the oral tradition are short and have fast-moving plots, they are especially appropriate for the read-aloud sessions which are a central feature of the Focus Unit model. The fact that traditional tales can be found to meet the needs and interests of children of all ages and diverse backgrounds is another reason for including these tales in a Focus Unit collection. The highly patterned nature of folktales is also an important factor. As children discover recurring character types, story types, plot patterns, and themes, they can use these basic patterns as literary tools to make sense of folklore as a whole.

[7]Favat, p. 58.
[8]Favat, p. 64.

Finally, I decided to give special attention to traditional literature because in recent years so many gifted artists have used these old tales to create some exquisite illustrated editions for children's aesthetic enjoyment.

It is my hope that the readers of this book will be inspired to become active explorers in the world of literature and will serve as guides for the children whose lives they touch.

ONE

Theory into Practice

WHOLE LANGUAGE: A PHILOSOPHY OF LEARNING AND TEACHING

A growing interest in whole language philosophy in recent years has been accompanied by the publication of numerous books and articles on the subject. Diverse support groups and inservice programs designed to explore the meaning of whole language and its implications for classroom practice have also emerged. The whole language classroom is characterized by its focus on meaning, making sense of print, and creating meaning to accomplish specific purposes. The whole language classroom is created as teachers explore ways to translate into practice theoretical models of literacy and literacy learning. Turning theory into practice is informed by the teacher's knowledge and experience as a professional educator who observes students engaged in the process of becoming literate. The curriculum is constructed out of a dynamic interaction between the teacher as a professional, theory and research, and student input. Although all whole language classrooms will be comprehension-centered and learner-centered, each will have a unique identity shaped by the special needs and interests of the children and teacher who create it.

Whole language is not a method or an instructional sequence which can be outlined in a teachers' manual or neatly packaged as a program. It is a philosophy, not a recipe for teachers. "Whole language is first of all a lens for viewing, a framework that insists that belief shapes practice" (Altwerger, *et al.*, 1987, p. 148).

The whole language teacher assumes that children will become literate, and begins with the children's strengths and skills as language learners to help them develop literacy. The teacher provides children with many opportunities to use written language to make sense of the world and to communicate with others. Because no single program or set of materials or instructional package will be adequate for the whole language classroom, the teacher engages in an ongoing quest for effective learning experiences, materials, and teaching ideas which will help individual children enter the literate community. Active learners themselves, teachers create a rich environment designed to support literacy learning.

HISTORICAL AND THEORETICAL BACKGROUND

Prior to the 1970s, behaviorist theory, which is based on stimulus-response relationships, was a dominant force in reading research and practice. For example, Anderson and Dearborn's *The Psychology of Teaching Reading* (1952) consisted primarily of research on visual perception and eye-movement behavior in reading, and explained learning to read as a process of forming S-R (stimulus-response) associations and then using these associations to perceive written words. Comprehension received very little attention in this popular text.

According to behaviorist theory learning is habit formation; and habits are established by reinforcing a response to a stimulus. Learning is a passive, associative process. In order to teach a task it must be divided into its smallest units and taught in a prescribed sequence.

The basic premise of most of the reading research carried out between the late 1920s and 1960s was that reading is based in the stimulus, and that the core of the reading process is identifying letters and words on the page. Thus, learning to read is essentially a matter of learning letter-sound relationships and accurate word identification skills. Research during this period was designed to determine the best method for teaching reading. In her book, *Learning to Read: The Great Debate*, Jeanne Chall, Harvard Professor of Education (1967), reports on her critical analysis of existing research, comparing different approaches to beginning reading. Her review of the research from 1912 to 1965 led to the conclusion that a code-emphasis method produces better results than a meaning-emphasis method for beginning reading instruction; that is, instruction should begin with the smallest units of language. Chall's recommendation for a change in beginning reading methods from a meaning-emphasis to a code-emphasis, or emphasis on phonic skills, program was supported by others in the reading field; and a consensus was reached about the critical role of decoding proficiency in learning to read. Reflecting this general consensus most commercial beginning reading programs designed after the late 1960s featured early and intensive phonics instruction.

In the 1970s there emerged a growing concern that early decoding was not the answer. For example, data from the National Assessment (NAEP, 1981) revealed that during the 1970s primary-grade children had made excellent progress in terms of decoding skills; but declining scores in the intermediate grades suggested significant problems with inferential and interpretive comprehension. Practitioners witnessed the slide in scores after Grade 3, and expressed concern about failures in comprehension in spite of proficiency in decoding. At the same time reading educators began to turn their attention to reading comprehension, and psychologists returned to the study of reading. Not since the turn of the century had psychologists such as James M. Cattell (1886), Edmund B. Huey (1908), and Edward L. Thorndike (1917), three reading research pioneers, seriously addressed the question: "What is reading?" In the 1970s cognitive psychologists, who study ways of knowing, began to challenge behaviorists' assumptions about the reading process, and new reading research and theoretical models emerged. Harry Singer, a reading theorist, begins his review of psychological research on reading from 1879 to 1980 with this statement: "In the past two decades we have witnessed a virtual explosion of theories and research in the psychology of reading" (Singer, 1985, p. 920).

Noam Chomsky, a linguist, developed a model of language acquisition which paved the way for much of this research and theory building. He described language acquisition as "a kind of theory construction" in which "the child discovers the theory of his language with only small amounts of data from that language" (Chomsky, 1968, p. 284). Chomsky rejected the behaviorist notion of language learning as passive and imitative, and emphasized instead the creative nature of this process. Children create hypotheses about the structure of language as they gather data from their linguistic environment. Children test these hypotheses by producing novel sentences: "I rided my bike" reflects the formation of a generalization about the rule systems of language. Ample and appropriate feedback allows children to revise and refine their theories of language until they approximate the ideal. Language learners actively construct their language as they engage in meaningful verbal interactions with mature language users.

The comprehensive theories of cognitive development formulated by Jean Piaget, Swiss psychologist (1952, 1969), and Lev Vygotsky, a Soviet cognitive psychologist (1962), contributed significantly to the theoretical models of language acquisition and reading development which appeared in the 1970s. They, too, challenged the behaviorist picture of the passive language learner. For example, Piaget stressed the *active* nature of learning and offered a creative conception of the process of human knowing. According to Piaget, children progressively construct and reconstruct reality out of their experiences with the environment until this reality approximates that of adults. "What the child understands reality to be is never simply a copy of what he has received by his sense impressions; it is always transformed by the child's own ways of knowing" (Elkind, 1976, p. 59).

Vygotsky's (1962) analysis of the nature of verbal thought, as based on word meaning and the complex and dynamic relationships between thought and word, opened the way for an entirely new way of studying cognitive processes. His study of inner speech led him to challenge "the behaviorist concept of thought as speech minus sound. . . ." (p. 152). According to Vygotsky "the relationships between thought and word is a living process; thought is born through words. . . . The connection between them, however, is not a preformed and constant one. It emerges in the course of development, and itself evolves" (p. 153).

Vygotsky (1962, 1978) contributed to our understanding that language learning begins in social interaction. Language acquisition is facilitated by opportunities for dialogue between the child and mature speakers. The concept of language learning as a sociopsycholinguistic process has significant implications for the creation of an environment to support literacy learning.

In the 1970s a reconceptualization of reading emerged from "the explosion of research" noted by Singer. The visual information on the page was no longer seen as the driving force of the reading process. The concept of reading expanded from a restricted notion of decoding proficiency leading to accurate word recognition to a view of reading as a cognitive process leading to comprehension. Cognitive and linguistic factors were emphasized instead of perception and conditioning.

P. David Pearson, reading researcher (1985), discusses this impressive change in view of comprehension and text:

No longer do we regard text as a fixed object that the reader is supposed to "approximate" as closely as possible as he reads. Instead we now view text as a sort of blueprint for meaning, a set of tracks or clues that the reader uses as he builds a model of what the text means. . . . In short, this view suggests that readers play a much more active-constructive role in their own comprehension than our earlier passive-receptive views dictated (Pearson, 1985, p. 726).

Cognitive theorists have demonstrated that reading involves an interaction between readers and a text in which readers actively generate meaning by relating their prior knowledge and experiences to the text (Rumelhart, 1976, and Adams and Collins, 1977). That is, readers make sense of text by bringing what they know about language, literature, and the world to the text. Frank Smith, education researcher, introduced the term "nonvisual information" to refer to this prior knowledge used to generate meaning (1978, p. 5).

THE CUING SYSTEMS OF LANGUAGE

Whole language is based on the premise that the three cuing systems—*graphophonic* (sound and letter patterns), *syntactic* (sentence patterns), and *semantic* (meanings)—are interrelated and function interdependently and simultaneously in any instance of language in use. These cuing systems are within the text and the reader. They are the three aspects of the reader's linguistic competence that affect comprehension, and all three information systems must be used to make meaning. The child learning to read must gain control over and internalize these systems and their interactions.

A major whole language goal is to help children use, not sever, these interrelationships among cuing systems. The means for achieving that goal is to engage children with authentic texts and in authentic reading and writing. A Whole Language framework insists that we become "skilled language users" *not* that we "learn language skills" (Altwerger, *et al.*, 1987, p. 148).

Readers use all three cuing systems to make predictions about what will occur in the text, monitor their reading to determine the accuracy of these predictions, and correct themselves to insure that they are making sense as they interact with and construct the text.

Over twenty years ago Kenneth Goodman, a psycholinguistic theorist, challenged the notion of reading as a precise process involving "exact, detailed, sequential perception and identification of letters, words, spelling patterns, and larger language units" (Goodman, 1967). He applied *psycholinguistics* (how people learn and use language) to the reading process and developed a model which emphasized meaning:

Reading is a selective process. It involves partial use of available minimal language cues selected from perceptual input on the basis of the reader's expectation. As this partial information is processed, tentative decisions are made, to be confirmed, rejected or refined as reading progresses (K. Goodman, 1967, p. 126).

Readers use cognitive strategies, such as sampling and selection, inference, prediction, confirming and disconfirming, and correction. Goodman introduced the notion that readers' oral *miscues* (points where observed and expected response to the text do not match) offer significant insights about reading strategies and selective use of graphophonic, syntactic, and semantic information.

The extent to which miscues result in meaningful text or are self-corrected if they disrupt meaning gives strong indications of a reader's concern for and ability to make sense of the text (Goodman, 1985, p. 831).

Thus, readers interact with a text and actively generate meaning by bringing their graphic, syntactic, semantic, literary, and world knowledge to the text.

SCHEMA THEORY AND STORY COMPREHENSION

According to this reconceptualization of reading, meaning is not in the text but in the reader: "The text has a potential to evoke meaning but no meaning in itself" (Goodman, 1985, p. 815). Cognitive theorists have demonstrated that the quality of reading comprehension is determined in large part by the quality of prior knowledge or nonvisual information the reader/listener brings to the text. This knowledge is organized; the term *schema* is used to refer to one's organized knowledge or mental model of the world. In terms of schema theory readers comprehend a message when they are able to retrieve relevant schemata from their memory stores and make appropriate connections to new information in the text. When readers interact with a text they use relevant schemata to make inferences.

The concept of schema was postulated by Frederic C. Bartlett (1932) in his study of memory. The notion of schemata also plays a key role in Piaget's theory of cognitive development, a process in which the schemata become elaborated, differentiated, and coordinated with other schemata (Piaget, 1952).

Story comprehension researchers developed a "story schema," which influences the comprehension process. It is based on the assumption that stories have an internal structure, or "grammar," made up of a network of categories and logical relationships (Stein and Glenn, 1979, p. 58). By listening to written stories children develop a story schema.

This implicit knowledge of "story grammar" helps children comprehend narratives. Children expect a story to have a structure; they make predictions prior to reading the story and recall it accordingly. Teachers can formulate questions to help children search for and use story structure as a basis for comprehension (Guthrie, 1977, p. 577).

READING AS TRANSACTION

Interactive models of reading stress the cognitive nature of the reader's encounter with text, but give little attention to the context or affective dimensions of the encounter. Louise Rosenblatt, New York University professor emeritus, introduced a transactional model of reading (1978). She portrays reading as "a transaction, a two-way process, involving a reader and a text at a particular time and under particular circumstances" (Rosenblatt, 1982, p. 268). According to Rosenblatt the nature of this transaction is determined by the reader's stance or "mental set." She uses the term *efferent* to refer to the stance of the reader who "focusses on accumulating what is to be carried away at the end of the reading" (p. 269). If a reader chooses an *aesthetic* stance, "his attention will shift inward, will center on what is being created *during* the actual reading" (p. 269). Thus the reader may choose to efferently attend to facts or "live through" a text by responding with personal feelings, ideas, and attitudes. "In aesthetic reading, we respond to the very story or poem that we are evoking during the transaction with text" (p. 270). The reader enters into the story, identifies with the characters, empathizes with their feelings, and cares about what happens to them. The aesthetic reader responds to the sounds and rhythms of the language and evoked images; appreciates an interesting literary technique or device; makes judgments about the moral behavior of one character or the wisdom of another's decision; enjoys a feeling of satisfaction about a new insight or emotional connection to the story or poem. Readers transform the text in the act of reading aesthetically by responding to it out of their personal histories, feelings, beliefs, concerns.

Rosenblatt stresses the importance of developing the habit and capacity for aesthetic reading, especially in the teaching of literature.

Precisely because every aesthetic reading of a text is a unique creation, woven out of the inner life and thought of the reader, the literary work of art can be a rich source of insight and truth (p. 277).

EARLY READER STUDIES

For the past two decades there has been a growing interest in "early readers," preschool children who have learned to read without formal school instruction (Clark, 1976, Durkin, 1966; Sutton, 1969). After reviewing numerous studies of early readers William Teale (1978) identified four factors as being repeatedly associated with the environments in which these children learned to read:

1. *An availability and range of printed materials in the environment* . . . enabled children to use and get used to written messages (p. 925).
2. *Reading is "done" in the environment* . . . That is, the child must initially learn that print is meaningful . . .

    Understanding the function of written language is greatly facilitated when the variety of printed materials is accompanied by interpretation (p. 926).

    [Frank Smith (1977) suggests that children develop this awareness of the function of print as they read and respond to "environmental print": signs, television commercials, labels on cans, bottles, and jars.]

    Reading books or stories to children . . . sensitizes [them] to the structure and nature of written language (p. 927).

    Of all the facets of the environment mentioned in the studies of early reading, reading to children is probably most cited. . . . Most investigators also found that one or both of the parents were readers themselves. . . . In this way it seems, the parents acted as models for reading behavior (p. 298).
3. *The environment facilitates contact with paper and pencil.* The evidence from these studies of early readers [suggests] that learning to read is reinforced by simultaneous experience in writing (p. 929).
4. *Those in the environment should respond to what the child is trying to do.* The studies of early readers demonstrate that a positive environment for learning to read is one in which a parent or sibling or other significant person in the child's life responds to the child's attempts to make sense of the printed word (p. 930).

These studies of early readers offer valuable insights to whole language teachers engaged in creating a classroom environment conducive to and supportive of literacy learning.

Insights about the way young children teach themselves to read have also emerged from these early reader studies. For example, most early readers began with whole language in order to generate meaning. They did *not* analyze language into its smallest units. They expected language to make sense and to have a predictable structure. They used the written language in their environment to learn to read, just as they used spoken language to learn to speak.

Children build their own system of rules for creating and comprehending language by listening, speaking, playing with it, and getting feedback from adults responding to their experimentation with language. Children use information from their language environment in their own way to teach themselves oral language.

The key theoretical premise for whole language is that, the world over, babies acquire a language through actually using it, not through practicing its separate parts until some later date when the parts are assembled and the totality is finally used. The major assumption is that the model of acquisition through real use is the best model for thinking about and helping with the learning of reading and writing and learning in general (Altwerger, *et al.*, 1987, p. 145).

As children interact with written language they construct a system of structures and rules which they use to teach themselves to read and write. They listen to stories read aloud, discover the nature and function of book language, and learn to make sense of written language to generate meaning. They use paper and pencil to communicate meaning, and in the process discover and experiment with the conventions of written language and the relationship between letters and sounds. Young children's invented spellings reveal their grasp of the phonic principle (Read, 1981). Their search for patterns, order, and rules is reflected in their spontaneous writing to communicate meaning. According to Kenneth Goodman (1986): "Language use begins with a function and then involves experimenting with the language forms necessary to fulfill that function" (p. 19). He demonstrates that language is learned from whole to part and that form follows function.

Studies of early readers suggest that social interaction is the key to natural literacy development:

In an important sense the child's literacy environment does not have an independent existence; it is constructed in the interactions between the child and those persons around him or her. . . . In fact, the whole process of natural literacy development hinges upon the experience the child has in reading or writing activities which are mediated by literate adults, older siblings, or events in the child's everyday life. . . . [Such interactive literacy events] serve an absolutely essential role in both triggering and furthering development (Teale, 1982, p. 559).

Recently, researchers have called attention to young children's ability to recreate favorite stories which have been read and reread to them by parents who encourage participation (Bissex, 1979; Cohn, 1981; Gardner, 1970). In his book, *The Foundations of Literacy* (1979), Don Holdaway examines this "reading-like behavior" and its relationship and contribution to the process involved in learning to read. As children retrieve and reproduce favorite stories which had been introduced during shared book experiences in the home, they engage in critical learning to read strategies: They are beginning to self-direct, self-monitor, and self-correct their own interactions with text to generate meaning.

Holdaway and a group of New Zealand teachers experimented with the notion of bringing shared book experiences associated with parents and children in the home to teachers and students in the classroom. They accomplished this by developing enlarged, or "big books," so that all the children could share both visually and vocally in the reading experience. The stories are read and reread, and children are encouraged to participate and eventually to "reread" them independently in order to engage in reading-like behavior as a way of developing and practicing the strategies involved in reading.

In the last two decades theory and research in literacy learning have resulted in a gradual movement toward development and learning rather than teaching. Margaret Clark, reading researcher (1976), posed a question for all reading teachers:

. . . to what extent and in what ways [is] learning to read a developmental process and [are] there sequential steps? . . . It may be necessary to consider whether those steps which are frequently regarded as sequential are so only because of the structure within which we *teach* rather than the pattern within which children *learn* to read. . . . It is . . . dangerous to assume without firm evidence to support it that the way we teach is the way children learn (p. 105).

READING AND WRITING RELATIONSHIPS

Studies of the relationship between reading and writing demonstrate that both are meaning-generating processes. Readers construct meaning by using their prior knowledge in conjunction with author's cues. Writers construct meaning by using prior knowledge in conjunction with hypotheses about the nature of the prior knowledge their readers bring to the text.

After a review of the findings from correlational and experimental studies on reading/writing relationships, Sandra Stotsky (1983) concluded that "reading experience seems to be a consistent correlate of, or influence on, writing ability. Thus, it is possible that reading experience may be as critical a factor in developing writing ability as writing instruction itself" (p. 637). Frank Smith emphasizes that one learns to write by reading. In his article, "Reading Like a Writer" (1984), Smith explains: "But to learn to write we must read like a writer. . . . To read like a writer we engage with the author in what the author is writing. We anticipate what the author will say, so that the author is in effect writing on our behalf, not showing how something is done but doing it with us" (pp. 52–53).

The knowledge that writers require resides in texts, so reading like a writer helps students build a background of writers' knowledge. Children also need to learn to write like readers. According to Smith (1982) the writer becomes a reader during the rewriting phase of the composing process. "Rewriting is the writer's own response to what has been written. . . ." (p. 127). Young writers need to become critical readers of their own writing from the viewpoint of their potential audiences.

Thus, comprehension and composition are so closely interrelated it would seem counterproductive to separate them in the curriculum. Pearson (1985) comments, "Were I to make a prediction about the single most important change in language instruction that will take place in the next decade, it would be that we will no longer separate instruction in reading and writing" (p. 736).

In the whole language classroom instruction in reading and writing focusses on whole pieces of text so that each interaction with text reinforces the notion that reading and writing are processes of constructing meaning. Young readers and writers can develop and practice meaning-generating strategies only in the context of predictable, whole language discourse.

THE WRITING PROCESS

Given this new focus on the critical role of writing in literacy learning, it is not surprising to note the considerable interest in the writing process itself among whole language theorists and practitioners.

In order to ensure that children's writing will be meaningful and relevant children are given opportunities to choose what they will write. They are encouraged to experiment with language in order to express what they want to express, to communicate with others. Risk-taking is supported and valued as a natural and important part of the learning process. Communication is emphasized rather than mechanical correctness. In his book *Writing and the Writer* (1982) Frank Smith distinguishes between two broad aspects of writing: *composition*, "what is said in writing," and *transcription*, "what has to be done to say it . . . the conventions of spelling, punctuation, grammar, and neatness" (p. 2). According to Smith "composition and transcription can interfere with each other, especially for the beginning writer" (p. 21). His solution to this conflict is to separate these two aspects of writing. "Composition and transcription must be separated, and transcription must come last" (p. 24).

Children in the whole language classroom are encouraged to construct meaningful texts for real audiences. Carole Edelsky and Karen Smith, elementary school-level educators, distinguish between authentic writing, which has meaning and purpose at its core, and inauthentic writing, associated with compliance to a teacher assignment and concerns about evaluation. They suggest that authentic writing is reflected in children's level of caring about their work: "As they began to trust their work would really be read and discussed by their peers along the same dimensions other writing was discussed (character, plot, theme, believability, author's voice) they began to write about topics and characters they cared about" (1984, p. 27).

As children begin to see themselves as authors their relationship to their writing becomes one of enjoyment and ownership. Motivated to engage in extensive authentic writing as a natural activity in the literate environment of the whole language classroom children gain confidence as well as competence as writers. The conventions of print and grammar are learned in the context of producing and revising meaningful texts.

INTEGRATING THE LANGUAGE ARTS

In the whole language classroom literacy is developed in conjunction with oral language experiences. "Integrating the language arts means providing natural learning situations in which reading, writing, speaking, and listening can be developed together for real purposes and real audiences" (Wagner, 1985, p. 557). The children become immersed in language experiences as they listen, speak, read, and write throughout the school day.

Diverse studies of language learning carried out during the last two decades have provided impressive evidence to support the integration of the language arts in the classroom (Bissex, 1980; Clay, 1975; Graves, 1983; King and Rentel, 1981; Scollen and Scollen, 1981). These studies indicate that listening, reading, speaking, and writing complement, reinforce, and build on each other when brought together in the context of literacy learning.

LITERACY ACROSS THE CURRICULUM

Reading and writing are tools for learning, not simply end points for instruction. They are processes for generating and shaping ideas, vehicles for exploring our world. Reading and writing should serve as the core of learning across the curriculum. In the process of learning about a particular content area through language, the student learns ways to *use* language and learns *about* language. Literacy learning and content learning are complementary and inter-related.

The "authoring curriculum" (Harste, 1988; Harste *et al.*, 1984; Rowe and Harste, 1986) is a useful conceptualization of literacy across the curriculum. Jerome C. Harste and his col-leagues concluded from their careful and extensive observations of children that all modes of language can be viewed as authorship and children as authors. They define authoring as much more than writing and composing: "It involves 'making' meanings through any of the available communication systems (language, art, drama, etc.) in order to achieve personal and social goals" (1986, p. 126). In this view of the authoring process emphasis is placed on meaning generation. "Authoring is a form of learning" (1986, p. 130). In the authoring curriculum literacy is multimodal. Meaningful learning occurs when students are exposed to and use different communication systems to generate meanings about a particular subject. They are encouraged to experiment with different ways of expressing their meanings. Harste uses the term *transmediation* to describe the process in which ". . . meanings formed in one com-munication system are moved to an alternate communication system (*e.g.*, from reading to art)" (1986, p. 132). In their observations of children these researchers found free movement between writing and art in children's attempts to generate meaning. "Involvement of alterna-tive, available expressions of language (speaking, listening, reading, writing) and communi-cation systems (language, art, math, music, drama, etc.) allows language users to psychologically and sociologically shift stances and get a new perspective on their knowing" (Harste *et al.*, 1984, p. 216). These new perspectives help students form and refine problems.

The authoring curriculum is based on the assumption that students will engage in critical thinking to define and solve problems and will take ownership of this process. It is grounded in the belief that learning is social and that social interaction is a critical feature of the environment in which children engage in authoring, making meaning.

Literacy across the curriculum means that students will read and write diverse forms of discourse and will move from one form to another. Content learning is facilitated by the use of both fiction and nonfiction. The exploration of a topic—in science, math, social studies, or the arts—can begin with stories or poetry, and then move into informational books and first-hand experiences and observations. Literature can serve as a springboard for inquiry and exploration. The authoring curriculum provides the form for this inquiry and exploration, inviting the child to engage in the process of meaning-making through different communication systems, alternative ways of knowing.

QUESTIONS

The transactional model of reading comprehension has significant implications for the nature of questioning as a teaching tool in the classroom. Observations of teachers and examinations of teacher manuals reveal that the majority of questions are designed for assessment purposes, require literal level thinking skills and a single correct answer, and that there is little coherence between questions (Beck *et al.*, 1979; Durkin, 1978–1979; 1981). In recent years investigators have focussed on the role of questioning in molding the quality of thinking done by students as they read or listen to written discourse (Ausubel, 1960; Carroll and Freedle, 1972; Frase, 1967; Pollack, 1988; Rothkopf, 1970). Such studies have demonstrated that questioning can be used as a valuable tool to teach and guide reading comprehension and to stimulate higher-level thinking. Teacher-initiated questions can suggest ways to interact with texts in order to generate meaning and serve as models for students to internalize. The ultimate goal is for students to generate their own questions to guide the reading/thinking process and help them to become critical readers and independent learners.

While listening to a story or poem during a read-aloud session children are encouraged to react spontaneously, verbally or nonverbally. Afterward they are invited to share personal meanings generated by this aesthetic experience or to transform the written text into other media (art, drama, dance) in order to recreate and deepen the experience. Using these spontaneous reactions as a starting point the teacher can introduce questions which encourage children to reflect on these reactions and suggest various ways to think about the story or poem as a literary piece and its connection to other literary pieces. As writers the children will find it natural to "read like writers" (Smith, 1984) and to discuss a literary selection *as* writers. They can identify and appreciate conventions and elements of style which the professional writer has used to create a believable character, to elicit emotional responses from potential readers, or to build an absorbing plot which captures the reader's attention. They can identify recurring literary patterns, motifs, and themes and, in the process, discover again and again the way "story leans on story, art on art" (Yolen, 1981, p. 15).

Teacher-initiated questions are designed to invite children to enter into the story, live through it, and then to stand back and enjoy it from another perspective. Ultimately they generate their own questions to guide their exploration of the world of literature and to enhance the quality of that journey.

LITERATURE AND LITERACY

These insights from reading research and studies of natural readers point to the importance of literature in the development of literacy in the elementary school. Literature provides children with language experiences which enhance their ability to generate meaning from literary texts.

Bernice Cullinan comments, "Children learn from the language they hear; it makes sense that the richer the language environment, the richer the language learning" (1987, p. 5). If the quality of reading comprehension is determined largely by the quality of prior knowledge or schemata brought to a text, then it would make sense that the richer the language background the richer the reading experience.

Experiences with literature also acquaint children with narrative structures. Margaret Meek, lecturer in English at the London Institute of Education, advocates teaching reading through reading stories, because stories teach the rules of narrative organization (1982). Listening to stories is not only important in learning to read literature but in learning to read in general. A recent review of research supporting the significant contribution of literature to reading development suggests that teaching the strategies necessary to interact with narrative texts is essentially a way of teaching the processes of reading comprehension (Sawyer, 1987).

Reading Strategies

Gerald Duffy and Laura Roehler, reading teachers and researchers, distinguish between strategies and skills used in reading:

Strategies are *plans* readers use flexibly and adaptively, depending on the situation. Skills, in contrast, are *procedures* readers overlearn through repetition so that speed and accuracy are assured every time the response is called for. . . . In teaching skills, the object is to create automatized accuracy through drill and practice activities (such as workbooks) which call repeatedly for the same response. . . . In teaching strategies, on the other hand, the object is to develop thoughtful and conscious reasoning about problems encountered in real text . . . where each situation demands a slightly different response (1987, p. 415).

Experienced and competent readers use a variety of reading strategies as they interact with text: activating relevant prior knowledge, schemata, and appropriate concepts; predicting; questioning; inferencing; allocating attention; creating mental images; comprehension monitoring; relating new information to old; using the author's organizational framework; and restructuring schemata or accommodation.

Frank Smith (1978) defines comprehension in terms of prediction and asking questions: "Prediction is a matter of asking specific questions . . . and comprehension means getting those questions answered" (p. 66). Prediction is based on the prior knowledge or schemata one brings to a text. The quality of comprehension is largely determined by the quality of questions the reader poses to guide the comprehension process and generate meaning. For example, the reader who has knowledge of story grammar can make predictions and initiate significant questions before and during interaction with a narrative text. Story comprehension is enhanced when the reader (or listener) is able to focus on narrative elements (setting, plot, characters, theme, style) and their interrelationships, as well as the logical organization of major events and ideas in the story.

Duffy and Roehler (1987) discuss two kinds of reading strategies:

The first kind is activated before reading actually begins. For instance, before reading a text, good readers use what they know about the topic, the type of text, the author's purposes, and their own purposes to make predictions about the content of the text. . . . Other strategies, called repair strategies, are activated during reading whenever meaning is blocked by unknown words, by predictions that turn out to be incorrect, or by a disruption in the reader's train of thought (p. 416).

Judith Newman, teacher educator, describes three basic types of reading strategies: predicting, confirming, and integrating:

Predicting strategies consist of generating expectations on the basis of information from any or all of the available cue systems [syntactic, orthographic, and semantic]. Confirming strategies are the result of asking ourselves if what we're reading makes sense. Integrating strategies are involved in the complex process of incorporating the meaning we're constructing into the knowledge we bring to the reading situation (1985, p. 105).

Writing

The critical role of literature experiences in the development of writing has been demonstrated in studies of reading/writing relationships. Literature is a rich natural resource for learning about written language. One learns to read like a writer in order to become a writer.

Motivation

A reading program should be designed not only to teach children how to read but to ensure that they want to read. This latter goal can be achieved by providing meaningful experiences with good literature on a regular basis in the classroom. Cullinan (1987) defines an *aliterate* as a "person who knows how to read but who doesn't choose to read" (p. 11). She expresses concern about the prevalence of aliteracy in our society today. In order to prevent both aliteracy and illiteracy language experiences must be created to support the process of learning to read and becoming a reader. Authentic literary experiences serve as powerful motivational factors in encouraging children to become readers. To grow as readers children must have a great deal of practice. Wide reading requires the availability of diverse reading materials, as well as plenty of time set aside for independent reading. The student who develops the "reading habit" discovers the value of books for providing enjoyment, challenge, and growth.

FOCUS ON LITERATURE

The primary thesis of this book is that the enjoyment and study of literature in its own right should be an integral and significant part of the elementary-school curriculum. A literature program which is incorporated into the school schedule suggests to children that literature is valued and is an important part of school life. The program is designed as an invitation to enter the world of books, a rich world of language, ideas, and human experience in the form of poetry, fable, myth, legend, folktale, fairytale, adventure, contemporary and historical realism, fantasy, mystery, biography, and so on. The central purpose of the literature program is to provide aesthetic experiences which are pleasurable and enjoyable for the child. As children "live through" aesthetic experiences they gain understanding of themselves and others, of human nature and the human condition. The aesthetic event provides a context for stretching the mind and the imagination and for exploring moral and ethical values. In a collection of essays about the importance of folklore and fantasy Jane Yolen, children's writer, stresses that myth, legend and folklore are vital to our intellectual and human growth: ". . . when we deny [our children] access to their inheritance of story . . . or deprive them of the insights and poetic vision expressed in words that humans have produced throughout human history, we deny them—in the end—their own humanity" (1981, p. 20).

Transactions with literature enrich the inner life of the child. The visual experiences provided by gifted artists who have illustrated children's books are a significant part of this enrichment. Children learn to appreciate such creative expression as they experience a rich variety of style and media, from the exquisite representational art of Tasha Tudor to the bright vivid colors of Brian Wildsmith, the folk art of Paul Goble, the cartoons of William Steig, the woodcuts of Marcia Brown, the majestic oil paintings of the landscape artist Thomas Locker, or the superb watercolors of Warwick Hutton.

Encounters with literary works become part of the literary background readers bring to their transactions with literary texts. The literature program offers a series of cumulative experiences that contribute to and shape readers' literary histories, which in turn contribute to their comprehension of current literary texts. The teacher invites children to join in an extended journey into the world of literature and acts as a guide along the way. As children explore this world the teacher helps them look closely at story to discover different levels of meaning and new perspectives; and to learn about literary patterns, conventions, and devices, narrative structures, the use of language, and the development of character. As children become aware of and recognize the elements of story and the threads which bind one story to another they gain a fuller understanding of literature and are better able to enjoy their transactions with it.

The literature program described in this book features a series of Focus Units (Moss, 1984) in which diverse but related literary selections are introduced to children in a planned sequence so that responses to each new selection are informed by prior literary experiences. Reading and writing are integrated and complementary components of the program. Children respond to literature as writers and become increasingly aware of the author's craft, an awareness which enhances their appreciation of literature and the quality of their own writing as well. Dialogue, the focus of Chapter 2, is a central feature of the literature program.

The purpose of this book is to offer examples of Focus Units that illustrate ways in which theoretical models and insights that have emerged from the research of the past two decades can be translated into practical ideas for building literary and literacy skills in the context of the literature program.

References

Adams, Marilyn J., and Allen Collins. *A Schema—Theoretic View of Reading*. Boston: Bolt, Beranek, and Newman, 1977.

Altwerger, Bess, Carole Edelsky, and Barbara Flores. "Whole Language: What's New?" *The Reading Teacher*, vol. 41, no. 21, November 1987, pp. 144–154.

Anderson, I. H., and W. F. Dearborn. *The Psychology of Teaching Reading*. N.Y.: Ronald, 1952.

Ausubel, D. "The Use of Advance Organizers in the Learning and Retention of Meaningful Verbal Material" in *Journal of Educational Psychology*, 51, 1960, pp. 267–272.

Bartlett, Frederic. *Remembering*. Cambridge: Cambridge University Press, 1932.

Beck, Isabel, Margaret G. McKeown, Ellen McCaslin, and Ann Burkes. *Instructional Dimensions that May Affect Reading Comprehension: Examples from Two Commercial Reading Programs*. Pittsburgh: University of Pittsburgh, Learning Research and Development Center, 1979.

Bissex, Glenda L. *GNYS at WRK: A Child Learns to Write and Read*. Cambridge, MA: Harvard University Press, 1980.

———. "Learning to Write and Learning to Read: A Case Study," doctoral dissertation, Harvard University, 1979.

Carroll, J., and R. Freedle. *Language Comprehension and the Acquisition of Knowledge*. Washington, D.C.: Winston, 1972.

Cattell, J. McK. "The Time It Takes to See and Name Objects." *Mind*, 1886, 11, pp. 63–65.

Chall, Jeanne. *Learning to Read: The Great Debate*. N.Y.: McGraw-Hill, 1967.

Chomsky, Carol. "Write Now, Read Later." *Language in Early Childhood Education*, C. B. Cazden, ed. Washington, D.C.: NAEYC, 1972, pp. 119–126.

Chomsky, Noam. "Language and Mind." *Psychology Today*, 2, 1968, pp. 280–286.

Clark, Margaret. *Young Fluent Readers*. London: Heinemann, 1976.

Clay, Marie. *What Did I Write?* Exeter, N.H.: Heinemann, 1975.

Cohn, M. "Observations of Learning to Read." *Language Arts*, 58, May 1981, pp. 549–556.

Cullinan, Bernice, ed. *Children's Literature in the Reading Program*. Newark, DE: IRA, 1987.

Duffy, Gerald G., and Laura R. Roehler. "Teaching Reading Skills as Strategies." *The Reading Teacher*, vol. 40, no. 4, January 1987, pp. 414–418.

Durkin, Dolores. "Children Who Read Before Grade One." *The Reading Teacher*, 14, 1961, pp. 163–166.

———. *Children Who Read Early*. N.Y.: Teachers College Press, 1966.

———. "Reading Comprehension Instruction in Five Basal Reading Series." *Reading Research Quarterly*, vol. 16, no. 4, 1981, pp. 515–544.

———. "What Classroom Observations Reveal about Reading Comprehension Instruction." *Reading Research Quarterly*, vol. 14, no. 4, 1978–1979, pp. 481–533.

Edelsky, Carole, and Karen Smith. "Is that Writing—Or Are Those Marks a Figment of Your Curriculum?" *Language Arts*, vol. 61, no. 1, January 1984, pp. 24–32.

Elkind, David. *Child Development and Education*. N.Y.: Oxford University Press, 1976.

Frase, L. "Learning from Prose Material: Length of Passage, Knowledge of Results, and Position of Questions." *Journal of Educational Psychology*, 58, 1967, pp. 266–272.

Gardner, K. "Early Reading Skills." *Reading Skills: Theory and Practice*, K. Gardner, ed. London: Ward Lock, 1970.

Goodman, Kenneth. "The Know-More and the Know-Nothing Movements in Reading: A Personal Response." *Language Arts*, vol. 56, no. 6, September 1979, pp. 657–663.

———. "Reading: A Psycholinguistic Guessing Game." *Journal of the Reading Specialist*, 4, May 1967, pp. 126–135.

———. "Unity in Reading." *Theoretical Models and Processes of Reading*, 3rd ed. Harry Singer and Robert B. Ruddell, eds. Newark, DE: IRA, 1985.

———. *What's Whole in Whole Language?* Portsmouth, N.H.: Heinemann, 1986.

Graves, Donald H. *Writing: Teachers and Children at Work*. Exeter, N. H.: Heinemann, 1983.

Guthrie, John. "Research Views: Story Comprehension." *The Reading Teacher*, vol. 30, no. 5, February 1977, pp. 574–577.

Harste, Jerome, Virginia Woodward, and Carolyn Burke. *Language Stories and Literacy Lessons*. Portsmouth, N.H.: Heinemann, 1984.

Harste, Jerome, Kathy Short, and Carolyn Burke. *Creating Classrooms for Authors: The Reading-Writing Connection*. Portsmouth, N.H.: Heinemann, 1988.

Holdaway, Don. *The Foundations of Literacy*. Sydney: Ashton Scholastic, 1979.

———. *Stability and Change in Literacy Learning*. Exeter, N.H.: Heinemann, 1984.

Huey, E. B. *The Psychology and Pedagogy of Reading*. N.Y.: Macmillan, 1908.

King, Martha L., and Victor Rentel. *How Children Learn to Write: A Longitudinal Study*. Final Report to the National Institute of Education (NIE-G-0039), 1981. ED 213 050.

Meek, Margaret. *Learning to Read*. London: Bodley Head, 1982.

Moss, Joy. *Focus Units in Literature: A Handbook for Elementary School Teachers*. Urbana, IL: NCTE, 1984.

National Assessment of Educational Progress. *Three National Assessments of Reading: Changes in Performance (1970–1980)*. Report No. 11-R-01. Denver, CO: Education Commission of the States, 1981.

Newman, Judith. *Whole Language: Theory in Use*. Portsmouth, N.H.: Heinemann, 1985.

Pearson, P. David. "Changing the Face of Reading Comprehension Instruction." *The Reading Teacher*, vol. 38, no. 8, April 1985, pp. 724–738.

Piaget, Jean. *The Origins of Intelligence in Children*. N.Y.: International Universities Press, 1952.

Piaget, Jean, and Barbel Inhelder. *The Psychology of the Child*. N.Y.: Basic, 1969.

Pollack, Hilary L. "Questioning Strategies to Encourage Critical Thinking." *Insights into Open Education*, vol. 21, no. 1, September 1988.

Read, Charles. "Pre-school Children's Knowledge of English Phonology." *Harvard Educational Review*, 41, 1971, pp. 1–34.

Rosenblatt, Louise. "The Literary Transaction: Evocation and Response." *Theory into Practice*, vol. 21, no. 4, Autumn 1982, pp. 268–277.

———. *The Reader, The Text and the Poem*. Carbondale, IL: Southern Illinois University Press, 1978.

Rothkopf, E. Z. "The Concept of Mathemagenic Activities." *Review of Educational Research*, 40, 1970, pp. 371–393.

Rowe, Deborah, and Jerome Harste. "Reading and Writing in a System of Knowing—Curricular Implications." *The Pursuit of Literacy*, M. Sampson, ed. Dubuque, IA: Kendall-Hunt, 1986.

Rumelhart, David E. *Toward an Interactive Model of Reading*. Technical Report No. 56. San Diego, CA: Center for Human Information Processing, University of California, 1976.

Sawyer, Wayne. "Literature and Literacy: A Review of Research." *Language Arts*, vol. 64, no. 1, January 1987, pp. 33–39.

Scollen, Ron, and B. K. Suzanne Scollen. Chapter 4, "The Literate Two-Year-Old: The Fictionalization of the Self." *Narrative, Literacy and Race in Inter-ethnic Communication*. Norwood, N.J.: Ablex, 1981.

Singer, Harry. "Hypotheses on Reading Comprehension in Search of Classroom Validation." *Theoretical Models and Processes of Reading*, Harry Singer and Robert Ruddell, eds. Newark, DE: IRA, 1985.

Smith, Frank. "Reading Like a Writer." *Composing and Comprehending*, Julie Jensen, ed. Urbana, IL: Eric, NCRE, 1984, pp. 47–56.

———. "Learning to Read by Bringing Meaning to Text." Unpublished mimeo. Ontario Institute for Studies in Education, Toronto, Canada, 1977.

———. *Understanding Reading. A Psycholinguistic Analysis of Reading and Learning to Read*, 2nd ed. N.Y.: Holt, Rinehart and Winston, 1978.

———. *Writing and the Writer*. N.Y.: Holt, Rinehart and Winston, 1982.

Stein, Nancy, and C. G. Glenn. "An Analysis of Story Comprehension in Elementary School Children." *New Directions in Discourse Processing*, vol. 2, R. O. Freedle, ed. Norwood, N.J.: Ablex, 1979.

Stotsky, Sandra. "Research on Reading/Writing Relationships: A Synthesis and Suggested Directions." *Language Arts*, vol. 60, no. 3, May 1983, pp. 627–642.

Sutton, M. "Children Who Learned to Read in Kindergarten: A Longitudinal Study." *The Reading Teacher*, 22, 1969, pp. 596–602, 683.

Teale, William. "Positive Environments for Learning to Read: What Studies of Early Readers Tell Us." *Language Arts*, vol. 55, no. 8, November/December, 1978, pp. 922–932.

————. "Toward a Theory of How Children Learn to Read and Write Naturally." *Language Arts*, vol. 59, no. 6, September 1982, pp. 555–570.

Thorndike, E. "Reading as Reasoning: A Study of Mistakes in Paragraph Reading." *Journal of Educational Psychology*, 1917, 8, pp. 323–332.

Vygotsky, Lev S. *Thought and Language*. Cambridge, MA: MIT Press, 1962.

————. *Mind in Society: The Development of Higher Psychological Process*. M. Cole, V. John-Steiner, S. Scribner, and E. Souberman, eds. Cambridge, MA: Harvard University Press, 1978.

Wagner, Betty Jane. "ERIC/RCS Report: Integrating the Language Arts." *Language Arts*, vol. 62, no. 5, September 1985, pp. 557–560.

Yolen, Jane. *Touch Magic: Fantasy, Faerie and Folklore in the Literature of Childhood*. N.Y.: Philomel, 1981.

T W O

Dialogue:
The Connecting Thread

DIALOGUE IN THE CLASSROOM

A classroom in which enjoyment and study of literature is an integral part of the curriculum is one in which teachers and students collaborate to make sense of print, to construct meaning from and to communicate meaning with authentic, whole language. In such a classroom literature is viewed as a source of aesthetic experience, as well as a context for literary and literacy learning.

Dialogue is a central feature of the literary and literacy events in this setting. Teachers and students enter into many kinds of dialogues as they engage in the process of making meaning. For example, as readers and writers they enter into a dialogue to generate meaning—the reader with the author, and the writer with the implied audience. Just as readers generate meaning by using their knowledge background in conjunction with author's cues, writers create meaning by using their knowledge background in conjunction with assumptions about the knowledge background of the implied reader (Tierney and Pearson, 1983).

The nature of the relationship between teacher and students affects the quality of the dialogues generated in the classroom community. Teachers and students collaborate as partners as they encounter challenging material and engage in intellectual inquiry in the literature program. In the context of this partnership the teacher encounters each student as a whole and unique individual with a rich background of experience and knowledge. Just as each reader brings cultural and social experiences and linguistic and conceptual knowledge to the text to engage in a dialogue with the author, so, too, does each student bring a unique background of experiences and understandings into the classroom and into the dialogue with the teacher. The dialogue serves as a cooperative learning experience.

As teachers and students engage in dialogue students are provided with a model to emulate as they interact with their peers. Students learn to encounter each classmate as a unique and whole individual, to make an effort to understand and respect the viewpoint of others, and to stand in the shoes of one whose background is different than their own. This involves some degree of dialogical thinking: *i.e.*, the ability to see things from another's point of view or to perceive a problem from a new and different perspective (Sternberg, 1985, pp. 53–54). Dialogue provides a context for language experiences which are meaningful and purposeful and related to the needs and experiences of individual children.

The regular read-aloud sessions which are an integral part of the Focus Unit set the stage for an ongoing literary-based conversation which begins before a story is read aloud, continues at appropriate points during the reading of the story, and takes up again after the story has been completed. Teacher and students engage in a dialogue as they "live through" the text together, and respond with feelings, ideas, and attitudes as the story unfolds. Together they explore the story world they evoke as they share the literary piece.

THE DIALOGUE BEFORE READING

Readers make sense of text by bringing prior knowledge to the text. The quality of readers' comprehension is determined in large part by prior knowledge they are able to relate to the text and utilize in order to make predictions and pose questions while they read. Prior to reading a story aloud the teacher introduces questions which will facilitate comprehension by prompting retrieval of relevant information from children's memory store and inviting them to bring their prior knowledge to the text as they listen to the story unfold. This prereading dialogue is intended to help both teachers and students become aware of what prior knowledge is available for comprehension of the text and what knowledge is needed to make sense of it. Dialogue serves to bridge the gap between what readers know and what they need to know to anticipate and predict meanings.

Other questions introduced into the prestory dialogue invite children to make predictions and pose questions about the story based on the title, the cover illustrations, the genre, and what they know about the author or illustrator. The teacher uses prestory dialogue to show children how they can use their prior knowledge to formulate predictions and questions about content and organization in order to enhance their comprehension.

THE DIALOGUE DURING READING

During the oral presentation of the story the teacher might stop at a significant point to ask: "What do you think will happen next?" This question is intended to help children develop an anticipatory attitude toward print and to make predictions as they read in order to facilitate comprehension. They need to understand that the author provides information that makes subsequent parts of the narrative more predictable and comprehensible. They learn to gather clues to meaning by looking for information or events in the story which support the development of the characters or plot or theme. They learn to construct a working interpretation of the story, and then to refine and modify this interpretation as new information is gathered.

The teacher might also interrupt the story to ask a question such as, "What did that character mean when he said '_____'?"

This type of question helps children build the habit of translating key words or phrases which contribute significantly to the meaning of the text. For example, in *The Great Quillow* by James Thurber (1944) the town council members refer to the toymaker as the "Great Quillow." The reader must use the author's clues to understand that "great" is used as a form of mockery in one context and to express scorn in another. By the end of the tale Quillow the toymaker has managed to save the town from a giant and has earned the respect of his fellow townspeople. The meaning of the word "great" changes significantly as the story unfolds and new information is provided.

The children are invited to interrupt the story with significant and relevant comments, predictions, or questions. More often, depending on the nature of the piece, they respond nonverbally as they evoke the story or poem, preferring it to unfold without interruption.

THE DIALOGUE AFTER THE STORY

After each story children are invited to respond spontaneously with comments and questions. They are encouraged to share their personal experiences, feelings, and knowledge. In the initial session of the Focus Unit sequence the teacher follows this spontaneous input with questions which suggest additional ways to think about and respond to the story or poem, and thus new ways to enjoy the literary experience. Some of these teacher-initiated questions are designed to encourage evaluation, confirmation, or revision of earlier predictions. Others call attention to story ideas, patterns, themes, and elements; layers of meaning; the language of literature; the author's craft; and diverse literary genres. Some questions invite children to make connections with other stories they've heard or to relate the story to their own lives. The purpose of these teacher-initiated questions is to set into motion a long-term, cumulative process of enjoying and learning about literature in the context of an ongoing dialogue which provides the connecting link between various literature units throughout the school year. The public dialogue is intended to serve as a model for the internal dialogue which solitary readers carry on with the author as they interact with and respond to a text. This public dialogue also generates a background of knowledge about literary craft and content from which the student-as-writer can draw to compose original narratives.

After these initial story sessions, in which the teacher introduces questions to demonstrate ways of reflecting on texts, students are ready to pose their own questions and to assume more responsibility for the content and direction of the dialogue. They draw from their expanding literary background, enriched by their experiences with related texts introduced in the Focus Unit sequence, to formulate questions and to construct meanings which shape the dialogue. This cumulative oral dialogue is the context for critical and creative thinking and active involvement in the learning process.

The Ongoing Dialogue

The oral dialogue which evolves as part of the group read-aloud sessions is complemented and extended by dialogues between the teacher and individual students in one-to-one conferences and in dialogue-journals in which teacher and students carry on written conversations about group or independent reading experiences, as well as any personal issues or questions which may emerge. The dialogue-journal, in which teacher and child respond to literature and to each other, is often the starting point for the conference discussion. A story can be the catalyst for turning children's own experiences into language. Children share personal concerns in a supportive environment which allows them to bring their lives to school (*see* Chapter 9 for a discussion of literary dialogue-journals).

Dialogues between students in small study groups or in informal social interactions provide further opportunities to exchange ideas about stories read aloud or independently, or about stories they are composing. A student's dialogue-journal can be shared with a classmate to initiate a new written conversation and new opportunities for learning.

These dialogues, public or private, oral or written, are encounters between persons who bring their inner feelings, personal histories, and special interests and strengths to their responses to literature and to each other. Dialogue becomes a shared experience in which teacher and students collaborate to study, explore, and respond to literature in a social context. The term "community of readers" describes children working together to become readers of literature and to explore and build meanings together (Hepler and Hickman, 1982). Such a "community of readers" is a consequence of and a context for the literature program in the curriculum.

The Dialogue and Literary Selections

The quality and nature of the dialogue is determined in large part by the quality and nature of the literature selected for each Focus Unit. The teacher chooses literary material that has the potential to stimulate questions, reflection, and exploration; that provides a context for learning about diverse literary genres and discovering significant truths about human experience inherent in all genres; and that suggests new possibilities for independent reading and writing. The teacher introduces children to fine authors and artists to provide enjoyable aesthetic experiences, to help them develop literary and artistic appreciation, and to stretch their minds and imaginations. The teacher introduces children to traditional literature, their literary heritage, to provide a sense of connection to the past and to other cultures, and to expose them to the building-borrowing process which shaped and reshaped the old oral tales. As children gain experience in analyzing and comparing the diverse tales introduced in the Focus Units they begin to see that each story or poem is part of the larger story which is world literature, the story of human experience told with insight and poetic vision.

The following chapters present a series of Focus Units in which dialogue serves as a vehicle for integrating the language arts, a context for language learning, and the vital link between exposure to literature and the development of literary and literacy skills. Dialogue is the connecting thread which weaves its way from diverse informal and formal, oral and written, teacher-student and peer interactions into the literature sessions and out again into the life of the classroom. It serves as a bridge between the study of literature and the generation of meaning in related reading and writing activities, as well as other forms of creative expression. And through this dialogue each literature session is connected to all prior and subsequent sessions, such that these sessions are bound into a long-term, cumulative process of exploring the form and content of diverse literary selections and discovering the fundamental unity of literature.

Responding to literature together and sharing the pleasure of aesthetic experience contribute to the enjoyment teachers and students derive from their exploration of the world of literature.

References

Hepler, Susan I., and Janet Hickman. "'The Book Was Okay. I Love You'—Social Aspects of Response to Literature." *Theory into Practice.* 21, 1982, pp. 278–283.

Sternberg, Robert. "Critical Thinking: Its Nature, Measurement, and Improvement." *Essays on the Intellect.* Frances R. Link, ed. Alexandria, VA: ASCD, 1985, pp. 45–65.

Thurber, James. *The Great Quillow.* N.Y.: Harcourt Brace Jovanovich, 1944.

Tierney, Robert, and P. David Pearson. "Toward a Composing Model of Reading." *Language Arts*, vol. 60, no. 5, May 1983, pp. 568–580.

THREE

Transformation Tales:
The Learner-Centered Classroom

THE LEARNER-CENTERED CLASSROOM

In the last two decades research in literacy learning has generated a shift in focus from teaching to development and learning. Attention has shifted from the central role of the classroom teacher to the central role of the learner. When Piaget (1952), Vygotsky (1962), Chomsky (1968), and other developmental and cognitive theorists challenged the behaviorists' picture of the passive language learner, they opened the way for the emergence of a new picture of an active, creative learner at the very center of the learning process. The theoretical models of language learning which have contributed to this picture provide the foundation for the learner-centered classroom.

The reconceptualization of reading which emerged in the 1970s drew attention to the central role of the reader who interacts with a text and generates meanings by relating prior knowledge and experiences to it. Louise Rosenblatt's transactional model of reading (1978) highlighted the role of the reader in recreating and interpreting a literary work of art. The reader engages in an aesthetic transaction with the text and creates something new: the poem. "The poem comes into being in the live circuit set up between the reader and the text" (p. 14). According to Rosenblatt:

> The transaction will involve not only the past experiences but. also the present state and present interests or preoccupations of the reader (p. 20). [The reader brings a] body of cultural assumptions, practical knowledge, awareness of literary conventions, and readinesses to think and feel (p. 88).

The recent interest in the writing process among whole language theorists and practitioners has also been associated with this emphasis on the central role of the learner in the classroom. In the learner-centered classroom children are given opportunities to choose what they will write and to experiment with language to express what they want to express. They are encouraged to produce meaningful and authentic texts. Risk-taking is supported and valued as a natural and important part of the learning process. Communication is emphasized rather than mechanical accuracy. In such a classroom children see themselves as writers whose work is taken seriously.

In the learner-centered classroom the teacher begins with children's strengths as language learners, rather than their deficits. The teacher builds on what children already know. Yetta Goodman, a professor of education, uses the term "kidwatching" to describe the process of learning about children by watching how they learn. "Through observing the reading, writing, speaking, and listening of friendly, interactive peers, interested, kidwatching teachers can understand and support child language development" (1985, p. 9). Current knowledge about language learning provides the basis for informed observation, interpretation, and evaluation of children's language behavior in the classroom and in other natural settings. Using a "child as informant" perspective, the teacher learns about children's concepts of language, their strategies for processing language, their uses of language, and their progress as language learners. This information serves as the basis for planning rich learning experiences and for creating an environment which allows language learning to occur naturally.

Jane Hansen, in her book *When Writers Read* (1987), describes the use of a "response approach" in reading-writing classrooms. The teacher listens to students to discover what they know, instead of what they don't know. The teacher then responds to what children are trying to do as they engage in meaning-making. A primary goal of this response approach is to get children to assume responsibility for their own learning; to respond to their own reading and writing and to each other.

The shift in emphasis from teaching to learning has been reflected in a growing interest among classroom teachers in becoming active learners themselves, and thoughtful observers in the context of the classroom. Observation of students is initiated and shaped by the teacher's questions about learning and concerns about current classroom problems. The teacher as observer engages in a process of discovery and learning which, in turn, informs curriculum development. The purpose of the inquiry is to seek solutions to problems and improve the quality of learning. Teachers who continue to learn and grow benefit not only their students but themselves as professionals.

Our work cannot become stale because we are continually redefining it. And this process of continual redefinition and renewal helps us retain the enthusiasm and commitment that brought us into this profession in the first place (Odell, 1987, p. 158).

Thus, both teachers and students engage in inquiry and learning in the learner-centered classroom. The classroom becomes a community of learners, a laboratory for inquiry. The literature curriculum described in this book was developed and implemented in the context of a learner-centered classroom. Each of the Focus Units was designed to allow teachers to observe children responding to literature and to each other in the process of enjoying and learning about literature. Each Unit was designed to allow and encourage students to participate as active, creative learners at the very center of the learning process.

A primary purpose of the Focus Units described in this book is to provide literary experiences which will enrich children's transactions with and responses to literary texts. The question, "What kinds of experiences will enrich the child's literary transactions?" guides the planning phase. The question, "What is the effect of these literary experiences on the child's transaction with and response to literary texts?" guides the evaluation phase during which the teacher studies the information gathered from observation of children engaged in these literary experiences. Insights and information gained from the evaluation phase are fed back into the planning phase. Thus, the planning, implementation, and evaluation of curriculum is an ongoing process informed by the teacher's continual inquiry and learning.

TRANSFORMATION TALES

The Focus Unit described here draws attention to a common literary motif: transformation. It was selected by the teacher because of her students' current interest in a popular toy known as the "Transformer." Since transformation is a literary motif found in many traditional and modern tales, the teacher decided to develop a Focus Unit around it, using a familiar and concrete object to introduce an abstract literary concept and the children's knowledge as the starting point for learning. Although this Focus Unit was initially developed for and with a group of seven- and eight-year-old children, it has been adapted for younger and older children by revising the list of books selected for reading aloud and/or for independent reading in accordance with the needs and interests of each age group. Specific children quoted in this chapter ranged in age from seven to nine years.

The central question guiding the planning, implementation, and evaluation of the Focus Unit was: To what extent will the study of a literary motif, transformation, found in traditional and modern stories, enhance the quality of a child's response to more complex narratives featuring "dynamic characters" whose transformation is associated with growth and change in personality and outlook. The dynamic character matures; gains insights; and develops new traits, attitudes, and values in the course of the events of the story.

The teacher planned activities which allowed the children to respond to literature orally and in writing. Through close observation of their responses to literary texts read in group settings and/or individually, the teacher sought answers to this question. For example, she looked for evidence that suggested readers had utilized the literary background derived from the cumulative dialogue which is the cornerstone of the Focus Unit. She looked for evidence that this dialogue provided children with questioning strategies which they used to guide their reading and writing of literary texts. She looked for answers to her question in records of group dialogue; individual dialogue-journal entries; narrative writing; student-teacher conferences; peer conferences; and recreation of stories through retellings, drama, art, and dance.

Session One

After printing the words TRANSFORM, TRANSFORMER, and TRANSFORMATION on the board the teacher asked the children if they could give the meaning of any of these words. Almost all of them recognized the second word and defined it in terms of their knowledge of the popular toy. Using this prior knowledge they were able to figure out meanings of the other two words:

- A TRANSFORMER is a thing that changes from a super jet to a robot and back.
- Mine changes from a race car to a robot.
- There's a real big one at the toy store that's supposed to transform from a space shuttle to a sky lynx super robot!
- *Transform* must mean the same as *change*! Like when you change the robot into a car, you *transform* it.
- That long word [*i.e.*, TRANSFORMATION] has *transform* in it, so it probably means to change, too.

Soon, the children reached a general consensus that these three words were associated with various types of change. Consultation with a dictionary confirmed this and added to their understanding of the use of each word. The stage was set for responding to a series of new texts: transformation tales. The children were invited to identify the "transformation" in each tale read aloud or independently during the literature unit.

The tale read in the first group session was *Solomon the Rusty Nail* (Steig, 1985), the story of a young rabbit who discovers he can change himself into a rusty nail. During prereading discussion the children were asked to predict what the story might be about. Several children suggested that there could be a mistake in the title:

- There should be an "and" after Solomon. The rabbit on the cover is probably Solomon.
- And he probably finds a rusty nail.
- Maybe it's a magic nail!

As the story unfolded, they discovered that Solomon was able to change *into* a rusty nail; and they made appropriate adjustments:

- The title was right! There wasn't supposed to be an "and"!
- But the rabbit's name *is* Solomon.
- And there *is* magic—He's *transformed*.

At the end of the story several questions were asked about the nature of the transformation and its relationship to the plot.

- What can you say about the transformation in this story?
- How did the transformation *solve* a problem?
- How did the transformation *cause* a problem?

The children easily identified Solomon's transformation and the formula used to achieve it. They noted that Solomon used his ability to change himself into a nail to escape from the villain in the story, but unfortunately he soon discovered that he might be unable to return to his normal shape and to his loving family. One child summed it up: "It solved one problem, but caused another. So the story had to keep going!"

Session Two

Sylvester and the Magic Pebble (Steig, 1969) was read aloud in the second session after the children were given an opportunity to make predictions about the nature of the transformation in this story. Most of the children agreed that the magic pebble would be used to achieve the transformation, but there was sharp disagreement about its nature. Several children observed that the animals on the book cover dressed and walked like humans and "looked sort of sad." They concluded that these animals had once been humans who were changed into animals. Other children disagreed. They noted that the first story was by the same author and was about animals who behaved like humans. As they listened to the story they evaluated and revised their predictions. Those who had predicted that Steig would write another animal story were pleased to have their predictions confirmed.

After the story was read aloud and spontaneous comments shared, the children were asked to compare it to the first story. They noted that in both stories the central character effects his own transformation to escape danger and discovers he cannot return to his original shape or to those he loves. The children noted with pleasure that both stories ended happily: The transformation is finally reversed and the main characters are reunited with their families.

After this comparative analysis the children were asked to try to explain how Steig had selected the pictures for the front and back covers.

- Well, the front cover shows Sylvester's parents trying to find him. That shows the main problem in the story . . . that Sylvester is missing.
- He could have used the picture of the rock that Sylvester was changed into. That was the *real* problem—for *him*!
- But that wouldn't be a good picture for the cover because you'd just think it's a book about *rocks*!
- The back cover is perfect. It shows the family hugging together. That shows the happy ever after ending when the problem gets all solved and everyone's happy!

This analysis reflected the children's knowledge of story structure and their ability to use this knowledge to actively generate meaning. (*See* Chapter 6 for a discussion of story schema.)

Session Three

A third story by William Steig, *Caleb and Kate* (1977), was introduced in the next group session. By this time the children were ready to initiate the discussion before and after the story was read aloud. They made predictions about the story, evaluated and revised these predictions as the story unfolded, and then compared it with the two stories read in previous sessions. They noted with some surprise that this third story featured human characters instead of animals; and that the transformation is caused by a witch who decides to test a new spell and changes poor Caleb into a dog. The children observed that in all three stories the transformed characters have difficulty returning to their original shapes and cannot communicate with loved ones even though they are not far away. One child exclaimed, "That's the *worst* thing—not to be able to get people to listen to you!" The children responded empathetically to the frustration experienced by the characters in these three stories.

When the discussion turned to Steig, the author/illustrator, one child commented on a common theme she had discovered: "I like his books because he always writes about people who love each other. My favorite picture is the one of Mr. and Mrs. Duncan hugging

Sylvester!" Several children supported this statement by referring to other books by William Steig with this basic theme.

The first two sessions prepared the children for assuming more responsibility for the nature and direction of the discussion in subsequent sessions. They had apparently begun to develop significant strategies for generating meaning: making predictions, evaluating and revising these predictions, making connections with other literary texts, applying their knowledge of story structure, relating the literary text to their own emotional and social experiences, and asking questions. The group story sessions were becoming learner-centered explorations of literary selections as the children lived through, responded to, and discussed each text, and then searched for connections with their own literary histories.

INDEPENDENT READING AND WRITING

After the third group story session a collection of transformation tales, selected to meet the diverse reading needs and interests in this group, was arranged on a large table (*see* the bibliography of transformation tales at the end of this chapter). The children were invited to choose any of the books from this collection to read independently or with a friend. They talked to each other about the stories and convinced others to read the ones they had enjoyed. They discovered transformation tales in their own personal libraries and in books in their local public libraries. These "discoveries" were brought to school to share and to add to the classroom collection. The children were becoming active participants in the process of creating the literary environment.

The book-sharing activity was a critical feature of the literary experience, reflecting the social aspect of reader response (Hickman, 1980, 1981). The children became part of a "community of readers," working together to become readers of literature (Hepler and Hickman, 1982). The learner-centered classroom supports the establishment of such a community of readers.

The children were given spiral notebooks in which to record their responses to literary selections heard in the group sessions or read independently (*see* Chapter 9 for a discussion of the literary dialogue-journal). Emphasis was placed on meaning-making, not mechanics. The entries in these literature journals provided important information about each child's interaction with and response to literary texts. It became apparent that the children had formulated and incorporated questions and answers of their own to guide their comprehension and interpretation. They had used the dialogue in the group story sessions as a catalyst for these questioning strategies. Many of the entries reflected the children's questioning and thinking about the nature of the transformation, literary themes and patterns, connections with other tales, and links to personal experience. These journals provided a cumulative record of each child's involvement in literary response and the learning process. The teacher's responses to the entries supported children's learning and often generated further reflection and extension of the meaning-making process.

These journals were used as the starting point for sharing literary responses in student-teacher conferences and in small response groups working together without a teacher. When Suzanne Brady, a teacher in Monterey, California, reviewed videotapes of the response groups in her classroom, she found that the groups working on their own took their responsibility more seriously and had more ideas than the groups meeting with her (Newkirk and Atwell, 1988, p. 142).

Discussions in conferences with the teacher and in response groups with peers often set the stage for rich interactions in the large group sessions which, in turn, contributed to the content of the informal interactions. As the children gained experience and confidence as participants in these diverse social interactions, the very nature of the discussions changed. In early group sessions, although chairs were arranged in a circle, the majority of student comments were directed to the teacher. Gradually, the children began to direct their comments to each other, to listen and respond to what others said. They began to engage in the give-and-take of genuine dialogue.

Session Four

In the fourth large group session *Big Bad Bruce* (Peet, 1977) was read aloud, discussed, and compared with other transformation tales. Bruce, a big bully of a bear, is shrunk to the size of a chipmunk by a witch who is determined to teach Bruce a lesson. The children were very excited about detecting the differences, as well as the similarities, between this and the other stories they had read.

- This time the witch does a transformation as a punishment!
- And Bruce *stays* transformed. He doesn't go back to his regular size.
- He deserved it! But the characters in the other stories deserved to be changed back.

The children were asked if they thought Bruce had changed *inside* as well. They decided that he had definitely not cha..ged inside because he continued to tease and scare small creatures.

- He's still just a great big bully, even though he's small in size!

During the discussion of this story the children began to distinguish between "inside transformation" and "outside transformation." They had discovered a basic literary concept which would contribute significantly to their understanding of dynamic characters they would encounter later in more complex narratives. The stage was set for the teacher to study the influence of this transformation unit on children's literary abilities. The central research question was: To what extent will the study of transformation as a literary motif enhance the quality of children's response to narratives featuring dynamic characters?

Session Five

The Donkey Prince (Craig, 1977) was introduced as the first of a series of *traditional* tales featuring transformation. After a discussion of the oral tradition and the critical differences and connections between traditional and modern literature, this adaptation of a Grimm Brothers tale was read aloud. The children identified *The Donkey Prince* as another example of a transformation associated with punishment and revenge. In this case, however, the transformation was reversed by the power of love. One child, drawing from her own literary experience, noted, "It's like 'Beauty and the Beast'!"

Sessions Six and Seven

Three other traditional tales were read aloud in these sessions: *The Frog Princess* (Isele, 1984), *The Hedgehog Boy* (Langton, 1985), and *The Crane Wife* (Yagawa, 1981). The children discussed each story and then made connections with the other stories they had heard or read independently as part of this unit. They had developed the habit of reading each new text in light of previous ones, using their prior knowledge to make predictions and ask significant questions to generate meaning. Their literary experiences were integrated into each new literary event.

In the context of these cumulative literary sessions the children demonstrated their active involvement in the process of constructing meaning from texts as they moved from analysis of single texts to synthesis of multiple texts. They assumed increasing responsibility for their own learning as they engaged in listening, talking, reading, and writing which they used as tools for learning and as processes for generating and shaping meaning.

Session Eight

When *Prince Sparrow* (Gerstein, 1984) was read aloud, the children were puzzled at first. They insisted this was not a transformation tale. After some time to think, they were able to uncover the "transformation" in this modern story.

- Oh, I get it! The transformation is not on the outside. It's that *inside* transformation.
- That spoiled, selfish princess learned how to take care of the sparrow and be nice to him.
- She started to think about someone else instead of just her.
- She *changed*! She didn't have tantrums anymore. I liked her at the end of the story.
- When she changed *inside*, it sort of made her change outside, too. She *looked* nicer and she acted nicer.
- It reminds me of the book I just read. It's called *The Old Woman Who Lived in a Vinegar Bottle* [Rumer Godden, 1970]. She got so greedy and mean-looking. But then at the end, she changed back to *herself*!
- I read that too. When she changed *inside*, her face showed it—just like that princess.
- I read *another* story like this. It's about this real selfish girl that gets changed into a fish ["The Enchanted Fish," Lang, 1964]. But then she helps save the fish-queen and she changes back to herself. She changed *inside*, too, because she's not selfish and obnoxious any more!

Session Nine

The children's response to the moving story of *Crow Boy* (Yashima, 1955) reflected their growing literary abilities developed in the context of this unit. They were able to detect the subtle "inside" and "outside" transformation of the main character as he changed from the shy child who crouched in fear in "the dark space underneath the school house floor" on the first day of school to the confident, happy youth who "set off for his home on the far side of the mountain, stretching his growing shoulders proudly like a grown-up man." They also noted the transformation in the attitude of his classmates, and identified the character in the story who was largely responsible for these transformations: Mr. Isobe, the new teacher. This sensitive, caring man made a significant difference in the life of another individual. One child observed, "Mr. Isobe *caused* the transformation because he helped Crow Boy realize he was special and that the things he could do were important. Mr. Isobe *appreciated* Crow Boy!"

At the end of this session the children were asked to look at the endpapers of the book and suggest possible reasons for the author/artist's decision to feature a butterfly on the first endpaper and a cherry blossom on the last. After a lively discussion the children concluded that Yashima intended to highlight the transformation which was the theme of the story:

- At first Crow Boy was closed and curled up like a bud or a cocoon. Remember when he was crouching under the school? Then he blossomed—like a butterfly or a flower opening up!

Several children recreated this metamorphosis through an impromptu mime performance. They were able to capture the body language of Crow Boy as he gradually achieved a more positive self-concept.

Session Ten

The Changing Maze, a haunting tale by Zilpha Snyder (1985), was introduced in the final read-aloud session. After living through this dramatic story of good and evil, the children responded with appreciative observations about the poetic language, the beautiful illustrations by Charles Mikolaycak, and the mythical nature of this unusual tale.

The narrative begins with an ancient legend told by Hugh's granny:

Long ago, in the far-off gone-away days, the wizard-king of the Ragged Lands prepared a secret evil plan for a marvelous green thorn maze.

Hugh, the central character, finds himself trapped in this maze and nearly succumbs to its evil spell. The children were especially interested in the way this legend was woven into the story and the nature of the mysterious transformation described.

. . . for none who walked the king's maze remained the same. Some wept while the world sang. Some stared while the world slept.

The children were asked why the boy, Hugh, was able to escape the evil power of the maze.

- He didn't go in to get the treasure. He went in to save his pet lamb.
- He didn't go into it for greed like the others.
- But then he *almost* gets tempted by the gold.
- But when he hears his lamb crying, he runs to find him. It's like that princess who cared more about her pet sparrow than being greedy and selfish.

- Also—he said a prayer and that was more powerful than the evil power.
- It's like using a cross to protect yourself against Dracula.
- This is like those old myths where the evil forces try to win over the good forces.
- I liked the ending where Hugh is safe at home with his granny. He knows that he *could* have been tempted by the gold. He said to his granny, 'I might have, but the black lamb cried.'
- Maybe he *was* sort of changed after that. I bet he'll be more careful not to get greedy.

EXTENDING THE RESPONSE TO LITERATURE

As the class became immersed in listening to, reading, talking, and writing about transformation tales several children began to create illustrations of favorite tales. Using this spontaneous activity as a starting point the teacher invited the rest of the children to think of other ways to extend these literary experiences through creative expression. A brainstorming session yielded a list of project ideas which gave the children a wide range of possibilities from which to choose.

Working individually or with partners the children produced murals, dioramas, mobiles, posters, poetry, prose, dance, puppets, and mime. Opportunities for choice allowed for a sense of ownership and encouraged active engagement in the meaning-making process through alternative modes of communication. It was interesting to note that most of the children who chose to compose original transformation tales produced stories which featured "inside" transformation, a more challenging task than creating a tale of "outside" transformation, but excellent as preparation for future reading experiences involving narratives probing the inner growth of central characters. These stories also provided the teacher with evidence that their composers had a firm grasp of this important literary concept.

STUDYING DYNAMIC CHARACTERS

In order to identify a dynamic character as one who grows and changes, and to understand the nature and causes of the "inside transformation" associated with dynamic characters, the reader is usually required to make inferences about motives, feelings, thoughts, and attitudes which are implicit in the story. The reader draws from a story schema (*see* Chapter 6) to infer a character's internal responses and reactions and the logical relationship between events and changes in the inner life of the character. Because the teacher had previously observed that many children seemed to have difficulty making such inferences, she decided to draw attention to the inner lives of dynamic characters in the context of the children's independent reading experiences. To this end she used the transformation unit as the background for the study of dynamic characters.

The first step was to select a number of stories with dynamic characters and to set aside a special shelf for them. Also on this shelf was a loose-leaf notebook for recording responses to the stories. The children were invited to jot down any comments they wanted to share with others. Initially, they simply rated the book with one to five stars, although a few wrote lengthy explanations about why they would or would not recommend it. The teacher recorded some of the interesting statements and interpretations various children had made orally about a particular story character's growth or change. Gradually, more children began to write down their discoveries and analyses of specific dynamic characters. This record of books and comments proved to be especially useful for those children who generally had difficulty selecting a book for quiet reading time. Some chose a book from the list based on its recommendation by a well-liked classmate. Others made their decisions because comments about the characters made the book sound interesting. The books were also discussed in informal response groups, student-teacher conferences, and occasional whole-class sessions; and the children continued to write in their journals.

The collection of "dynamic character" stories was initially a small one set up by the teacher as the starting point for the development of a larger and richer collection. The responsibility for the collection was handed over to the children. As usual, they were given the freedom to choose whatever book they wanted to read for quiet reading time. However, they were now asked to consider each story they had selected in light of their growing awareness of dynamic characters and their understanding of "inside transformation."

When children identified stories in this category, they recorded the title, author, and comments in the notebook and added the book to the collection of dynamic character stories. Since many of these books had been borrowed from local public libraries, the collection changed frequently. Gradually the list and collection grew, and it continued to grow throughout the school year, long after the "transformation unit" had been completed. As the collection grew, so did the children's ability to make inferences about the growth of story characters and the significance of the changes in their inner lives. The quality of the children's discussions, journal entries, and narrative compositions reflected this literary learning.

THE DYNAMIC CHARACTER STORIES

Some of the oral and written comments about the books which became part of the dynamic character collection will be included here to illustrate the nature of the children's responses to these texts and the types of connections they discovered. (A list of some "5-star favorites" can be found at the end of the chapter. This list suggests the wide range of reading levels and diverse reading interests represented by these 2nd-, 3rd-, and 4th-grade children.)

Sam, Bangs and Moonshine (Ness, 1973) generated a great deal of discussion about the nature of truth and "moonshine." The children explored the possible origins of Sam's habit of lying and what caused her finally to face up to the difference between "REAL and MOON-SHINE." Only when she was confronted with the serious consequences of her actions was she ready to let go of this habit.

Those who had also read *Julian's Glorious Summer* (Cameron, 1987) recognized the common theme which connected these two stories.

- Julian and Sam both told lies. And they both learned something about the consequences of not telling the truth.
- But Julian told stories because he didn't want to let people know he was afraid of bikes.
- But it's sort of the same. I think Sam told stories because she was lonely and didn't want to

face the truth that her mom was dead, and Julian didn't want to face the truth about being afraid of bikes.

- He changes in the end, too. He's just about to tell another lie, but then he sees it's easier to just tell the truth. He realized that he got himself into lots more trouble whenever he said stuff he didn't mean.
- What a mess he got himself into! He had to spend all his time hiding his first lie so he never had any fun. I'm glad he finally changed at the end!

The Sparrow's Song (Wallace, 1986) was selected by many of the children because of its familiar setting: Niagara Falls (near Rochester, New York). In this brief but poetic tale Katie finds an orphan bird and learns that her brother, Charles, had killed its mother with his slingshot. When Katie is able to forgive her brother, he joins her in caring for the little sparrow and watching it grow. Toward the end of the story they decide it is time to let their bird fly free. Wallace describes the scene this way:

Beating its wings against the fateful wind, the bird soared, triumphantly, long and high. From his pocket Charles pulled his slingshot. Katie gasped in fear, but instead of aiming the slingshot, Charles hurled it away. End over end it tumbled through the air until the river swallowed it.

The children were impressed by the moment of tension captured in this brief scene and Charles' symbolic gesture revealing his transformation.

- Charles learned to *care* about the bird. He didn't just see it as a target to hit with his slingshot.
- It's like in the other stories. He saw the *consequences* of what he did to a living thing.

The children who had read *Fox in a Trap* (Thomas, 1987) compared it to *The Sparrow's Song*:

- Daniel [in *Fox in a Trap*] thinks it would be so great to trap foxes and hunt bears with his uncle. But *then* when he finds out the bait is little kittens, he gets really upset. And when he *sees* his uncle kill a fox they trapped, he gets *sick*!
- I think the change came when he realized he really *cared* about animals and couldn't stand to see them in pain or killed.
- I liked the part when he goes out alone at night to spring all the traps.
- That's like when Charles threw away the slingshot. You just *know* they have a different attitude now.
- It's kind of like that boy in *The Biggest Bear* [Ward, 1952]. At first he wanted to shoot a bear to show off a bearskin but then he found a little bear cub and makes him a pet. So he changes his mind about shooting bears!
- In *The Cry of the Crow* [George, 1980] a girl takes care of an orphan crow but then she doesn't want to let it go free. She wants to keep it as a pet.
- Those stories are alike. The bear got huge and was eating all the food and crops. So the boy had to get rid of it. And the crow got bigger and tried to *hurt* the girl's brother because *he* was the one who shot the crow parents. So, she had to *kill* her pet to save her brother.
- At the end of that story she seemed a lot more grown up. She realized how selfish she had been to keep him a pet.

- But *The Biggest Bear* has a different ending. The boy doesn't *have* to kill the bear because the zoo people take it. So it's a happy ending for younger kids to read. But the crow book is for *older* kids. Mandy really has to shoot her pet. It's so sad. But you know she *has* to do it to save her brother.

The Fisherman and the Bird (Levitin, 1982) was identified as another story in which a central character changes because of a bird. Rico the fisherman chose to live a solitary life until a large rare bird builds a nest on the mast of his boat. The village teacher convinces Rico not to destroy the nest but to allow the bird and its mate to hatch their eggs there. As Rico guards the nest the villagers join him. He begins to care about the bird and to enjoy the company of the villagers. On the last page of the story Rico sings with happiness, and the artist shows him smiling for the very first time.

The Boy Who Held Back the Sea (Locker and Hort, 1987) is an unusual retelling of the famous story of the Dutch boy who held his finger in the dike and saved Holland from a flood. The children who read this new version of an old story were especially impressed by Thomas Locker's striking paintings which reflect the influence of the great Dutch masters. One third-grade boy wrote in his journal:

Last summer I went to Holland with my Mom and Dad to visit my Aunt. And we went to a very large museum. And we saw paintings just like the ones in this book!

In response to this entry the teacher brought in a book of Dutch paintings so the class could see the works of Rembrandt and Vermeer, the Dutch masters who apparently inspired Locker as he created the illustrations for this remarkable picture book. The children were also interested in the significant difference between Lenny Hort's retelling and earlier adaptations of this legend first told by Mary Mapes Dodge over a hundred years ago.

- Mr. Hort made the Dutch boy a dynamic character in this story. In the other one, the boy doesn't change.
- This one is sort of like "The Boy Who Cried Wolf" because no one believed him about the hole in the dike because he was *always* telling lies. Then he changed in the end.

In *A Toad for Tuesday* (Erickson, 1974) Warton the Toad is captured by an owl who plans to eat him on Tuesday, his birthday. While waiting for Tuesday to arrive, the owl learns to care about Warton and to enjoy his company. He discovers he'd rather have him as a friend than as a meal. The owl learns what it means to have a friend and to be a friend in this suspenseful and humorous animal tale.

As the story unfolded, the children were able to identify the subtle clues which foreshadowed the owl's remarkable metamorphosis. Several children compared it to *We'll Have a Friend for Lunch* (Flory, 1974) in which a group of cats observe a family of robins they plan to have for lunch. As they watch, the five eggs hatch and the mother and father care for their babies, and the cats begin to care about the robin family. In the end, they decide not to eat them. "We can't eat a family we *know*" (p. 29).

A Bundle of Sticks (Mauser, 1987), selected by a number of older readers, is the story of Ben Tyler who is threatened by the class bully and sent to a martial arts school to learn the art of kajukenbo. By the end of the book Ben has gained the insight necessary to grasp the meaning of the words of Sifu, his teacher:

Kajukenbo is something you wear inside of you, not around your waist. The cloth is only a symbol. . . . What you know of yourself is more important than what anyone else thinks (p. 68).

By the time he had completed the physical tests required to achieve the Purple Belt, Ben was filled with pride and self-respect. He knew this belt was "a symbol of what you wear inside" (p. 167). He had learned about different kinds of strength and discovered his own inner strength as an individual who hates the idea of fighting "but could do it if he had to" (p. 167). The children identified Ben as a dynamic character who "changed inside *and* outside."

They contrasted this thoughtful and realistic tale with Lois Duncan's *Wonder Kid Meets the Evil Lunch Snatcher*,[1] another story about a bully. Four of his victims collaborate to create and carry out a plan to frighten the bully. The problem is solved with a great deal of imagination and humor. However, the central character does not show any real growth and was not identified by the children as a dynamic character.

Sarah, Plain and Tall (MacLachlan, 1985) is a gentle, sensitive tale about Sarah who answers an ad in the paper for a wife; leaves her home in Maine; and travels to the prairie home of Papa, Anna, and Caleb for a trial visit. As they adjust to each other and learn to love and trust one another all four of these central characters change. One young reader commented that the story "started out with four separate people and ended with a family!" This comment drew attention to the kind of change associated with the growth of human relationships.

Stories about the building of friendships were frequently selected for independent reading by third- and fourth-graders. They observed that individual growth was generally necessary for establishing and nurturing a long-term friendship. In *Teacher's Pet* (Hurwitz, 1988) Cricket eventually gains significant insight about herself as she begins to see herself through the eyes of others. This perspective enables her to let go of her competitive attitude and her attempts to prove her superiority and gain approval which have contributed to her rejection by her peers. She learns to respect and appreciate the talents of a new classmate instead of feeling threatened by her. This change in Cricket allows her to enter into more enjoyable social interactions and opens the way for establishing a friendship with the new student, Zoe.

All the children were familiar with *Charlotte's Web* (White, 1952) and were able to identify Wilbur the pig as the dynamic character in this remarkable story.

- At first he's just a baby and only thinks about food. But then he starts to think about Charlotte and her babies and he acts like a grown up.
- At the end he sounds sort of like Charlotte.

A few of the children saw the connection between this and the friendship stories mentioned above. They noted that having a devoted friend like Charlotte enabled Wilbur to *become* a devoted friend, and to develop the dependability, steadfastness, and caring associated with friendship. Others compared Wilbur to the princess in *Prince Sparrow*. Both characters started out as immature and self-centered, and gradually matured as they began to care about others and to assume the responsibilities of a caring relationship.

[1]Lois Duncan. *Wonder Kid Meets the Evil Lunch Snatcher*. Boston: Little, Brown, 1988.

E. B. White has provided us with a fine example of the dynamic character. Wilbur's growth occurs gradually, and the change from the immature, self-centered piglet described in the first pages to the mature, responsible, thoughtful character we see at the end of the narrative is convincing and believable. Wilbur is one of those memorable characters developed in the classics, books that continue to be read because of their enduring interest and appeal.

As new dynamic character stories were identified and added to the collection the children were reinforcing their understanding of the meaning of the literary term, "dynamic character." Most of the children were developing the habit of searching for evidence of change in a particular character and clues about the reasons for and nature of the change. They were making inferences about the inner lives of central characters and about the "inside transformation" that distinguishes the dynamic character from the static character, the one who does not change or grow in the course of the narrative sequence.

TEACHERS AND STUDENTS AS LEARNERS

The central question which guided the planning, implementation, and evaluation of this two-part unit was: To what extent will the study of a literary motif, transformation, found in traditional and modern stories, enhance the quality of a child's response to more complex narratives featuring "dynamic characters"? Oral and written responses to the stories read aloud and independently over the course of this extensive literary experience, provided ample evidence that the literary background developed during the cumulative dialogue in the group sessions did, indeed, enrich the children's subsequent responses to more complex texts. For example, their discovery of the difference between "outside" and "inside" transformation provided them with the conceptual framework to explore the idea of the "dynamic character." They had begun to develop the language necessary to engage in literary analysis. Their oral and written comments suggested that most of the children had internalized the basic questioning strategies demonstrated in group sessions. This was revealed in their inferences about the internal responses of a central character and their search for evidence of transformation in that character. Highlighting the idea of change and growth in diverse story characters seemed to help the children focus on and understand distinguishing features of the dynamic character, and to enable them to identify dynamic characters in relatively complex narratives.

The narrative writing of many of the older children also reflected an understanding of and interest in the dynamic character. Their narratives suggested that they were learning to "read like writers to become writers" (Smith, 1984). They were becoming increasingly aware of the author's craft and were acquiring from these literary texts the knowledge that writers require. By building up a background of writer's knowledge they were enhancing their literary appreciation, as well as the quality of their own writing.

The teacher and students were engaged as active learners in the context of this Transformation Focus Unit. The teacher learned about her students as meaning-makers and found evidence to support the notion that selected literary experiences have the potential to enhance the quality of students' transactions with and responses to literary texts. The students learned about literature and acquired new strategies for generating meanings as thoughtful readers and writers.

References

Chomsky, Noam. "Language and Mind." *Psychology Today*, 2, 1968, pp. 280–286.

Goodman, Yetta. "Kidwatching: Observing Children in the Classroom." *Observing the Language Learner*, Angela Jagger and M. Trika Smith-Burke, eds. Newark, DE: IRA and Urbana, IL: NCTE, 1985, pp. 9–18.

Hansen, Jane. *When Writers Read*. Portsmouth, N.H.: Heinemann, 1987.

Hepler, Susan I., and Janet Hickman. "'The Book Was Okay. I Love You'—Social Aspects of Response to Literature." *Theory into Practice*, 21, 1982, pp. 278–283.

Hickman, Janet. "Children's Response to Literature: What Happens in the Classroom." *Language Arts*, vol. 57, no. 5, May 1980, pp. 524–529.

———. "A New Perspective in Response to Literature: Research in an Elementary School Setting." *Research in the Teaching of English*, 15, 1981, pp. 343–354.

Newkirk, Thomas, and Nancie Atwell. *Understanding Writing: Ways of Observing, Learning and Teaching*, 2nd ed. Portsmouth, N.H.: Heinemann, 1988.

Odell, Lee. "Planning Classroom Research." *Reclaiming the Classroom—Teacher Research as an Agency for Change*, Dixie Goswami and Peter Stillman, eds. Upper Montclair, N.J.: Boynton Cook, 1987, pp. 128–160.

Piaget, Jean. *The Origins of Intelligence in Children*. N.Y.: International Universities Press, 1952.

Rosenblatt, Louise. *The Reader, the Text and the Poem*. Carbondale, IL: Southern Illinois University Press, 1978.

Smith, Frank. "Reading Like a Writer." *Composing and Comprehending*, Julie Jensen, ed. Urbana, IL: ERIC, NCRE, 1984, pp. 47–56.

Vygotsky, Lev S. *Thought and Language*. Cambridge, MA: MIT Press, 1962.

Bibliography of Transformation Tales

Andersen, Hans Christian, Anthea Bell, trans. *The Swineherd*. Lisbeth Zwerger, illus. Morrow, 1982.

———. *The Ugly Duckling*, R. P. Keigwin, trans., Johannes Larsen, illus. N.Y.: Macmillan, 1967.

———. *The Wild Swans*. Marcia Brown, illus. Scribner's, 1963.

Bang, Molly. *Tye May and the Magic Brush*. N.Y.: Greenwillow, 1981.

Barber, Antonia. *The Enchanter's Daughter*. N.Y.: Farrar, Straus & Giroux, 1988.

Bomans, Godfried. "Maraboe and Morsegat." *The Wily Witch and All the Other Fairy Tales and Fables*. Owings Mills, MD: Stemmer House, 1977.

Brown, Marcia. *Once a Mouse . . . A Fable Cut in Wood*. N.Y.: Scribner's, 1961.

Cohen, Caron Lee. *The Mud Pony*. N.Y.: Scholastic, 1988.

Conover, Chris, reteller. *The Wizard's Daughter—A Viking Legend*. Boston: Little, Brown, 1984.

Cooney, Barbara, reteller. *Little Brother and Little Sister* (Grimm tale). Garden City, N.Y.: Doubleday, 1982.

Coville, Bruce, and Katherine Coville. *The Foolish Giant*. Philadelphia: Lippincott, 1978.

Craig, M. Jean, reteller. *The Donkey Prince* (Grimm tale). Garden City, N.Y.: Doubleday, 1977.

D'Aulnoy, Marie C. *The White Cat and Other Old French Fairy Tales*. Rachel Field, trans., Elizabeth MacKinstry, illus. N.Y.: Macmillan, 1928, 1967.

Eichenberg, Fritz, reteller. *Poor Troll—The Story of Ruebezahl and the Princess*. Owings Mills, MD: Stemmer House, 1983.

Gág, Wanda, trans. *Jorinda & Joringel*. N.Y.: Coward, McCann & Geoghegan, 1978.

Gerstein, Mordicai. *Prince Sparrow*. N.Y.: Four Winds Press, 1984.

Goble, Paul. *The Girl Who Loved Wild Horses*. Scarsdale: Bradbury, 1978.

Godden, Rumer, reteller. *The Old Woman Who Lived in a Vinegar Bottle*. N.Y.: Viking, 1970.

Grimm, Jacob, and Wilhelm Grimm. "The Frog Prince." *Favorite Fairy Tales Told in Germany*. Virginia Haviland, reteller. Boston: Little, Brown, 1959.

——. *Snow White and Rose Red*. Adrienne Adams, illus. N.Y.: Scribner's, 1964.

——. *King Grisly-Beard*. Edgar Taylor, trans., Maurice Sendak, illus. N.Y.: Farrar, Straus & Giroux, 1973.

——. *The Frog Prince*. Paul Goldone, adaptor and illus. N.Y.: McGraw-Hill, 1975.

——. *King Thrushbeard*. Felix Hoffman, illus. N.Y.: Harcourt, Brace and World, 1969.

——. *The Seven Ravens*. Elizabeth D. Crawford, trans., Lisbeth Zwerger, illus. N.Y.: Morrow, 1981.

——. *The Three Feathers*. Mankato, MI: Creative Education, 1984.

——. *Wanda Gág's The Six Swans*. Wanda Gág, reteller, Margot Tomes, illus. N.Y.: Coward, McCann & Geoghegan, 1982.

Hastings, Selina, reteller and illus. *The Singing Ringing Tree*. N.Y.: Henry Holt, 1988.

Hogrogian, Nonny, reteller and illus. *The Glass Mountain*. N.Y.: Knopf, 1985.

Isele, Elizabeth, reteller. *The Frog Princess*. N.Y.: Crowell, 1984.

Lang, Andrew, reteller. "The Enchanted Fish." *The Orange Fairy Book*. Andrew Lang, compiler. N.Y.: Random House, 1964.

Langton, Jane, reteller. *The Hedgehog Boy—A Latvian Folktale*. Harper, 1985.

Laurin, Anne. *Perfect Crane*. N.Y.: Harper, 1981.

Mayer, Marianna, reteller. *Beauty and the Beast*. Mercer Mayer, illus. N.Y.: Four Winds, 1978.

McDermott, Gerald, adaptor. *The Stonecutter: A Japanese Folktale*. Viking, 1975.

Otsuka, Yuzo, reteller. *Suho and the White Horse* (Mongolia). N.Y.: Viking, 1981.

Oxenbury, Helen. *Pig Tale*. N.Y.: Morrow, 1973.

Pearce, Phillipa, reteller. *Beauty and the Beast*. Alan Barrett, illus. N.Y.: Crowell, 1972.

Peet, Bill. *Big Bad Bruce*. Boston: Houghton Mifflin, 1977.

Severo, Emoke dePapp, trans. *The Good-Heartest Youngest Brother—An Hungarian Folktale*. Scarsdale, N.Y.: Bradbury, 1981.

Snyder, Zilpha. *The Changing Maze*, Charles Mikolaycak, illus. N.Y.: Macmillan, 1985.

Steig, William. *Caleb and Kate*. N.Y.: Farrar, Straus & Giroux, 1977.

——. *Solomon the Rusty Nail*. N.Y.: Farrar, Straus & Giroux, 1985.

——. *Sylvester and the Magic Pebble*. N.Y.: Simon and Schuster, 1969.

Tripp, Wallace, adaptor. *The Tale of a Pig: A Caucasian Folktale*. N.Y.: McGraw-Hill, 1968.

Turkle, Brinton. *Do Not Open*. N.Y.: Dutton, 1981.

Wetterer, Margaret. *The Mermaid's Cape*. N.Y.: Atheneum, 1982.

Winter, Jeanette, reteller. *The Magic Ring—A Tale by the Brothers Grimm*. N.Y.: Knopf, 1987.

Yagawa, Sumiko, reteller. *The Crane Wife*. Katherine Paterson, trans. N.Y.: Morrow, 1981.

Yashima, Taro. *Crow Boy*. N.Y.: Viking, 1955.

Yolen, Jane. *Greyling—A Picture Story from the Islands of Shetland*. William Stobbs, illus. N.Y.: Collins World, 1968.

——. *The Simple Prince*. N.Y.: Parents' Magazine Press, 1978.

"Dynamic Character" Stories

Alexander, Lloyd. *The Four Donkeys*. N.Y.: Holt, Rinehart and Winston, 1972.

Callen, Larry. *Dashiel and the Night*. N.Y.: Dutton, 1981.

Cameron, Ann. *Julian's Glorious Summer*. N.Y.: Random House, 1987.

Carrick, Carol. *Dark and Full of Secrets*. N.Y.: Clarion, 1984.

——. *What a Wimp!* N.Y.: Clarion, 1983.

Christopher, Matt. *The Hit-Away Kid*. Boston: Little, Brown, 1988.
Cleary, Beverly. *Dear Mr. Henshaw*. N.Y.: Morrow, 1983.
Crofford, Emily. *A Matter of Pride*. Minneapolis: Carolrhoda, 1981.
Erickson, Russell E. *A Toad for Tuesday*. N.Y.: Lothrop, Lee & Shepard, 1974.
Flory, Jane. *We'll Have a Friend for Lunch*. Boston: Houghton Mifflin, 1974.
George, Jean. *The Cry of the Crow*. N.Y.: Harper, 1980.
Hewitt, Kathryn, reteller and illus. *King Midas and the Golden Touch* (Nathaniel Hawthorne). N.Y.: Harcourt Brace Jovanovich, 1987.
Hughes, Shirley. *Alfie Gives a Hand*. N.Y.: Lothrop, Lee & Shepard, 1983.
Hurwitz, Johanna. *Teacher's Pet*. N.Y.: Morrow, 1988.
————. *Tough-Luck Karen*. N.Y.: Morrow, 1982.
Keats, Ezra Jack. *Peter's Chair*. N.Y.: Harper, 1967.
Levitin, Sonia. *The Fisherman and the Bird*. Boston: Houghton Mifflin, 1982.
Lexau, Joan. *Benjie*. N.Y.: Dial, 1964.
Lifton, Betty Jean. *Good Night Orange Monster*. N.Y.: Atheneum, 1972.
Locker, Thomas, illus. *The Boy Who Held Back the Sea*, Lenny Hort, reteller, Mary Mapes Dodge, adapter of *Hans Brinker, or the Silver Skates*, 1865. N.Y.: Dial, 1987.
MacLachlan, Patricia. *Sarah, Plain and Tall*. N.Y.: Harper, 1985.
Mauser, Pat Rhoads. *A Bundle of Sticks*. N.Y.: Macmillan, 1987 [1982].
Ness, Evaline. *Sam, Bangs and Moonshine*. N.Y.: Holt, Rinehart and Winston, 1973.
Norris, Gunilla. *The Friendship Hedge*. N.Y.: Dutton, 1973.
Paterson, Katherine. *Bridge to Terabithia*. N.Y.: Crowell, 1977.
————. *The Great Gilly Hopkins*. N.Y.: Crowell, 1978.
Preston, Edna Mitchell. *Squawk to the Moon, Little Goose*. N.Y.: Viking, 1974.
Rylant, Cynthia. *Miss Maggie*. N.Y.: Dutton, 1983.
Steig, William. *The Real Thief*. N.Y.: Farrar, Straus & Giroux, 1973.
Steptoe, John. *Stevie*. N.Y.: Harper, 1969.
Thomas, Jane Resh. *Fox in a Trap*. N.Y.: Clarion, 1987.
Uchida, Yoshika. *A Jar of Dreams*. N.Y.: Atheneum, 1981.
Wallace, Ian. *The Sparrow's Song*. N.Y.: Viking Kestrel, 1986.
Ward, Lynd. *The Biggest Bear*. Boston: Houghton Mifflin, 1952.
White, E. B. *Charlotte's Web*. N.Y.: Harper, 1952.

FOUR

Baba Yaga Tales:
Comprehension to Composition

READING AND WRITING RELATIONSHIPS

Literacy learning is supported in a classroom in which the language arts are integrated. The focus of this chapter is on the interrelationships between reading and writing in the context of a Focus Unit featuring Baba Yaga, a unique witch character found in Russian folklore.

Recent research has demonstrated that reading and writing are complementary and inter-related processes. Both readers and writers engage in a composing process and share a common goal: to construct a coherent text (Jensen, 1984, p. 2). Many of the reading/writing studies have highlighted the significant influence of reading experiences on writing ability. After reviewing the findings from correlational and experimental studies of reading/writing relation-ships, Sandra Stotsky, writing consultant, concluded that ". . . it is possible that reading experiences may be as critical a factor in developing writing ability as writing instruction itself" (1983, p. 637).

Stotsky examined a four-year longitudinal study in which the composition skills of fourth-graders improved significantly as a result of a program of listening to or reading and then discussing children's literature (Mills, 1974). In a study of language acquisition in children between the ages of six and ten Carol Chomsky, researcher in language development (1972), found a strong correlation between children's exposure to written language and the rate of linguistic development. Chomsky concluded, "The child who reads (or listens to) a variety of rich and complex materials benefits from a range of linguistic inputs that is unavailable to the nonliterary child" (p. 23). Another study of the effects of children's reading on their writing revealed that second-graders' writing samples reflected the linguistic structures found in their basal readers (Eckhoff, 1983).

Frank Smith emphasizes that one learns to write by reading. The knowledge writers require resides in texts, so reading like a writer helps students build a background of writer's knowledge. As writers, students engage in the process of constructing their own texts and gain insights about the nature of written language which, in turn, enrich their subsequent reading experiences. There is a reciprocal relationship between comprehension and composing: One learns to write by reading; and one learns to read by writing.

THE BABA YAGA FOCUS UNIT

The unit described in this chapter was developed for eight-, nine-, and ten-year-old children, and has been adapted for use in a number of different classroom settings. Selected Russian folktales which included the Baba Yaga character were introduced to the children in these classrooms. This provided them with a literary background that served as a natural resource for composing their own narratives about this fascinating witch. The teacher's questions in the initial sessions were designed to draw attention to the rich language, story patterns, and motifs found in traditional literature and to demonstrate how to read like a writer. As children acquired this writer's knowledge, both their comprehension and composition of literary texts improved.

Session One

The folktale *Baba Yaga* (Small, 1966) was selected to introduce the Focus Unit to a third-grade class during the first group read-aloud session. After hearing this tale the children were invited to compare Baba Yaga with other witches they had encountered in previous literary experiences. Initially, the children identified specific similarities but soon focussed their attention on contrasting features which rendered Baba Yaga a unique story character. One child's comment illustrates the adjustment of her existing schema about witches to include this character: "Baba Yaga certainly isn't a *generic brand* of witch! She doesn't do what you expect a witch to do! She's a different *kind* of witch."

The children noted that instead of riding on a broom Baba Yaga traveled in a mortar, propelled herself along with a pestle, and swept away her tracks with a broom. They were intrigued with Baba Yaga's peculiar code of ethics: Like other witches of traditional folklore Baba Yaga is a cannibal witch who specializes in devouring children; she is particularly interested in Russian children. In this story Baba Yaga carefully discriminated between good and bad children and had an appetite only for *bad* Russian children. The detailed description of Baba Yaga's house was the source of pleasant shivers and giggles: the revolving hut on chicken legs, surrounded by a fence of human bones and skulls; and inside, the Russian stove, the samovar, and the remarkable cabinet filled with herbs and berries for magic brews and potions.

Session Two

At the second story session the children were introduced to *Vasilisa the Beautiful* (Whitney, 1970), a Russian variant of "Cinderella" in which Baba Yaga is a key figure. During the discussion following the story the children identified the now familiar characteristics associated with Baba Yaga: her hut, her habits, her mode of travel, and even the content of her dialogues.

They found in this text further evidence of Baba Yaga's complex personality and her adherence to a code of justice in which good is rewarded and evil punished. Several children recognized other connections with previous literary experiences. Some noted, for example, that Baba Yaga's respect for the power of a mother's blessing called to mind Dracula's reaction to a crucifix or holy water. Others recognized the dark forest as a common setting for wicked witches in the story world. In response to this observation about story setting, the teacher shared the comments of the Russian historian, Vasily Kluchevsky.

The silence of the sleepy, dense forest frightened the Russian; it seemed to harbour something evil in the fearful, soundless twilight of its ancient summits. . . . (Riordan, 1976, p. 269)

Again, drawing from their prior knowledge or schemata associated with fairytales, the children recognized the elements in *Vasilisa the Beautiful* which connected it to "Cinderella": the jealous stepmother and stepsisters, the magic doll in the role of fairy godmother, the marriage to the king, and the "happily ever after" ending. By reading one text in light of another they enriched their transaction with the text.

The group discussions about stories in this Focus Unit provided models for transactions with texts. In addition, the dialogue helped to build a "community of readers" to serve as the social context for talking about stories and exploring meanings (Hepler and Hickman, 1982). Within this community of readers the children and teacher worked together to make connections between prior literary experiences and present ones. In the process they moved toward an understanding of the fundamental unity of literature. The sequence of story sessions provided opportunities for this "intertextual tying" (Harste, 1984) and for building a rich literary background.

Session Three

Before reading *The Frog Princess* (Isele, 1984) aloud the teacher asked the children to suggest another story this title called to mind. Several children were familiar with "The Frog Prince" (Grimm Brothers) and shared some of the details they remembered about this famous tale of transformation. Then, as *The Frog Princess* was read aloud, they made predictions based on their prior knowledge. The children listened to this complex tale unfold without further comment until they heard the words: "Much later, the golden ball stopped before a hut in the forest. It was a strange house built on chicken legs, and it turned round and round continually" (p. 27). Immediately, almost in unison, they called out: "It's Baba Yaga! She's in *this* story, too!" As soon as the story reached its conclusion the children were ready and anxious to engage in intertextual tying:

- This Baba Yaga helps Ivan just like in *Vasilisa*.
- And she sits on top of the stove just like in the first story.
- And there's another part that's the same. You know when the frog-princess kept saying to Ivan, "Go to sleep, the morning brings more wisdom than the evening." Well, in *Vasilisa*, the doll kept saying, "Go to sleep, things always look brighter in the morning."
- Another thing is the white horse that could fly. In the other two stories those flying horses were Baba Yaga's servants. In this story she gave the white horse to Ivan and Vasilisa.

- In this story it said that this Baba Yaga was the *oldest* one. So there must be other Baba Yagas in the Russian forest.
- Maybe the other stories are about her children and grandchildren.

The question, "Why do you think Baba Yaga decided to help Ivan instead of eating him?" was introduced to call attention to a distinguishing feature of the Baba Yaga character.

- She said she liked his spirit!
- Ivan acted very brave and strong and not like a wimp.
- He had spunk.
- I think if he was shaky and scared, she probably wouldn't like him and might of decided to eat him!

At the close of this session the illustrations in all three single editions were examined more closely and compared. The children uncovered fascinating individual differences among the three illustrators and discussed the way each set of illustrations reflected the unique interpretation of the artist.

Session Four

"The Firebird" (Higonnet-Schnopper, 1973) was introduced in the fourth group session. After listening to the long, complex tale of Ivan Tsarevich (Ivan the Tsar's son) and his quest for the firebird, the children listed the recurring patterns they had identified.

- The hut on chicken legs.
- And it turns round and round.
- And there's a poem they say to get it to stand still so they can go in.
- Baba Yaga sits on the stove.
- And there are three Baba Yagas. Remember in the other story it said there was more than one.
- There're three Baba Yaga sisters.
- And they all help him and they give him magic things.
- It was because this Ivan was just like the other Ivan [in *The Frog Princess*]. And I think the witches liked his spirit so they were nice to him.
- But he also prayed like Vasilisa did. That would protect him, too!

The teacher commented that this story was a good example of a quest tale and asked if anyone knew the meaning of the word *quest*. Since no one was familiar with this word, a dictionary was consulted. The phrases "to make a search" and "involving an adventurous journey" were selected as most appropriate for describing the story.

- Ivan made a search for the firebird because then he'd get the kingdom!
- And he certainly had a lot of adventures on his journey!

When asked to name another example of a quest tale several children identified the quest in *The Frog Princess*:

- When Ivan went off to search for his lost wife, that was the quest.
- And he went on a journey.
- And he meets an old man who gives him the golden ball.
- And then he meets the bear and the duck and the fish.
- And Baba Yaga!
- And then the next adventure is when he has to get rid of Old Koshchey. And those animals help him because he was nice to them.

Session Five

When "Ivan Young in Years, Old in Wisdom" (Riordan, 1976) was introduced in the fifth session, the children were asked to try to explain the meaning of the title.

- I bet it's another story about the *youngest* son!
- And he's going to be the smartest even though he's the youngest.
- He has wisdom—he's wise like an old man. But he's not *old*.

After the story was read aloud they noted that their predictions were accurate and that this was another example of a quest tale.

- Ivan—they really like that name in Russia!—had to go on a quest for the Harp, the Goose, and the Cat.
- And Baba Yaga and her sisters helped him just like in the other stories.
- That ball of yarn that he follows is just like that golden ball that the other Ivan [in *The Frog Princess*] followed!
- The *best* part was when he gets to the end of his quest and has to get the magic things from the Mountain Dragon.
- And it's her *son*. The dragon is Baba Yaga's son! What a weird family!
- But she helped him so the Dragon wouldn't eat him.
- I loved the part when Ivan and the dragon played cards, and the dragon says, "The winner eats the loser!"
- But I *knew* that it would end okay—because Ivan's the *hero*.

Session Six

After listening to *Anna and the Seven Swans* (Silverman, 1984) the children observed that this was another example of a quest tale.

- Anna had to go search for her baby brother, Ivan.
- Ivan, again!
- But you could tell the swans were going to steal him because the mom and dad *warned* Anna about Baba Yaga's swans! Also—on the front cover it shows the baby flying off on one of them [swans].
- This quest is like the one in *The Frog Princess* because everything Anna helps on her way,

helps *her* escape from Baba Yaga. Ivan [in *The Frog Princess*] helped those animals on the way, and then later they helped him.

- But this Baba Yaga was different. She was *really* wicked. She was really going to *eat* little Ivan!
- And the swans were different too. They were kidnappers!
- They were working for Baba Yaga getting innocent kids for her dinner.
- She's like those witches in most other stories.

When asked to find other significant differences between this tale and the Baba Yaga tales presented in previous sessions, the children focussed on other characters.

- This time it's a girl who goes on a quest.
- And she's just ordinary. The others were usually princes or at least they ended up marrying a princess.
- Vasilisa married a king. She went on a quest—to get the light from Baba Yaga.
- Anna had a regular family. And the happy ending was that they all got together again instead of getting married at the end.
- She was younger than the others. She wouldn't get married yet!
- She's sort of like Marusia in the first Baba Yaga story. She's just ordinary, too, and the ending is the same. She gets back with her family safe and sound.

Session Seven

The front cover of *Bony-Legs* (Cole, 1983) elicited a number of comments before this easy-to-read adaptation was read aloud in the seventh session. The children appreciated the artist's details on the cover: the hut on chicken legs, the dense forest, the bats, the curtains decorated with skulls and flowers, and Baba Yaga herself grinning out at them.

They decided that the author had used the name "Bony-Legs" to refer to Baba Yaga because these were the words used by other storytellers to describe this distinctive Russian witch. After listening to the story the children immediately pointed out the similarities between Anna in *Anna and the Seven Swans* and Sasha in this story. Both were ordinary girls whose acts of kindness were repaid during their attempts to escape from Baba Yaga. They compared Sasha to Marusia in the first Baba Yaga story: both girls had been sent on an errand and had encountered Baba Yaga when they entered the forest.

They also noticed the connection between *Bony-Legs* and "The Firebird":

- They both got magic objects that changed into things to help them escape. Like the mirror changed into a lake, and the comb got like a big tree fence. And in "The Firebird" the boot heel changed into a mountain, and the comb turned into a dense forest, and the brush changed to a fiery river.
- But in that story Ivan got the magic things from the three Baba Yagas.

Several children noted with interest that this was the only story that started out with an introduction to Baba Yaga on the first page. After some discussion they reached the conclusion that the other stories were better:

- I think it was better when you didn't *know* when Baba Yaga was going to appear in the story.
- It was more suspenseful that way.
- And you didn't know if she was going to be the evil Baba Yaga or the one who helps the good people.

The group discussions, which were such an integral part of these story sessions, served as oral rehearsals for written responses to independent reading experiences by suggesting ways to interact with texts and to read new texts in light of previous texts. Students' oral responses revealed that they were learning to read like writers and to focus on the author's craft. Thus, the group discussions prepared them for composing their own narratives. Independent reading and writing activities followed these story sessions featuring Baba Yaga.

INDEPENDENT READING AND WRITING

Other tales in which Baba Yaga plays a role were collected and placed on a display table in the classroom along with the seven tales which had been read aloud (*see* bibliography of Baba Yaga tales at the end of this chapter). The children were invited to select at least one of the new tales for independent reading and to record their interpretations and reactions in their Literature Journal. This Literature Journal was a spiral notebook given to each child to record individual responses to literary experiences over the course of the school year. The teacher responded to Journal entries with comments or questions, so that a written conversation or dialogue between the teacher and the student was established. The content of these Journal entries varied according to the interests, experiences, and style of each journalist. Most of the children made use of the oral discussions as models for written responses. For example, almost all the children included comparisons between the Baba Yaga tales and other stories in their literary background (*see* Chapter 9 for a discussion of literary dialogue-journals).

Although the children were expected to read only one story independently most decided to read additional tales recommended by their peers. Within this "community of readers" the children talked informally about what they had read, enthusiastically "selling" a favorite tale or sharing a new insight or discovery gleaned from it. The end result was extensive voluntary independent reading and requests for "more witch tales" or "another Cinderella tale from a different country" or "other stories about flying horses."

Sharing Independent Reading

After these independent reading and writing activities had been set into motion the children met as a group to share and compare their Baba Yaga stories and to discuss narrative elements, similarities and differences, literary connections, illustrations, interesting words and phrases, and Baba Yaga herself. For example, a boy who had read *Teeny-Tiny and the Witch Woman* (Walker, 1975) said:

- My story wasn't from Russia. It was from Turkey. But I think the witch could be Baba Yaga because she lived in a dark forest and her house had a bone fence—*little people* bones! And when she chased the children they threw down three magic objects to stop her just like in *Bony-Legs* and "The Firebird."

A child who had read "I-Know-Not-What of I-Know-Not-Where" (Downing, 1956) observed that the archer's wife, the Dove Maiden, gave the archer a golden ring which would lead straight to the object of his quest. The child compared this to the golden ball in *The Frog Princess* and the ball of yarn in "Ivan Young in Years, Old in Wisdom."

Another child who had read that story added, "She also gave him a ball of wool which leads him to her mother's house. Guess who? It's Baba Yaga! And then he says that magic formula so he can get inside: 'Izba, Izba! Turn thy door to me!' Remember in the first Baba Yaga story we read, she says 'Izbushka, Izbushka, lower your door to me!'"

A third child who had shared this and other stories with his grandfather contributed some interesting information to the group. He explained that his grandfather speaks Russian and translated the Russian words in this formula: "My grandpa said that 'Izba' means 'an old house' and that 'Izbushka' means a 'cute little house' or a 'cozy little house.' So I think the Baba Yaga in that story ["I-Know-Not-What of I-Know-Not-Where"] had a much bigger house than the other one."

A fourth child who had read the story made another interesting discovery. She noted that the archer's wife, the Dove Maiden, reassures her husband with the words: "Go to bed and rest now, for morning is wiser than evening" (Downing, 1956, p. 118). Later in this story Baba Yaga, the Dove Maiden's mother, says to her son-in-law: "But go now to sleep for the morning is wiser than evening" (p. 130). This child was very excited about finding another literary connection: "Remember when the Frog Princess kept saying that to her husband so he wouldn't be so worried! And the doll said it to Vasilisa when *she* was given those hard tasks!"

This discovery prompted a number of students to attempt to explain the meaning of the phrase and its repeated use by different storytellers. Some of the children connected it to the reassuring words of their own parents. One girl commented, "Whenever I'm feeling unhappy or mad, my mom always says, 'Well, go to sleep now. You're going to feel much better in the morning.'"

Several advanced readers discussed *The Dream Stealer* (Maguire, 1983) in this group session. This is an original tale drawn from the stories about Vasilisa the Beautiful and her magic doll, Baba Yaga, and the Firebird. The children shared many of the literary connections they had found in this magical story. It was obvious that they had enjoyed the process of intertextual tying. One child concluded that the author must have read all the Baba Yaga tales when *he* was in school and had been inspired to create a modern fantasy based on these Russian folk stories.

One student brought Jay Williams' modern fairytale, *The Silver Whistle*[1] to this sharing session. Most of the students in this group had been introduced to this story and others by Jay Williams the previous year as part of a Focus Unit on modern fairytales. The student was questioned about his choice of a story that did not seem to have any connection to the Baba

---

[1]Jay Williams. *The Silver Whistle*. N.Y.: Parents' Magazine Press, 1971 (unpaged text).

Yaga tales. In response he opened the book and read aloud that part of the story in which the heroine sets off to make her way in the world.

> She traveled for many a day and many a mile and at last she came to a house that stood on four legs in the middle of a wood. The house turned round to face her, and out came an old witch.

As soon as he read these lines his classmates responded as he had expected.

- That witch must be Baba Yaga!
- I never noticed that.
- Mr. Williams must have read the Baba Yaga tales, too, and then put her in one of his own stories.
- I think he must have read the ones about the evil Baba Yagas. *This* one sure isn't nice like a lot of the ones in the Russian tales.
- I bet that artist didn't know that the hut is supposed to be on *chicken* legs.
- But when you make up your own story or pictures you can do it however you want. You can use some of the ideas from the old stories and some of your own, too.

Descriptive Writing

Following this oral dialogue, which added to their growing store of "Baba Yaga knowledge," the children were asked to create word portraits of Baba Yaga in order to give them practice in descriptive writing. For these verbal portraits of Baba Yaga the children were encouraged to draw upon information they had gathered about her external features in order to generate a mental picture for potential readers who might be unfamiliar with her. The next step was to paint a portrait of Baba Yaga, using the verbal portrait as a guide for translating their words into another form of communication. Most of these young artists chose to include Baba Yaga's famous hut, her mortar and pestle, and her three horsemen.

An outgrowth of this "portrait project" was the production of Baba Yaga poems by those interested in experimenting with this form of written language. To provide some literary background for those engaged in this optional project, a number of "witch poems" were gathered from various collections of poetry. When the Baba Yaga poems were completed, they were mounted on the bulletin board along with the portraits. Arrangements were made to share this work with other classes in the school.

Analysis of Story Character—A Group Writing Project

The purpose of the next project was to give the children an opportunity to work together in small groups on another form of writing: an analysis of the story character, Baba Yaga. The preparatory or planning phase of this composing process involved gathering information about aspects of Baba Yaga's personality communicated explicitly or implicitly in the stories they had heard or read. This collection of ideas generated some lively debates as children argued over conflicting interpretations about this complex, many-sided character. They struggled to explain their views and to reach consensus in their attempts to classify Baba Yaga as either good or evil.

In these debates some children argued that Baba Yaga was really a good witch who assisted heroes and protected the innocent; they supported their arguments with excerpts from: "The Firebird" (Higonnet-Schnopper, 1973), *Vasilisa the Beautiful* (Whitney, 1970), "I-Know-Not-What of I-Know-Not-Where" (Downing, 1956), *Baba Yaga* (Small, 1966), and "Ivan Young in Years, Old in Wisdom" (Riordan, 1976).

On the other side were those who insisted that Baba Yaga was the personification of evil, typical of the tribe of malevolent witches found all over the world. To prove their case they cited *Anna and the Seven Swans* (Silverman, 1984), "Baba Yaga and the Little Girl with the Kind Heart" (Ransome, 1974), "The Black Geese" (Lurie, 1980), *Bony-Legs* (Cole, 1983), and "Marya Morevna" (Riordan, 1976) as examples of stories in which Baba Yaga is portrayed by the storyteller as a wicked old witch with no redeeming qualities.

Finally, one youngster observed, "Maybe Baba Yaga isn't good *or* bad, but both . . . sort of like people who sometimes act good and sometimes act bad." This contribution was shared with other groups and stimulated the children to move beyond their initial attempt to classify Baba Yaga as either good or evil and to view her as the complex, multidimensional character she has become through generations of retellings of traditional Russian tales.

With this new perspective, the children decided to compare those stories in which Baba Yaga appears in a helper role with those in which she is portrayed as destructive or evil. They noticed that in the latter stories Baba Yaga is generally not a well-developed character and, except for brief references to details such as the hut and mortar and her name, she appears to be almost synonymous with other witches in traditional literature. In contrast, in stories such as "The Firebird," *Vasilisa the Beautiful*, and "The Three Ivans," Baba Yaga is developed as a unique personality through dialogue, references to her family, and various descriptive details. In "The Firebird" the reader/listener is introduced to Baba Yaga's two sisters; in "I-Know-Not-What of I-Know-Not-Where" Baba Yaga reveals that the archer's wife is her daughter and welcomes him as her son-in-law; in "Ivan Young in Years, Old in Wisdom" Baba Yaga informs the hero that the Mountain Dragon is her nephew, the son of her eldest sister. The children also observed that Baba Yaga showed respect for hero characters who displayed boldness, self-confidence, and spirit; and she assisted them in their quests. In "The Three Ivans," for example, Baba Yaga responds to such a hero with the words: "Greetings, my hero, where would you go, and how can I serve you?" (Manning-Sanders, 1973, p. 71).

Thus, during the planning or prewriting phase of the composition process, the children pulled together relevant information and clarified their ideas in preparation for writing an analysis of the Baba Yaga character. The next step was to select a title which would provide a focus for their composition. The children in one group came up with the title "Who *Is* Baba Yaga?" This seemed to help them make the leap from talk to written language, and to focus on the development of structure and cohesion in their written texts (Rentel and King, 1983).

Members of this group decided to develop a brief outline to guide the composing process. This outline took shape as a series of key questions, which were later turned into topic sentences for each of the paragraphs of the essay. This approach parallels the strategy in which the reader turns a topic sentence into a question and then reads the paragraph to find the answer. As writers, these children used a similar strategy: They developed each paragraph as an explanation or elaboration of the topic sentence. The key questions were:

Who is Baba Yaga?
What does she look like?
Where does she live?
How does she travel?
How is she different from other witches?
Is she good or evil?
What kinds of things does she say?
What magic powers does she have?
Who are her relatives?
What opinions and attitudes does she have?

When the children composed their first drafts they reread and revised along the way. They worked together, striving to choose appropriate words and to develop logical connections between sentences and between paragraphs. They reexamined, added, deleted, and substituted words and phrases in their effort to produce meaningful and cohesive prose. They considered the evolving text in terms of intended meanings and their potential audience. When the members of this group were finally satisfied with their essay each child was given a copy of the final draft to keep in his/her folder of written work produced for the Baba Yaga Unit. Some of the groups borrowed this "key question" idea for composing their own analysis of Baba Yaga; other groups used different strategies.

The purpose of this group writing project was to provide all the students with an opportunity to engage in the process of composing expository prose and to discover ways of making meaning with this prose form.

Narrative Writing

Following this experience with the composing process in a group context, the children were asked to work independently on a final writing project for this Unit: the creation of a new story featuring Baba Yaga as a central character. By this time they had read and talked about the Baba Yaga tales sufficiently to develop a rich background for creating their original folktales.

Although this was an independent writing project it did involve a good deal of sharing and verbal interaction. Writing, like reading, occurred in a community context. In addition to informal and spontaneous interactions, more formal and planned "partner conferences" were established to insure that each writer enjoyed the feedback and support of a peer during the story-production process. Students shared their work with partners who functioned as critical readers/listeners; in turn, partners shared their writing with the first students who now assumed the role of readers/listeners. The purpose of these writer-reader partnerships was to allow writers to see their compositions through the eyes of others who would ask for clarification, focus on missing links, suggest improvements, laugh at the humor, or show appreciation for a good story. This helps writers to consider their potential audiences as they write, and to respond to their writing as critical readers. The partners worked together to revise and edit their respective narratives and provided mutual support throughout the composing process.

These excerpts taken from the introductory segments of narratives composed by third-grade students reflect their use of story language and patterns:

Baba Yaga and the Unicorn
by Jennifer

Once upon a time there lived a mean witch named Baba Yaga. One day she was flying in her mortar and pestle when she saw a gold and silver unicorn. So she landed in the woods and began to chase the unicorn.

Now this unicorn happened to belong to a little girl named Heather. Heather was playing in the woods when suddenly she saw her unicorn running and Baba Yaga running after her. Heather did not know what to do! She ran to her unicorn, but Baba Yaga saw her and caught her while she was running and immediately pushed her into the mortar and flew away. Before she knew it, Heather was outside a hut with chicken legs. . . .

Kim's Wish
by Kim

Once upon a time there was a little girl named Kim. One night her dad told her a story about Baba Yaga. Kim said to her dad, "I wish I could be *in* that story."

Well, in the middle of the night, there was a shooting star. And it turned into a woman. The star-woman went right to Kim's window and woke her up. Kim thought it was a dream, but it wasn't. The star-woman said, "I will grant you one wish." Kim said, "This is my chance! I wish to be in the Baba Yaga story." Then Kim got smaller and smaller. The next thing she knew she was in the book. She was walking in a dense forest. She saw a little *candy* house. "Oh, no," she said. "This is the wrong story!" So she walked and walked to a house on chicken legs. . . .

Baba Yaga and the Knights
by Tom

Once upon a time there was a party of knights. Their names were Sir Lancelot, Sir Galahad, and King Arthur. They were venturing into a dense forest in Russia. One day they came upon a hut on chicken legs. No sooner had they walked into the clearing than a black horseman flew by through the air. It was night and the knights knew that this was one of Baba Yaga's faithful servants. . . .

The Aunt Who Was a Witch
by Doris

Once upon a time there was a little girl who lived in a dense forest with her Aunt. Now her Aunt was really a witch who called herself Baba Yaga the Beautiful. Of course, she was really very ugly, but she thought the name would pull it off. Well, whenever Baba Yaga wanted to cast some spells, she sent her niece off to pick berries. But one day the little girl came back *very* quietly, and she heard her aunt singing, "Ruble, ruble, make my niece a lot of trouble." Then she knew her aunt was really a witch, and she became very frightened. . . .

When these original Baba Yaga tales were completed, they were illustrated, bound into individual books, and shared in the next group meeting. These stories were discussed in much the same way that published works had been discussed during previous story sessions. The children responded with appreciative comments about texts and illustrations, questions about confusing parts, comparisons with other literary selections, and analysis of literary elements. The teacher had prepared an environment in which these young authors knew their work was taken seriously.

COMMUNICATING THROUGH ART FORMS

To complete the Baba Yaga unit the children were invited to participate in various artistic experiences which would allow them to move from literature into drama, dance, music, and art. The children responded enthusiastically to the invitation and generated many ideas for small-group and individual projects. The Baba Yaga literature provided a natural stimulus for creative expression. It wasn't long before favorite story characters, episodes, and settings were recreated in paintings, murals, plays, a puppet show, and a dance-drama by these young artists, dancers, actors, actresses, and musicians.

COMPREHENSION AND COMPOSITION

The Baba Yaga Focus Unit provided a context in which reading, writing, speaking, and listening were allowed to interact, to complement, reinforce, and build on each other in a community of literary learners. In this context the children were given opportunities to learn to write by reading and to learn to read by writing. As they explored and accumulated literary ideas and insights, their capacity to comprehend, compose, appreciate, and enjoy literature expanded accordingly.

References

Chomsky, Carol. "Stages in Language Development and Reading Exposure." *Harvard Educational Review*, 42, 1972, pp. 1–33.

Eckhoff, Barbara. "How Reading Affects Children's Writing." *Language Arts*. vol. 60, no. 5, May 1983, pp. 607–616.

Harste, Jerome. "Cognitive Universals in Literacy and Literacy Learning: Toward Practical Theory." Presented at the Spring Conference on Teaching English and the Language Arts, Columbus, OH: April 14, 1984.

Hepler, Susan, and Janet Hickman. "The Book Was Okay. I Love You—Social Aspects of Response to Literature." *Theory into Practice*, vol. XXI, no. 4, Autumn 1982, pp. 278–283.

Jensen, Julie M., ed. *Composing and Comprehending*. Urbana, IL: ERIC and NCRE, 1984.

Mills, E. "Children's Literature and Teaching Written Composition." *Elementary English*, 51, 1974, pp. 971–973.

Rentel, Victor, and Martha King. "Present at the Beginning." *Research on Writing—Principles and Methods*. Peter Mosenthal, Lynne Tamor, and Sean Walmsley, eds. N.Y.: Longman, 1983.

Smith, Frank. "Reading Like a Writer." *Composing and Comprehending*. Julie Jensen, ed. Urbana, IL: ERIC and NCRE, 1984, pp. 47–56.

Stotsky, Sandra. "Research on Reading/Writing Relationships: A Synthesis and Suggested Directions." *Language Arts*, vol. 60, no. 3, May 1983, pp. 627–642.

Bibliography of Baba Yaga Tales

Afanas'ev, Aleksandr, collector. *Russian Fairy Tales*. "Baba Yaga and the Brave Youth," pp. 76–79; "Baba Yaga," pp. 194–195; "The Three Kingdoms," pp. 49–53; "The Maiden Tsar," pp. 229–234;

"Prince Danila Govorila," pp. 351–356; "Baba Yaga," pp. 363–365; "King Bear," pp. 393–398; "The Sea King and Vasilisa the Wise," pp. 427–437; "Go I Know Not Wither, Bring Back I Know Not What," pp. 504–520; "Maria Morevna," pp. 553–562; "Ilya Muromets and the Dragon," pp. 569–575. N.Y.: Pantheon, 1945.

Buck, Pearl S., ed. *Fairy Tales of the Orient.* "The Death of Koschei the Deathless," pp. 35–46. NY: Simon and Schuster, 1965.

Carey, Bonnie, adaptor and trans. *Baba Yaga's Geese and Other Russian Stories.* "Baba Yaga's Geese," pp. 92–95. Bloomington: Indiana University Press, 1973.

Cole, Joanna. *Bony-Legs* (easy-to-read adaptation). N.Y.: Four Winds, 1983.

Dolch, Edward. *Stories from Old Russia.* "Vasilisa the Beautiful," pp. 99–107; "The Hut of Baba Yaga," pp. 109–113; "Vasilisa Gets Fire," pp. 115–119; "Shirts for the Tsar," pp. 121–129. Champaign, IL: Garrard, 1964.

Downing, Charles, reteller. *Russian Tales and Legends.* "I-Know-Not-What of I-Know-Not-Where," pp. 116–137. London: Oxford University Press, 1956.

Fenner, Phyllis, selector. *Giants and Witches and a Dragon or Two.* "Baba Yaga," pp. 79–92. N.Y.: Knopf, 1943.

Haviland, Virginia, reteller. *Favorite Fairy Tales Told in Russia.* "Vasilisa the Beautiful," pp. 20–42. Boston: Little, Brown, 1961.

Higonnet-Schnopper, Janet, compiler. *Tales from Atop a Russian Stove.* "The Firebird," pp. 93–108. Chicago: Albert Whitman, 1973.

Hoke, Helen, selector. *Witches, Witches, Witches.* "Baba Yaga and the Girl with the Kind Heart," pp. 19–30. N.Y.: Franklin Watts, 1958.

Isele, Elizabeth, reteller. *The Frog Princess.* Michael Hague, illus. N.Y.: Crowell, 1984.

Lurie, Alison, reteller. *Clever Gretchen and Other Forgotten Folktales.* "The Black Geese," pp. 17–22. Crowell, 1980.

Maguire, Gregory. *The Dream Stealer.* N.Y.: Harper, 1983.

Manning-Sanders, Ruth. *A Book of Sorcerers and Spells.* "The Three Ivans," pp. 69–90. N.Y.: Dutton, 1973.

Ponsot, Marie, trans. *Russian Fairy Tales.* Benvenuti, illus. "Vasilisa the Beautiful," pp. 21–30; "Maria Marina," pp. 51–64. N.Y.: Golden Press, 1960.

Ransome, Arthur. *Old Peter's Russian Tales.* "Baba Yaga and the Little Girl with the Kind Heart," pp. 68–80. Baltimore: Penguin, 1974.

Riordan, James, reteller. *Tales from Central Russia—Russian Tales, volume one.* "Fair Vasilisa and Baba Yaga," pp. 11–19; "Fenist the Bright-Eyed Falcon," pp. 63–72; "Marya Morevna," pp. 148–160; "The Swan Geese," pp. 175–178; "Ivan Young in Years, Old in Wisdom," pp. 213–221; "The Archer Who Went I Know Not Where to Fetch I Know Not What," pp. 243–261. Hammondsworth: Kestrel Books, 1976.

Silverman, Maida, reteller. *Anna and the Seven Swans.* N.Y.: Morrow, 1984.

Small, Ernest, reteller. *Baba Yaga.* Boston: Houghton Mifflin, 1966.

Walker, Barbara. *Teeny-Tiny and the Witch Woman.* Michael Foreman, illus. N.Y.: Pantheon, 1975.

Whitney, Thomas, trans. *In a Certain Kingdom—Twelve Russian Fairy Tales.* "Marya Moryevna," pp. 107–120. N.Y.: Macmillan, 1972.

Whitney, Thomas, reteller. *Vasilisa the Beautiful.* N.Y.: Macmillan, 1970.

FIVE

Devil Tales:
Inquiry and Discovery

INQUIRY AND DISCOVERY

The work of developmental and cognitive theorists has provided a rationale for classrooms in which learners are at the center of the learning process, actively making sense of the world, seeking answers to their questions, and constructing meanings for themselves. Exploration, inquiry, and discovery are central strategies for learning in these classrooms. Listening, talking, reading, and writing are processes of meaning construction and serve as vehicles for building understanding and creating knowledge.

The Focus Unit model is designed to support active, independent learning. Teachers prepare the environment by bringing literature into the classroom and sharing it with their students. Students are encouraged to respond to literary texts as individuals and to draw from their prior knowledge and past experiences, their present interests and viewpoints as they engage in the process of constructing meaning. Literature serves as a springboard for exploration and inquiry. Students are encouraged to generate questions, to search for answers, to define and solve problems, and to experiment with different ways of interpreting literary selections by using different communication systems such as language, art, music, and drama. The spirit of curiosity is cultivated in this environment; the question is viewed as the starting point for learning. Each learner embarks on a personal journey of inquiry and discovery within a broader context of social interaction, a critical feature of the learning environment which supports the learning process.

THE DEVIL TALE FOCUS UNIT

The description of the devil tale Focus Unit highlights students' use of exploration, inquiry, and discovery as central strategies for learning. Devils come in all shapes and sizes and vary widely in their personality traits and behaviors. Because of this interesting diversity and the wide array of traditional and modern devil tales available in collections and single illustrated editions, the study of devil characters was chosen as the focus of a literature unit which would activate the spirit of curiosity and invite inquiry.

Students in various intermediate classrooms were invited to explore "devil literature," to generate questions, meanings, interpretations, and insights; to draw conclusions; and to move toward synthesis. As students explored the devil tales and engaged in inquiry and discovery, they gained experience as students of literature and as thoughtful readers and writers.

The Devil Tales

Devils appear in folktales and legends around the world, although storytellers in different countries have not necessarily agreed on the nature and distinguishing features of these supernatural characters. Dorothy Spicer, folklore specialist, introduces her collection of devil tales in this way:

> Everyone has his own notion about Devils. Once, when I was a child, a dear old friend told me of the *personal* Devil who plagues everyone. Then I was puzzled, but now I know what he meant. He was referring to the contrary spirit within that makes us do this, or say that—although we know very well it's horrid and mean.
>
> In the popular belief of every country, Devils and demons and wicked imps stand for the evil within man's heart. These creatures are servants of the Master Devil, the Prince of Hell, who sends them swarming over earth. They tempt man who, from greed for gold, lust for power, or some desperate need, makes a pact and promises his soul—*for a price* (1967, p. 6).

Some storytellers use the word "devil" to refer to an ogre, a creature with a taste for human flesh. For other storytellers the devil is connected to Satan, the devil of Christian theology. Devil characters, as collectors of souls, are generally portrayed as malevolent and cunning but lacking in intelligence, so they can usually be outwitted by the protagonist. These stories of the devil as adversary often begin with the devil's contract. The devil may set up a series of riddles for the hero to solve or impossible tasks for the hero to perform as part of the contract; but in most stories the hero manages to solve the riddles or perform the tasks in order to escape fulfillment of the contract and to save his soul. In some stories the devil is the personification of death, such as in *The Devil and Mother Crump* (Carey, 1987) and *Jack-O'-Lantern* (Barth, 1974). But not all devil characters are adversaries. Some prove to be valuable allies and helpers of those heroes and heroines who treat them with kindness and respect.

Students who became involved in the study of devil tales discovered many delightful stories which they might otherwise never have encountered. Their exposure to this one segment of world literature helped to expand their literary background and their horizons as readers. Many discovered or rediscovered the enjoyment associated with reading or hearing traditional literature, and returned again and again to that section of the library in which these old tales are shelved.

GROUP SESSIONS

To introduce the devil tale Focus Unit most teachers began by inviting students to share their notions of the devil. As students presented their personal ideas and understandings of the devil, it became clear in each group that no single picture or conceptualization was emerging. On the contrary, everyone seemed to have a different notion of the devil, as well as different emotional associations with the term. So, the stage was set to introduce students to the tales of many storytellers who had created devil characters according to their own notions of this supernatural being and his role in human experience.

In each classroom three or four tales were read aloud in a series of group sessions to expose students to a few examples of different types of devil characters and story patterns which can be found in devil tales around the world.

In one classroom the teacher started with three Russian tales—*The Devils Who Learned to Be Good* (McCurdy, 1987), "The Sign at the Smithy Door" (Spicer, 1967), and "The Sly Gypsy and the Stupid Devil" (Spicer, 1967)—because these students had recently engaged in a study of Russian folklore. In a bilingual classroom the teacher selected three tales from Spanish-speaking countries, since this was the cultural heritage of her students. She introduced the unit by reading aloud *Oté—A Puerto Rican Folk Tale* (Galdone, 1969), "How El Bizarrón Fooled the Devil" (Yolen, 1986), and "How the Devil Constructed a Church" (Carter, 1973). Her students enjoyed having the opportunity to draw upon their cultural backgrounds to construct the meaning of these texts. In a third classroom the teacher started with *Jack-O'-Lantern* (Barth, 1974), a legend of the first Jack-O'-Lantern, and the three short stories in *Mean Jake and the Devils* (Hooks, 1981) because the unit was introduced the week before Halloween.

During the group dialogues which evolved in response to these first few devil tales students were encouraged to focus on distinguishing features of the devil character and the protagonist in each tale and the relationship between these central characters. They were also invited to identify recurring story patterns and motifs in these and other tales read aloud and independently as part of the devil tale Focus Unit. As this story data was gathered, it was recorded on large charts, and was eventually used as a basis for categorizing the tales to assist in the inquiry and discovery process.

INDEPENDENT READING AND WRITING

Once students had been introduced to three or four devil tales in group sessions, and had begun to study the characters and story patterns and find significant differences as well as similarities, they were invited to continue the exploration on their own, with a partner, or in a small group. Single illustrated editions and collections of traditional and modern tales were displayed in each classroom to facilitate selection of devil tales for independent reading. When two or more students chose the same tale they were encouraged to form an informal dialogue group to discuss it and to compare it with those shared in large group sessions. The members of these small dialogue groups often chose to continue to work together, and to decide as a group which tales they would select for subsequent independent reading.

THE LITERARY JOURNAL

Each student was also given a "Literary Journal," a notebook for recording personal responses to these tales. (*See* Chapter 9 for a discussion of literary dialogue-journals.) These journals were sometimes passed around in the small dialogue groups so that classmates could respond in writing to a particular entry. The teacher also responded to individual entries with written comments. These written conversations played an important role in the oral dialogues which took place in small-group meetings and in student-teacher conferences. In many cases questions raised in a journal entry became the starting point for a discussion in these groups or conferences. In turn, ideas and insights gained in these oral interactions were often recorded in journals, and served as springboards for further reflection and inquiry. Listening, talking, reading, and writing were integrated and interdependent within the ongoing process of generating meaning and making sense of these literary selections. The literary journals provided students with opportunities to record their personal journeys as learners engaged in inquiry and discovery. The context for these personal journeys was the community of learners in which the ongoing interchange of ideas helped to generate new ideas, insights, and perspectives.

PROJECTS

These independent reading and writing experiences often generated a number of different individual or group projects in which other communication systems were used to make meaning. For example, several students translated lists of words describing specific devil characters into portraits of these creatures. Some portraits were apparently inspired by the artists who had illustrated various retellings; others were clearly original interpretations. When these portraits were displayed as a group it was not difficult to see the significant differences among them, not unlike the individual differences among the storytellers and artists who had created devil characters according to their own mental images.

Other students represented different story sequences with cartoons. The choice of this particular art form was explained by one student: "Some of these stories are so funny and the devil is such a comical character in them that it just seemed right to use cartoons!" One group put together a "Devil Tale Comic Book."

Other students used drama to represent story ideas. Some chose to dramatize a favorite story; others chose to recreate particular scenes from the stories. The two most popular scenes appeared to be the one in which the devil and the protagonist enter into a contract, and the one in which the devil is outwitted and realizes he will lose a soul. In every classroom students also worked independently or in small groups on various research projects guided by interests and questions that emerged during their study of the devil literature.

DISCOVERING DISTINGUISHING FEATURES AND CONNECTING LINKS

When students had become acquainted with a wide range of devil tales the whole class was called together to review the story data which had been gathered by individuals or small groups and recorded on charts. They also shared other discoveries and insights about these tales. In most classrooms students developed a number of categories in order to organize the mass of story data accumulated, as well as their insights, interpretations, and conclusions.

Devil Characters

First the data collected about devil characters were reviewed and discussed. Since descriptions of the physical appearance of these characters had generated a great deal of interest, and had stimulated some wonderful artwork, the examination of the data generally started with external characteristics. Students categorized one type of devil as "elegant" or "well-dressed." Evidence from particular texts was used to place a devil in this category. For example, in *The Devil's Bridge* (Scribner, 1978), a French tale, the devil is a tall stranger.

He looked like a nobleman in his fine suit of bright silk. He walked with a limp and leaned on a cane with a silver handle. He smiled and looked friendly enough, but the dogs growled and backed away when he came close to them [unpaged text].

In "The Devil's Field" (Holman and Valen, 1975), another French tale, the devil is described as "a gentleman of fashion," but "his laugh gave him away," as did the observation that "where the devil walked—clumps of garlic and onion grew" (p. 26).

In "The Devil and Daniel Webster" (Hoke, 1976) the devil is described as "a soft-spoken, dark dressed stranger" in a handsome buggy. But the protagonist "didn't like the looks of the stranger, nor the way he smiled only with his teeth. . . . And he didn't like it when the dog took one look at the stranger and ran away howling, with his tail between his legs" (p. 169).

In *The Magician of Cracow* (Turska, 1975) the devil is "an elegant figure dressed all in black," but is portrayed with horns, hooves, and tail by the illustrator.

Students discovered that in most of the stories featuring "elegant devils" the storytellers had included important but subtle clues about his real identity. They noted the devil's limp or smile or the terrified response of dogs. In *The Devil and Mother Crump* (Carey, 1987) the devil wears clothes of rich red velvet and red leather boots with shiny silver buckles, but "his eyes glowed like coals, and when Mother Crump looked into them, she saw no reflections" (p. 10). In *The Magician of Cracow*, the physical characteristics associated with the devil are shown in the illustrations, and he is identified in the text as soon as he appears in the story. One student observed: "I think it's better when the storyteller doesn't tell you right away who it is, but just gives a few clues. It makes it more interesting." Other students agreed, and many chose to use this "more interesting" technique when they created their own devil tales at the end of the unit.

Another type of devil character was classified as the "comic creature." For example, in *The Devils Who Learned to Be Good* (McCurdy, 1987) the devils are noisy, grotesque creatures with horns and tails. In *The Brave Soldier and a Dozen Devils* (Rudolph, 1970), the devils are more clearly of nonhuman shape, with hairy bodies, bat wings, horns, hooves, claws, and tails. The devil in *Jack-O'-Lantern* (Barth, 1974) sends his two sons to fetch Mean Jack, the blacksmith. His youngest son, Norman, is described as "a creature about the size of a woodchuck." The eldest son, Everett, is "a good deal bigger." Both are portrayed by the artist, Paul

Galdone, as fat, pig-faced creatures with horns and hooves, dressed like schoolboys. In *Duffy and the Devil* (Zemach, 1973), a variant of "Rumpelstiltskin," the devil is described as an "oogly little squinny-eyed creature with a long tail." To many of the students these devil characters were particularly appealing. They proved to be wonderful subjects for art and drama activities.

In addition to looking at the various physical characteristics of devils students focussed on the personality and behavior of different devils. Some were identified as "mischief-makers," as in *The Devils Who Learned to Be Good* (McCurdy, 1987), "The Schoolmaster and the Devil" (Spicer, 1967), *The Devil's Storybook* (Babbitt, 1974), and *Old Devil Is Waiting* (Van Woerkom, 1985). Other devil characters were identified as more powerful and serious agents of evil, some representing Satan himself. The devil characters in "The Devil's Field" (Holman and Valen, 1975) and *The Magician of Cracow* (Turska, 1975) were cited as examples of this type.

Students were surprised to discover that not all devil characters were adversaries of the protagonist. In "The Devil's Gifts" (Fillmore, 1958), a Czechoslovakian tale, a poor shoemaker gives some meat to Prince Lucifer, who in turn gives him some magic gifts which eventually bring him good fortune. However, Prince Lucifer punishes the farmer and his wife for their greed and wickedness.

In "The Devil's Granny" (Spicer, 1967), a similar tale from Germany, the Granny Devil, in her red-and-white-checkered apron and ruffled cap, is pleased with Hans' polite behavior toward her and the excellent sausages he gives her. In return, she protects him from her grandsons, seven young and hungry devils, and gives him enough gold to start his own sausage shop. When Fritz, his mean-spirited, jealous brother goes to Granny Devil, she allows her grandsons to have him for their supper. Granny comments at the end of the story: "It goes hard with the greedy once they reach Hell. Especially if someone who's generous and kind gets here first. Then we Devils can afford a choice!" (Spicer, p. 110).

The devil's old grandmother in *The Devil with the Three Golden Hairs* (Hogrogian, 1983), a Grimm Brothers tale, also protects an innocent boy from her grandson, another flesh-eating devil. The old woman also helps the boy accomplish the terrible task set by a wicked king, enabling the brave youth to return to his bride and to live with her happily ever after.

In *The Grateful Devil* (Spicer, 1967) the devil saves the life of young Prince Martinho, the heir to the throne of Brazil. Later, the Prince discovers the identity of his savior. It is the devil whose statue the Prince had rescued from the dust and had restored to its original elegance. Students were delighted to discover that even a Devil can show his gratitude.

Another favorite was "Tripple-Trapple" (Manning-Sanders, 1970) about a merry little devil who changes himself into a black pot and steals from a "rich man who sets his dogs on the poor" (p. 9). What this devil takes from the rich man, he gives to a poor man and his wife. In the end he takes the rich man off to hell. *The Magic Pot* by Patricia Coombs (1977) is a single illustrated edition of this tale.

Additional observations about these devil characters were related to differences in their behavior. Students noticed, for example, that "elegant devils" tended to have elegant manners and courtly speech. The "comic devils," and those whose outward appearance reflected their true identities, were associated with obnoxious and crude behavior. For example, the devils in *The Brave Soldier and a Dozen Devils* (Rudolph, 1970) and *The Devils Who Learned to Be Good* (McCurdy, 1987) seem to enjoy traveling in noisy groups. They are lively fellows who like to drink and smoke and dance and have not learned proper manners. The squinny-eyed devil in *Duffy and the Devil* (Zemach, 1973) spins and knits for Duffy for three years; at the end of this time he will take her away unless she can guess his name. When the three years are almost up "he started jibing and jeering at her, grinning and winking and behaving all cock-a-hoop . . ." On the last day his "eyes weren't squinny now—they were goggly. And his tail was twitching."

Students found examples of devil characters who behaved like ogres or giants. These were the flesh-eating creatures featured in "The Devil's Granny" (Spicer, 1967), *The Devil with the Three Golden Hairs* (Brothers Grimm, 1983), and "A Demon for Work" (Bond, 1982). Several students observed that in the first two stories each of the ogre-like devils had a grandmother who protected innocent characters from becoming the devil's meal. These students drew from their literary backgrounds to make connections between these devil tales and other traditional tales in which an ogress or giantess protects an innocent hero or heroine from danger. Students who had previously studied Russian folktales compared these grandmother devils to Baba Yaga, the Russian witch: "They're all very careful about who they help and who they punish—or eat! Baba Yaga only ate bad children and she helped Vasilisa because she was good and polite and had her mother's blessing." Another student responded with a comment which prompted a lively discussion about gender: "Maybe those female creatures are more humane and more sensitive because they're *mothers!*"

The Protagonists

Another important discovery made by these student researchers related to the relationship between the nature of protagonists and the pattern of the story in which they are central characters. They identified some protagonists as innocent victims, and others as greedy or wicked. Still others were perceived as basically good people who, in a moment of weakness or desperation, had succumbed to temptation. Some protagonists were rewarded for their kindness; others were punished for their wickedness.

Paper John (Small, 1987) is the story of a gentle, good-natured fellow who makes a living folding paper birds and masks and flowers, which he sells in the town square on market day. When a gray devil attempts to destroy the town and the innocent townsfolk it is Paper John who manages to save everyone.

In "The Schoolmaster and the Devil" (Spicer, 1967) a young devil decides to wreck havoc in a small peaceful village of contented farmers and fisherfolk. The villagers ask the old schoolmaster to help get rid of the Evil One in their midst. For three days and three nights the old man pours over ancient volumes on witchcraft and sorcery to learn how to outwit the devil. He makes a bargain with the devil: If the devil can do all three tasks named by the schoolmaster the old man must forfeit his soul. But if the devil fails, he must leave the village at once and return to hell. It is only the third task which the devil is unable to accomplish. At the conclusion of the tale, when the people learn that the schoolmaster has foiled the devil and restored peace to the village, he explains modestly, "'Twas not I, but the wisdom I found in books, together with God's help" (p. 71). And we are told, "no evil spirit dared visit the village again" (p. 71).

A second type of protagonist included those who were not really innocent victims of the devil but neither were they really bad persons. But these protagonists were tempted to enter into a pact with the devil. For example, "The Devil and Daniel Webster" (Hoke, 1976) is the story of Jabez Stone who lives at Cross Corners, New Hampshire. "He wasn't a bad man to start with, but he was an unlucky man" (p. 168). Although he works hard as a farmer, he is unable to earn enough to feed his wife and children. Once, when he is feeling desperate, Jabez says, "I vow it's enough to make a man want to sell his soul to the devil!" This is how it happens that the stranger dressed in dark clothes appears and makes a bargain with Jabez, who "had to prick his finger to sign" (p. 169). Jabez and his family enjoy prosperity and contentment after that, but in the last days of the last year of the contract Jabez decides to seek the famous lawyer and statesman Dan'l Webster to argue his case with the devil. In the end the eloquence of Webster saves the soul of Jabez Stone, and the contract with the devil is torn into four pieces.

In "The Three Clever Brothers" (Spicer, 1967) Pieter, Ebbel, and Jans are left penniless when their parents die. They work hard and are full of courage, but "most of the time their stomachs yawned like empty sacks, and their pantaloons, though clean, were frayed and patched . . . the three never had a copper to spare" (p. 83). One night, as they share their dreams of a better future, "a tall stranger in black" appears at their hovel. The devil, for it is he, tells them he will "grant each of you your fondest wish." In payment they are to give up their souls to him on the day each of them reaches "his three score—tenth birthday." The only way any one of them can be released from the bargain is to name a task the devil cannot do. In the end the three brothers, good men all, are able to outwit the devil and save their souls. When Ebbel's turn comes to give up his soul to the devil he names this task: "You're to turn all these planks and timbers back into trees, plant them in the forest again, and make them flourish as before I cut them down." The devil is furious and his face turns sickly green: "'Rascal—cheat!' he shrilled. 'What you propose isn't Devil's work. As you well know, God alone makes trees! And now you're free, while I—' He ended on a terrified screech. . . .'" (p. 88).

The third group of protagonists included those who failed to save their souls. The rich man who tried to get others to pay his debt to the devil in *The Brave Soldier and a Dozen Devils* (Rudolph, 1970) is finally caught in his own treachery and taken away by the dozen devils. The soldier who discovers the evil plan of the rich man uses three magic gifts—rewards for his kindness to three old men—to outwit the devils who would have taken him in place of the rich man. The story pattern is one in which the innocent character is saved and rewarded for his kindness, and the wicked character gets what he deserves. The devil, the collector of souls, adds one more to his collection. In "The Devil's Granny" (Spicer, 1967), "The Grateful Devil" (Spicer, 1967), and "The Devil's Gifts" (Fillmore, 1958) the wicked characters are punished by the devil but kindness is rewarded.

The elegant devil in "The Devil's Field" (Holman and Valen, 1975) has no association with the reward-punishment pattern. He convinces a poor but self-centered carpenter to sign an agreement to give up his soul in exchange for riches. The carpenter becomes a miser and spends the rest of his life amassing gold. In the end he offers his thirty barrels of gold to the devil if he will tear up the agreement. The devil responds, "Do you mean you are offering to buy your soul for thirty barrels of gold?" (p. 36). The carpenter answers, "No, No! I am simply offering you a gift of something finer than my soul." The devil throws back his head and laughs, and when he has stopped laughing says, "Carpenter, what is valuable to one may not be so valuable to another. Some, for example, collect gold. And I, for example, collect souls" (p. 37). In this story the soul collector is the victor.

Students observed that the majority of the protagonists were basically good people with a few human weaknesses. Some were tempted by the devil and entered into an agreement with him in a moment of weakness. These characters were able to outwit the devil and save their souls. In contrast, the stories in which devils were successful in their quest for souls featured characters who were inherently wicked. One student commented: "I was glad when those good characters got free. I think that 'escape clause' in the devil's contract is there to give good people a second chance. But it was different with the mean characters. They deserved what they got." Another student added, "These stories are like most fairytales. They're all about good and evil. The good people get rewarded or learn a lesson, but the evil ones get punished."

DISCOVERING PATTERNS AND CONNECTIONS

In the process of exploring various types of devil characters and protagonists, and the relationship between them, students made some interesting discoveries about story patterns, motifs, and themes, and found connecting links between particular stories and familiar folk- and fairytales.

One group of student researchers decided to focus on story motifs, the smallest elements within tales having the power to persist in tradition.[1] Many of the motifs they found in the devil tales they had also encountered in other traditional tales. For example, the "pattern of three" was familiar to most of the students. They found stories with three brothers, three sisters, three wishes, three tasks, and three gifts. They found "transformation" of Granny Devil's gray hair into gold ("The Devil's Granny" [Spicer, 1967]) and sweepings into gold ("The Devil's Sooty Brother" [Grimm, 1972]). They found "magic objects," such as the pipe that couldn't be smoked out, the bottle of wine that could not be finished, the sack that sucks in whatever is named, a stick that acts on command, and a tablecloth that provides food. They identified "impossible tasks," such as obtaining three golden hairs from the head of the devil. They found the "unfavorable prophesy" and the attempts to escape its fulfillment in *The Devil with the Three Golden Hairs* (Brothers Grimm, 1983) and "The Grateful Devil" (Spicer, 1967). They found many examples of "rewards and punishment," the "reversal of fortune," "supernatural helpers" in the form of old men and women, the "success of the youngest child," and "character traits" such as greed, generosity, cruelty, and kindness.

In their "catalogue of motifs" these students included a separate section of motifs which seemed to be associated more specifically with devil tales, such as the "bargain with the devil," the "seven-year contract," the "escape clause," and "selling one's soul" for riches. Of special

---

[1]Atelia Clarkson and Gilbert B. Cross. *World Folktales*. N.Y.: Scribner's, 1980, p. 4.

interest was the motif they called "the curse." In "The Devil's Gifts" (Fillmore, 1958) the farmer tells the shoemaker to "go to the devil!" In "The Devil's Granny" (Spicer, 1967) Fritz yells at his brother, "To the Devils in Hell with you and your sausages!" (p. 104). In "The Devil and Daniel Webster" (Hoke, 1976) Jabez Stone cries in desperation, "I vow it's enough to make a man want to sell his soul to the devil! And I would, too, for two cents!" (p. 168). In "Katcha and the Devil" (Yolen, 1986) Katcha thinks to herself, "Here I am getting old and yet I've never danced with a boy! Plague take it, today I'd dance with the Devil if he asked me!" (p. 369). All the words uttered in anger or frustration and often quite thoughtlessly cause the devil to appear. As one student put it, "You're just asking for trouble when you say stuff you don't mean. In these stories this kind of curse is like an invitation to the devil!"

A related motif was identified by this group as "meaner than the devil." When a character in a devil tale was described in this way by neighbors and townsfolk the devil generally became curious or angry enough to look into the matter. This group found these characters to be especially colorful and interesting: Mean Jack in *Jack-O'-Lantern* (Barth, 1974), Mother Crump in *The Devil and Mother Crump* (Carey, 1987), Mean Jake in *Mean Jake and the Devils* (Hooks, 1981), and Old John in "Wicked John and the Devil" (Yolen, 1986).

Another student research group shared with their class the results of their search for connecting links between the devil tales and other folk- and fairy-tales which went beyond motif connections. They looked for stories which seemed to be variants of or somehow reminded them of familiar traditional tales. For example, they recognized *Duffy and the Devil* (Zemach, 1973) as a variant of Rumpelstiltskin and noted that "The Sly Gypsy and the Stupid Devil" (Spicer, 1967) and "How El Bizarrón Fooled the Devil" (Carter, 1974) reminded them of "The Brave Little Tailor." They decided that "The Devil's Granny" was similar to other tales about a rich brother and poor brother, such as in "The Magic Mortar,"[2] a Japanese tale, and *The Three Magic Gifts*,[3] a Russian tale. They compared "Saint Sava and the Devil" (Spicer, 1967) to another familiar tale of "crop division," *Tops and Bottoms*.[4] The little devils in "Tripple-Trapple" (Manning-Sanders, 1970) and *The Magic Pot* (Coombs, 1977) were compared to Robin Hood, because they steal from the rich to give to the poor. In "Tsar Boris and the Devil King" (Spicer, 1967) the six brothers have supernatural powers which enable them to rescue Princess Maritza from the Devil King. The story was compared to tales such as *The Five Chinese Brothers*,[5] *Long, Broad and Quickeye*[6] and *The Fool of the World and the Flying Ship*.[7] They decided that "Bearskin" (Brothers Grimm, 1972) was similar to "Beauty and the Beast" because "the youngest daughter agreed to marry a man who *looks* like a monster but really is a handsome man." Those familiar with "Puss in Boots" noted that the boy in *The Boy and the Devil* (Magnus, 1986) uses the same trick Puss in Boots had used to outwit the ogre. The boy takes advantage of the devil's vanity and challenges him to show off his power

[2]Yoshiko Uchida, reteller. "The Magic Mortar." *The Magic Listening Cap: More Folktales from Japan*. N.Y.: Harcourt Brace, 1955.

[3]James Riordan. *The Three Magic Gifts*. N.Y.: Oxford University Press, 1980.

[4]Lesley Conger. *Tops and Bottoms*. N.Y.: Four Winds, 1970.

[5]Claire Bishop, reteller. *The Five Chinese Brothers*. N.Y.: Coward-McCann, 1938.

[6]Evaline Ness, adaptor. *Long, Broad and Quickeye*. N.Y.: Scribner, 1969.

[7]Arthur Ransome, reteller. *The Fool of the World and the Flying Ship: A Russian Tale*. N.Y.: Farrar, Straus & Giroux, 1968.

to make himself very large and very small. When the devil makes himself as small as a flea, the boy has him creep into the hole in a nut and then asks the blacksmith to crack it for him. In "Puss in Boots" the ogre is challenged to make himself as small as a mouse. The cat swallows him the moment the ogre proves he can perform this feat.

THE WRITER'S CRAFT

In one classroom, where reading and writing were very closely integrated, the teacher was interested in having her students focus their attention on the language of the stories. She hoped they would use the devil literature as a resource for learning about writing. To this end she invited them to look at the way each writer had used language to tell a story, to create a mood, and to stimulate the mind and imagination of the audience. Students were encouraged to search for interesting language and literary techniques which reflected the writer's craft. They were encouraged to read critically, to evaluate a lead sentence, for example, in terms of its effectiveness in pulling the reader-listener into the story. Gradually the students became collectors and critics of the language of literature. One small group set up a file box of 5 × 8 cards to collect "samples of writers' craft." Students contributed to this file throughout the school year. Although most of the samples were selected as models of "good writing," some were chosen on the basis of the poor quality of the writing. Students who selected a sample would be expected to explain why they had judged it as "good" or "poor" quality and to suggest ways to revise and improve poor writing.

These cards were often used in small or large group dialogues as the starting point for focussing on the language of literature and writers' knowledge. By examining the cards students began to see what writers do. They became aware that an opening sentence could be a powerful invitation to read on. They saw that opening lines could provide significant clues about the nature or mood of the story. They looked at samples of figurative language in terms of the richness of the mental images they evoked. They examined techniques used by writers to elicit humor, suspense, or terror.

On one of the cards a student recorded the introduction to "The Schoolmaster and the Devil" (Spicer, 1967):

On a certain dark night, long ago, a dejected young Devil in search of souls hovered above the secluded hamlet of Cockerham—close to Morecambe Bay, on England's west coast. His black wings drooped wearily, for he'd flown far, and with no luck at all for the effort. Catching sight of the old church tower, he decided to rest there and think over what to do next" (p. 64).

Another student wrote the lead sentence in "Wishes," one of the ten tales in Natalie Babbitt's *The Devil's Storybook* (1974):

One day when things were dull in Hell, the Devil fished around in his bag of disguises, dressed himself as a fairy godmother, and came up into the World to find someone to bother" (p. 3).

A third student selected the opening line of "The Devil in the Steeple" (Jagendorf, 1948):

This happened when no place in all America was so troubled by the Evil One as the State of Massachusetts, the state of the Pilgrim Fathers" (p. 153).

When these three students shared their cards in a group session the discussion centered around the differences between the opening lines on each card and the way they set the stage for different kinds of narratives. One student observed that "the first paragraph in 'The School-master' story is like a *written* story, but the first sentence in the 'Steeple' story makes it sound like someone is just *telling* it—like sitting in a rocking chair by the fireplace!"

Other cards contained samples of language that students had especially enjoyed. For example, in "Wicked John and the Devil" (Yolen, 1986) the devil sends one of his sons to fetch Old John. The little devil is described as "about a fifth-grade-size devil—little horns just startin' to bump up on his forehead" (p. 362). His older brother is described as "a little devil about high-school-size, little horns spike-in' up" (p. 362).

Many of the students recorded descriptions of the devil himself on their cards:

- the near-sighted devil
- his eyes glowed like coals
- his strange, glowing eyes
- his wicked eyes narrowing to slits
- sparks flew from his eyes, and his tale gave an angry lash
- his eyes were blazing

They were intrigued to discover how much attention was given to the eyes of the devils in these stories.

COMPOSING DEVIL STORIES

Reading and listening to devil tales, discussing them in large and small groups, writing about them in journals, and studying them in depth provided extensive preparation for composing original devil tales.

A review of the story data on the charts, journal entries, the samples of "writers' craft" on 5 × 8 cards, and the reports of research projects reminded students of the amount of literary knowledge they had accumulated and gave them the confidence and motivation to write devil tales.

The wonderful stories composed by these students reflected their grasp of the character types, patterns, and themes found in traditional devil tales. Their stories revealed their awareness of the language of literature and their willingness to experiment with literary techniques and styles they had encountered in their study. When these young authors shared their stories in group sessions the feedback was thoughtful and supportive. Many students interpreted the positive responses of classmates and teachers as invitations to continue to write and to share their work. Students often saw new respect in the eyes of their peers; and this made a significant difference for them as writers and as individuals.

SYNTHESIS

The students who studied devil literature developed special interests which guided their exploration. They formulated questions which generated inquiry and discovery. In the process they acquired the knowledge base necessary to move toward synthesis. They pulled together recurring patterns and themes in this collection of tales and looked for larger ideas which went beyond single texts to cover the collection as a whole. As one girl put it: "We need to find some way to tie all these stories together." In some classrooms students raised key questions which assisted this search for the threads that tied the stories to each other. One student asked, "Why did people tell devil tales all over the world?" Another question was, "What do the stories tell us about the storytellers?" In each classroom the majority of students were able to reach agreement about the nature of the connecting threads and the larger significance of the collection as a whole.

One group concluded that all these stories were essentially about good and evil.

- People all over the world talk about good and evil, so that's why the stories are told in a lot of different countries.
- It's something that started a long time ago—in the Garden of Eden—in the Story of Creation.
- Religion is about good and evil. That's why there are a lot of churches and priests in these stories.
- The devil is like a character that stands for evil like a flag stands for a country. And he tries to get people to be evil like him.
- But most times he fails. So the storytellers are saying that most people are good and won't get caught by the devil. And religion helps.
- But some people are really wicked and *those* are the ones that get caught.

In another classroom a student came to this conclusion: "The reason you have a conscience is so the devil *doesn't* win! Your conscience is like a voice that tells you that you shouldn't do something because it's wrong. And then the devil's voice fades away and he loses!" This prompted a classmate to suggest: "Maybe the devil looks around for people who don't have a conscience like Fritz who was so mean to his brother, or that farmer who thought more about money than his own family." A third student added: "So, the storytellers want their audience to *think* about this. To think about how they act and about the *consequences* of evil behavior. It's like they're teaching a lesson—like in church—but with a good story so you'll pay attention but still get the message!" Another student continued with the idea, "Probably a lot of people in different countries really believe in evil spirits like devils and demons, so the storytellers put devil characters in their stories. And people believe in God, too, so that's in the stories, too. It's a good way to teach about good and evil." This led to the observation that ". . . the good people get rewarded in these stories and they usually win over the devil. And in that one story about the soldier he even gets the devils to change so much they *like* doing good deeds!" This student was referring to *The Devils Who Learned to Be Good* (McCurdy, 1987), a story in which a group of devils "grew quite fond of the old soldier, and rather fond of helping those in need as well."

In one group students began to explore the idea of the "personal devil" within us described in Dorothy Spicer's introduction to her collection of devil tales. One girl expressed it this way: "It's like everyone has good in them and bad, too. It's like you have this little devil inside trying to get you to do stuff you *know* you shouldn't. Sometimes he's quiet a long time and then—he's there—and he's saying, 'Oh you won't get caught' or 'It won't matter' and stuff like that!" Another student took the idea a step further: "I think it's different than giants or dragons or monsters. *They're* the scary things out in the world or in the dark. But the devils are inside, like Marny said. They sort of tempt you to do stuff. But then when you *do*, it doesn't feel so great."

INQUIRY AND DISCOVERY

Excerpts taken from dialogues of intermediate-level students who studied devil literature reflect the quality of their thinking as they generated meanings, insights, and interpretations, drew conclusions, and moved toward synthesis. Their search for understanding led to discoveries about the unique features of individual tales, as well as patterns which connect these tales to each other and to folktales and legends in general. These discoveries prepared them to search for deeper meanings and to uncover significant connections between these tales and human experience. As they engaged in exploration, inquiry, and discovery, they gained experience as students of literature and as thoughtful readers and writers. These students learned to use inquiry and discovery as central strategies for learning as they constructed meaning and created knowledge and understanding for themselves.

Bibliography of Devil Tales

Alegria, Ricardo E., ed. *The Three Wishes: A Collection of Puerto Rican Folktales.* "The Young Girl and the Devil," pp. 80–83. N.Y.: Harcourt Brace and World, 1969.

Babbitt, Natalie. *The Devil's Other Storybook.* N.Y.: Farrar, Straus & Giroux, 1987.

———. *The Devil's Storybook.* N.Y.: Farrar, Straus & Giroux, 1974.

Barth, Edna, reteller; Paul Galdone, illus. *Jack-O'-Lantern.* N.Y.: Seabury, 1974.

Bond, Ruskin, reteller. *Tales and Legends from India.* "A Demon for Work," pp. 77–79. N.Y.: Julia MacRae, 1982.

Brittain, Bill. *Devil's Donkey.* N.Y.: Harper, 1981.

Calvino, Italo, reteller and selector. *Italian Folktales.* "Silver Nose," pp. 26–30; "The Devil's Breeches," pp. 167–172; "Lame Devil," pp. 586–588; "Jump into My Sack," pp. 708–713. N.Y.: Harcourt Brace Jovanovich, 1980.

Carey, Valerie Scho. *The Devil and Mother Crump.* N.Y.: Harper, 1987.

Carter, Dorothy, selector and adaptor. *The Enchanted Orchard and Other Folktales from Central America.* "How the Devil Constructed a Church" (Honduras), pp. 109–114. N.Y.: Harcourt Brace, 1973.

Carter, Dorothy, adaptor. *Greedy Mariani and Other Folktales of the Antilles.* "How El Bizarrón Fooled the Devil" (Cuba). N.Y.: Atheneum, 1974, pp. 23–29.

Chase, Richard, reteller and collector. *Grandfather Tales: American-English Folktales.* "Wicked John and the Devil," pp. 29–39. Boston: Houghton Mifflin, 1948.

Colwell, Eileen, reteller. *Round About and Long Ago: Tales from the English Counties.* "The Devil's Bridge" (Westmoreland), pp. 23–26; "The Wizard of Long Sleddale," pp. 27–29. Boston: Houghton Mifflin, 1974.

Coombs, Patricia. *The Magic Pot.* N.Y.: Lothrop, Lee & Shepard, 1977.

Fillmore, Parker, reteller. *The Shepherd's Nosegay: Stories from Finland and Czechoslovakia.* "Katcha and the Devil," pp. 160–171; "The Devil's Gifts," pp. 172–184. Eau Claire, WI: Hale, 1958 (1919).

Galdone, Paul. *Oté—A Puerto Rican Folk Tale.* N.Y.: Pantheon, 1969.

Grimm Brothers. *The Complete Grimm's Fairy Tales.* "The Devil's Sooty Brother," pp. 463–466; "Bearskin," pp. 467–472. N.Y.: Pantheon, 1972 (1944).

————. *The Devil with the Three Golden Hairs.* Nonny Hogrogian, reteller and illus. N.Y.: Knopf, 1983.

Harper, Wilhelmina, compiler. *Ghosts and Goblins—Stories for Halloween.* "The Witches' Ride" (a Costa Rican folktale, Lupe de Osma, reteller), pp. 228–233. N.Y.: Dutton, 1964 (1936).

Hoke, Helen, selector. *Devils, Devils, Devils.* "The Bottle Imp," Robert Louis Stevenson, pp. 11–57; "The Devil and Daniel Webster," Stephen Vincent Benet, pp. 166–191. N.Y.: Watts, 1976.

Holman, Felice, and Nanine Valen. *The Drac—French Tales of Dragons and Demons.* "The Devil's Field," pp. 19–39. N.Y.: Scribner's, 1975.

Hooks, William. *Mean Jake and the Devils* (three short stories based on folktales the author heard as a child in North Carolina). N.Y.: Dial, 1981.

Jagendorf, M. A. *New England Bean-Pot: American Folk Stories to Read and to Tell.* "The Smart Woman of Kennebunkport," pp. 26–29; "Three Times and Out," pp. 46–53; "The Devil in the Barrel," pp. 84–88; "Magic in Marblehead," pp. 139–146; "The Devil in the Steeple," pp. 153–157; "The Devil in Red Flannel," pp. 231–235. N.Y.: Vanguard, 1948.

Jagendorf, M. A., and R. S. Boggs. *The King of the Mountains—A Treasury of Latin American Folk Stories.* "Pancho Villa and the Devil" (Mexico), pp. 202–204. N.Y.: Vanguard, 1960.

Joyce, James. *The Cat and the Devil.* (Fable written by Joyce in 1936 in a letter to his grandson.) N.Y.: Dodd, Mead, 1964.

Lyons, Grant. *Tales the People Tell in Mexico.* "Ashes for Sale," pp. 71–79. N.Y.: Julian Messner, 1972.

Magnus, Erica. *The Boy and the Devil.* (Adapted from a Norwegian folktale.) Minneapolis: Carolrhoda, 1986.

Manning-Sanders, Ruth. *A Book of Devils and Demons.* "Tripple-Trapple" (Denmark), pp. 9–14; "Jack at Hell Gate" (Hungary), pp. 39–50; "The Blacksmith and the Devil" (Gascony), pp. 76–86; "Ride to Hell" (Denmark), pp. 98–109; "The Little Red Mannikin" (Carpathian mountains), pp. 110–116. N.Y.: Dutton, 1970.

————. *Scottish Folktales.* "The Shadow," pp. 21–28. London: Methuen, 1976.

McCurdy, Michael, adaptor. *The Devils Who Learned to Be Good* (Russian). Boston: Little, Brown, 1987.

Pino-Saavedra, Yolando, ed. *Folktales of Chile.* "The Unknown Bird," pp. 215–217. Chicago: University of Chicago Press, 1967.

Rudolph, Margeurita, reteller. *The Brave Soldier and a Dozen Devils—A Latvian Tale.* N.Y.: Seabury, 1970.

Scribner, Charles, Jr., reteller. *The Devil's Bridge.* N.Y.: Scribner's, 1978.

Small, David. *Paper John.* N.Y.: Farrar, Straus & Giroux, 1987.

Spicer, Dorothy Gladys, collector. *13 Devils.* "The Schoolmaster and the Devil" (England), pp. 63–70; "The Devil's Granny" (Germany), pp. 101–109; "The Sly Gypsy and the Stupid Devil" (Russia), pp. 43–52; "The Grateful Devil" (Brazil), pp. 71–81; "The Three Clever Brothers" (Netherlands), pp. 82–90; "The Sign at the Smithy Door" (Russia), pp. 91–100; "Saint Sava and the Devil" (Serbia), pp. 110–116; "Tsar Boris and the Devil King" (Russia), pp. 52–62. N.Y.: Coward-McCann, 1967.

Turska, Krystyna, reteller. *The Magician of Cracow* (Polish legend). N.Y.: Greenwillow, 1975.

Valen, Nanine. *The Devil's Tail.* (Old French legend.) N.Y.: Scribner's, 1978.

Van Woerkom, Dorothy. *Old Devil Is Waiting: Three Folktales.* (For beginning readers.) N.Y.: Harcourt Brace Jovanovich, 1985.

Yolen, Jane, ed. *Favorite Folktales from Around the World.* "The Peasant and the Devil" (Germany), pp. 358–359; "Wicked John and the Devil" (U.S.), pp. 359–366; "The Bad Wife" (Russia), pp. 367–368; "Katcha and the Devil" (Czechoslovakia), pp. 369–374; "The Lawyer and the Devil" (Ireland), p. 375; "Coals on the Devil's Hearth" (Ireland), pp. 376–377; "The Devil's Hide" (Finland), pp. 378–386; "How El Bizarrón Fooled the Devil" (Cuba), pp. 386–389; "Bearskin" (Germany), pp. 389–393; "The Lad and the Devil" (Norway), pp. 394; "Wiley and the Hairy Man" (U.S.), pp. 395–400. N.Y.: Pantheon, 1986.

Zemach, Harve, and Margot Zemach, reteller and illus. *Duffy and the Devil.* N.Y.: Farrar, Straus & Giroux, 1973.

Cat Tales:
Story Schema

STORY SCHEMA

If reading is viewed as a cognitive process in which readers interact with text and actively generate meaning by bringing their prior knowledge and experience to the text, then it follows that attention should be focussed on the nature of this prior knowledge and experience. This knowledge is organized, and the term *schema* refers to that organized knowledge or mental model of the world.

Schema theorists interested in story comprehension have demonstrated that there is an inherent logical structure or *grammar* made up of a network of categories and logical relationships in stories (Stein and Glenn, 1979, p. 58). Although schema theorists label the components of a story differently, a grammar usually includes these categories:

- A *setting* which introduces the characters and the time and place in the story;
- an *initiating event* which leads the main character to formulate his/her major goals and starts the sequence of actions and events;
- the *goal*, which is the major desire of the main character;
- a number of *attempts*, which are the actions of the characters;
- a series of *outcomes*, which are events or states produced by the character's actions;
- *internal responses*, which are the subgoals, thoughts and feelings of a character leading to his/her actions;
- *reactions*, which are thoughts or feelings produced by the outcomes of actions; and
- the *resolution*, or final consequence, of the story (McConaughy, 1980, p. 158).

These basic components are related causally or temporally. A story is defined as "a series of problem solving episodes centering on the main character's (or characters') efforts to achieve a major goal" (McConaughy, 1980, p. 58).

By listening to stories children develop a story schema, an implicit knowledge of story grammar. According to the results of story grammar research children use this knowledge of story organization to comprehend and recall stories, to make predictions about the story, and to generate their own stories. Children with better knowledge of story structure tend to be better readers (Fitzgerald, 1984). One important implication of the findings of story-grammar research is that incorporating knowledge of story structure into teaching strategies has the potential for improving reading comprehension in children. Results from several recent studies suggest the usefulness of instruction designed to strengthen children's awareness of story structure (Gordon and Braun, 1983; McConaughy, 1980; Rand, 1984; Sadow, 1982; and Spiegel and Fitzgerald, 1986).

Story grammar provides a conceptual framework for formulating questions that reflect the story as a whole and that focus on its internal logic and pattern of relationships. Questions initiated by the teacher demonstrate strategies for interacting with narrative texts and help students internalize story structure (Sadow, 1982).

THE CAT TALE UNIT

A Focus Unit featuring cats illustrates the translation of theoretical insights, which have emerged from story-grammar research, into classroom practice. Knowledge of story structure can be used to guide and facilitate the comprehension and discussion of stories; the reconstruction of stories through retellings, drama, and art; and the composition of new stories.

The cat tale Focus Unit was originally developed in response to the many cat lovers in a second-grade classroom. Subsequently, this unit was adapted for use with other age groups and in other classroom settings to share the many interesting cat characters which can be found in traditional and modern literature. In order to introduce the Cat Tale Focus Unit to these second-grade children many cat pictures were collected and displayed in the classroom. The collection was drawn from a variety of sources, from greeting cards and magazines and reproductions of the works of great artists. The display provided a survey of diverse artists' interpretations of cats from the dignified cat of ancient Egypt to the cartoon cat created for a commercial. Prior to the first group story session the children were invited to study the cat portrait gallery and to think of words which would best describe individual cats.

Session One

At the first session the children were anxious to share their descriptive words and defend their choice of a label for a particular cat. Eventually, group consensus was reached so that appropriate words could be printed on cards and each one mounted under the cat it was intended to describe. Then the children were asked to share their personal experiences with cats. Many had cat pets, and all had had some contact with felines. This oral sharing offered the children an opportunity to bring into focus their relevant knowledge background. Later they would draw from this background as they interacted with the texts selected for this Unit.

Nobody's Cat (Miles, 1969) was the first of a series of cat tales featured in this Unit. Before reading it aloud the teacher asked the children to consider the meaning of the title. They decided that the cat in the story must be without an owner; it was probably a stray or alley cat. Again, they were encouraged to draw on their knowledge to list what they knew about stray cats. They were asked to use the picture on the front cover of the book to determine if this would be a fantasy or realistic story. Most agreed with the child who responded, "It looks like it's going to be a real story." Later, as the story unfolded, they were able to confirm this prediction.

After the story was read aloud the children were invited to add new information about stray cats to the list generated earlier. A number of significant details associated with survival needs and behavior were identified and added to the list. The children were particularly interested in the strategies used by the cat in life-threatening situations.

The question: "Why did the stray cat leave a dead mouse on the school steps?" brought expressions of repulsion. "Yuck!" . . . "Ugh!" . . . "Gross." Several children expressed surprise that the cat didn't eat the mouse after killing it. Finally, a cat owner explained the significance of this gesture: "It was to say thank you for the food those children brought before school. That's just what *my* cat does."

This led to a discussion of the ways cats communicate with humans. Each illustration in the book was examined again and typical cat behaviors were identified. The children were able to "read" the body language that communicated fear, anger, affection, and contentment. In the process they were practicing an important reading strategy: making inferences about the meaning of overt behaviors of story characters based on information drawn from prior knowledge and the context in which the behavior occurred in the text.

The question: "What did you think about the way the story ended?" elicited these remarks:

- I thought he was going to become a pet.
- Yeah—I wanted that girl to adopt him. I didn't like the way the author ended the story.
- But I think it was more *real* this way. In real life there *are* stray cats and dogs . . . and not every one gets to be somebody's pet.
- I think he didn't even *want* to be a pet. I think he really just wanted to be on his own.
- And he seemed so happy at the end even though he has a pretty dangerous life.
- It's like people. Some people like to stay home and watch TV and other people like to do dangerous things—like Evel Knieval and Houdini.

Session Two

Puss in Boots, adapted and illustrated by Paul Galdone (1976), was introduced in the second group session. Holding the book up to show the charming front cover picture of a jaunty cat standing upright, arms folded, and wearing bright red boots, the teacher asked, "What kind of a story do you think this will be?" The children had no difficulty recognizing that the cat portrayed here would have to be a "make believe character."

- You can tell it's a pretend story 'cause of the red boots.
- And *that's* not the way cats stand!
- This is going to be different than *Nobody's Cat*.

As this story was read aloud a number of interruptions were necessary to clarify new words or complex language essential to the total meaning of the narrative. At appropriate moments children interrupted briefly to make predictions and to confirm or revise those made earlier.

At the end of the story, and after the children had responded spontaneously to it, the teacher initiated three questions:

1. "Why did Boots give three presents to the King?" (Intended to elicit inferential thinking about the motivation behind the cat's behavior.)
2. "Why did the King give his best suit to the miller's son?" (Intended to help children make logical connections between events occurring early and later in the story sequence.)
3. "How did Boots outwit the Giant?" (Intended to draw attention to a recurring pattern or motif found in traditional tales: *i.e.*, the challenge to a large creature to transform itself into a smaller one. In this case the giant is challenged to change himself into a mouse. When he does he is quickly snapped up by Puss in Boots.)

Session Three

The purpose of the third session was to introduce a strategy for interacting with a narrative text in terms of its basic structure or grammar. A series of questions derived from story grammar was used to draw attention to the categories of information and the logical relationships which make up a story's organization.

1. The children were asked to identify the main character(s) and the time and place of *Nobody's Cat*. This information was recorded on a chart under the heading, "SETTING."
2. "When did the story really begin?" Comments were elicited about the initiating event, internal response, goals, and attempts, although these specific terms were neither introduced to nor used by the children.

- It started when he felt hungry.
- So he says to himself, "I better go get food!" [This "internal response" was inferred from the text.]
- So he goes out to get food and he has all these adventures!
- The story tells how he tries to get food.

The information was summarized and recorded on the chart under the heading "BEGINNING OF THE STORY."

3. "What kinds of things happened to the cat as he tried to get food?" The focus was on the outcomes of various attempts.

- Well, one time he got chased by a bigger cat when he tried to drink the milk. And they fight. And he didn't give up.

- He was so brave!
- One time he got meat from that nice man.
- Then he gets caught in the school cafeteria. He was so scared.
- Cats don't like to be cornered like that.

These and other attempts and outcomes were identified and recorded under the heading, "WHAT HAPPENED?"

4. "What problem was solved?" Children easily recognized that the problem was hunger and the solution was the relief of that hunger.
5. "What else can you say about the ending?" Comments were made about the resolution.

- The cat liked the children and said thank you with the mouse, but he liked being a stray cat, too.
- Because in the end he went back home to his alley.

These answers were listed in THE ENDING category.

The same headings were printed on a chart to guide the analysis of *Puss in Boots*. This complex tale presented quite a challenge. For example, identifying the main character was no easy task. Some children thought it was the miller's son; others argued in favor of Puss in Boots.

- *His* name is the title so he must be important.
- He does all the work.
- He says more. The miller's son hardly says anything.
- The story tells a lot about the cat but not the boy. So, the cat is the main character!

Consensus was finally reached and Puss in Boots was printed on the chart. After the analysis of categories was complete the chart looked like this:

- SETTING
  Main character: Puss in Boots
  Time: Long ago
  Place: A kingdom
- BEGINNING OF STORY
  Miller's son has a problem—no way to earn a living.
  Cat sees he needs help and decides to help him get rich.
- WHAT HAPPENED
  Puss in Boots tricks King, people in field, and the Giant.
- ENDING
  The miller's son got rich and married the Princess and Puss in Boots got his own throne.

Attention then turned to the logical relationships between categories. The children noted that the story started with a problem which led to attempts to solve the problem which, in turn, led to a happy solution. Then they were asked to compare this chart with the one based on *Nobody's Cat*. One child shared her discovery: "Look! It's the same thing! Both [stories] started with a problem and ended getting it solved. And the middle tells how." Another added,

"But it was different, too. The stray cat solved his own problem and Puss in Boots solved the boy's [the miller's son] problem."

In this introduction to story-analysis strategies the teacher did not attempt to teach the language and rules of story grammar directly but used her knowledge of story grammar to plan an experience which would help children discover the way stories are organized.

Session Four

Do Not Open by Brinton Turkle (1981) was introduced in the fourth group session. When the teacher showed the illustrations on the book cover and the first two pages the children observed that this would probably be another real story, "because the pictures are like true life." Several children wondered out loud what the title could mean. Others made predictions. It is interesting to note that by the time this third story was presented, the children had apparently begun to internalize and use some of the strategies for interacting with texts demonstrated in previous sessions. After the discussion the teacher began to read this story of Miss Moody who liked to look for things on the beach, especially after a storm. When the teacher reached the page which told of the discovery of the purple bottle with the words "Do Not Open" scratched on it, one child whispered, "I bet it's a genie!" The next line in the text—"A voice said, 'What do you want more than anything in the world?'"—elicited a number of excited comments.

- See—it *is* a genie!
- Oh—this isn't a real story. It's a make-believe story.
- It started out like a real one and then it changed to the other kind . . . like a fairy tale.

The story continued without interruption until they reached the point at which Miss Moody challenged the terrible creature that had emerged from the purple bottle to "grow small like a little mouse." Immediately, hands went up as the children anticipated what would happen next.

- It's just like in Puss in Boots!
- He's going to show off his powers and change into a mouse!
- And then Miss Moody's cat is going to *eat* him!

They were delighted to find that they were right. They had used their literary background to anticipate events in this new story. They were making connections with past texts to assist comprehension of new ones.

When the story came to an end there were a number of requests to "make another story chart." At first the story analysis presented no difficulty for the children. They immediately identified the *beginning* of the story as the discovery of the bottle with its awful creature. They identified the *problem*, "to get rid of that thing," and Miss Moody's *plan* to outwit the monster and the *outcome* of her plan. Then one child observed, "But that wasn't the *end*. The *end* was when the banjo clock started to work again—just like she always *wanted*!" After the entire group puzzled over this for a while another child came up with a solution that seemed to satisfy everyone: "Maybe there are sort of two stories. One starts out when Miss Moody was unhappy that the clock didn't go—then she makes a secret wish with the genie that it would tick and bong, and *then* in the *end* her wish came true. The *other* story starts when the *monster* comes but they're [the stories] connected." The children decided to do the chart over again so that both "smaller stories" could be shown to be part of the "bigger story." By using red and blue markers the teacher was able to record their ideas of the way the "monster story" was embedded within the "clock story" to make a whole.

INDEPENDENT READING

At the close of the fourth session the children were invited to choose books from a set of display shelves for independent reading. The books on these shelves contained fiction, folklore, poetry, and nonfiction about cats (*see* Bibliography at the end of this chapter). The children were encouraged to draw from their independent reading experiences to contribute to discussions during subsequent group story sessions. The teacher also scheduled individual conferences to discuss students' independent reading. One strategy the teacher used to evaluate the children's overall understanding of story structure was having them retell the story they had read silently. This provided the teacher with some information about how the reader interacted with the text to generate meaning. The reconstruction of the story revealed what kinds of information related to story parts and what relationships were missing. This provided the teacher with a basis for developing specific questions to extend the child's interaction with a text (Ringler and Weber, 1982). For example, if a child did not spontaneously infer important story information during a retelling, the teacher introduced questions to elicit inferencing, an essential factor in constructing meaning from texts. The logical inferences required to understand character and plot development were elicited by "how" and "why" questions. Many of the children had difficulty with the "internal response" category. The teacher's questions helped them make inferences about a character's motives, feelings, and thoughts, which are implicit in a story and how these relate to the goals and actions which form the plot.

Although significant information can be derived from a child's retelling of a story, it is a time-consuming procedure. When an abbreviated version was necessitated by time constraints, the teacher asked the child to "tell about the most important parts of the story" and generally gained enough information about the child's grasp of the story structure to generate relevant and useful questions. In the group setting a round robin retelling of a story previously read aloud gave each participant a chance to share in the reconstruction of the story by contributing segments of the total narrative sequence, filling in gaps, and challenging the validity of a prior contribution. This activity served to reinforce and enhance the children's story comprehension and provided the teacher with clues about the nature of their interaction with a text.

SMALL-GROUP SHARING

Small groups were established to allow the children to talk about their independent reading with a few classmates. Jane Hanson, in her book *When Writers Read* (1987), discusses the value of "response sessions" in which children have a chance to share what they have read and to invite classmates to respond with comments and questions. Talking about a book helps children clarify their ideas as they think out loud. The children respond to each other, building on each other's comments and questions. These children are not grouped in terms of ability, and the content and direction of the discussion are not determined by the teacher but by the children, as they engage in a dialogue about books they have chosen to read independently.

Some of the children came to the small-group "response sessions" with something they had written about their books which they read aloud to initiate discussion. Others opened the session by reading "a really good part of the story" or a strong lead sentence aloud. Others started off with a brief retelling and their own interpretations of the meaning of the story or its connection to other tales or a personal experience. Those who had read nonfiction books generally began with what they had learned or something that surprised them or a question which was *not* answered in this book. These sessions were initiated and organized by the children who learned to respond to each other with mutual respect and support. In this context the children gained self-confidence and the motivation to engage in further reading and sharing experiences.

Session Five

Before reading *The Witch Who Lost Her Shadow* (Calhoun, 1979) aloud, the teacher asked the children to define the word *shadow*. They responded with descriptions of the appearance and behavior of a shadow.

- It's black.
- It's sometimes long and sometimes short.
- It follows you.
- It only follows you outside. It can't come in the house with you.
- It hides at night.
- Sometimes you play with it—like someone tries to step on your shadow.
- But sometimes it's creepy to see shadows.

The teacher prepared them for listening to the story by explaining that the "shadow" in the title is the name of a cat, and the "witch" would be referred to as a "white witch" in the story. The children were asked to think about why the cat was given the name Shadow as well as the possible meaning of "white witch" as they listened to the story. They were to "save their thoughts" for the discussion at the end. As the story unfolded, it was quite clear that they had come up with some significant thoughts to contribute to the discussion. The only time this quiet tale was interrupted was at the point when the little stray cat brings a dead mouse to Falinda, the white witch. The children were very excited about this episode. Rather than being repulsed by it they were able to draw from their previous literary experience with *Nobody's Cat* to comprehend the meaning of the gesture.

- That's a present!
- She wants to thank Falinda for the food.
- She has good manners!

At the end of the story the children shared their thoughts about Shadow and the white witch.

- Shadow is a *black* cat and he followed Falinda all day.
- But only outside.
- At night he went off on his own and didn't come inside.
- Falinda was a healing witch. She helped people.
- She used herbs. It was good magic—not black magic.
- And she never wore black. She wore regular clothes.
- She had a friendly face.
- Everyone liked her because she was a nice witch.

Several questions were introduced to extend the discussion. The first question was: "Why do you think she named the stray cat 'Homebody'?"

- Because it stayed home and liked to cuddle.
- She's just the opposite of Shadow who liked to wander around at night—alone.
- When she gave her a *name* she was a *pet*. She wasn't a stray anymore.
- It's like in my book. I read *Spooky Night* [Carlson, 1982]. It's about this cat who wanted to be a pet and the people took her in the house and gave her a *name*.
- You could tell how happy she [Homebody] was 'cause she purred. She felt at *home* so she's called *Home*body.

The next question, "What did you think about the way the author ended her story?" sparked some interesting and thoughtful comments.

- It was nice that the stray cat got a home, but she [the author] should've told about Shadow.
- What *happened* to Shadow? I didn't like that—I mean not knowing.
- Maybe he got killed in the forest.
- Maybe he went and met a lady cat and had babies.
- Maybe one of the *babies* was that little stray cat!
- Maybe he always *had* a wife and babies and that's why he went into the forest at night.
- Maybe he was just getting food for them.
- But she [the author] should've said it!
- Maybe he went to live with a *real* witch . . . like in *Spooky Night*!

At this point the teacher suggested that some of them might want to write a sequel about Shadow, using these ideas to explain the mysterious disappearance of the black cat. Several children volunteered to work on this project and a block of time was arranged for them to get started that afternoon. However, since there continued to be an uncomfortable feeling about the story, the teacher suggested that a "story chart" might help them understand the author's intentions. The following information was recorded:

- SETTING

Who: Falinda and the cats
When: Long ago
Where: A village

- BEGINNING

The day Shadow did not come home.

- WHAT HAPPENED

Falinda was sad. She missed Shadow. She thought about him all day. She thought *no* cat could take his place. She did not want the stray cat. She did not want the cats the children brought. But the stray cat made her stop feeling sad and mad. The stray cat made her happy.

- ENDING

Falinda had a cat to love and take care of. She knew Shadow was really gone. The stray cat took the place of Shadow.

After the chart was completed and read aloud one child observed:

I know! This story is all about Falinda. *She's* the important character. She thinks she's never going to love any cat but Shadow. But then pretty soon she does. When my dog died, I didn't think there could *ever* be a dog like her. But now we have another one, and I really love him.

Another child added:

So that's why she [the author] didn't say anything about Shadow—because he's not the main character. It's not really a story about Shadow. But the sequel *we're* going to write will be all about Shadow and his adventures!

Subsequent Sessions

During subsequent group sessions selected cat tales were read aloud, discussed, and compared with stories read in the group or independently during silent reading periods. Each tale shared with the group was selected for its quality as a good story in its own right and for its potential to stimulate thinking about the nature of stories in general. For example, in *Anatole and the Cat* (Titus, 1957) the cat is portrayed as the villain and the mouse as hero. When the children compared this story and its well-developed mouse character with earlier cat tales, they noticed the reversal in viewpoint. In this story they cared what happened to the mouse, whereas in previous stories they easily accepted the role of mouse as victim and its use as a thank you gift. The discussion centered on the kinds of techniques authors use to elicit particular emotional responses from their readers/listeners.

When introduced to *The Church Mouse* (Oakley, 1972) the children noticed that the large cat on the front cover was conversing with a mouse, suggesting an unusual relationship between the two. They also noticed that the story combined fantasy and realism in an interesting way.

- The pictures are so detailed. They look like real life.
- And the animals *act* like animals sort of . . . but they talk and think like people.
- And the people treat them like real mice.

They also observed that, like the mice in *Anatole and the Cat*, the mice in this story were the primary characters, but the cat was not portrayed as a villain.

The Chinese Storyteller (Buck, 1973) was selected for two reasons:

1. The author had used an interesting literary technique, the "story within a story."
2. It represented a particular literary genre, the pourquoi tale.

In this case the storyteller in the story within the story explains why cats and dogs fight.

The stories *All the Cats in the World* (Levitin, 1982) and *A Cat's Tale* (Cate, 1982) were selected because humans are featured as the central characters and the cats are secondary. They serve as interesting contrasts with many of the other cat tales shared in the group sessions or read independently.

Two other literary genres were introduced: *Dick Whittington and His Cat* (Brown, 1950), an old English legend, and "The Priceless Cats" (Jagendorf, 1956), an Italian folktale. Although the two stories are very different they share a common motif: A cat brought by merchants to a catless island plagued by mice takes on extraordinary value as an article of trade.

INDEPENDENT PROJECTS

A number of independent projects were generated and in progress during the weeks the cat tales were being read in group sessions and independently. Several children were interested in learning more about the history of cats; their findings were recorded and shared in a group session. They were especially impressed to discover that stories about cats have been told for almost 4000 years (Zaum, 1985).

Other children found riddles, proverbs, and poems about cats. Their favorites were copied, illustrated, and bound into a big book. One child created a book called, *How to Take Care of Your Pet Cat*. Another made a cat dictionary filled with a variety of facts about cats. A small group worked together to dramatize a favorite cat tale. Other children brought in snapshots of their cats and wrote stories about them. Each picture was mounted on construction paper with its story and included in another book for the class library.

GROUP WRITING PROJECT

At the conclusion of the cat unit the children were invited to create original cat tales. In preparation for this composing process the cat tales read to the group and/or independently were reviewed and the story charts reexamined. The schematic representation of story grammar recorded on the charts served as an aid for producing stories around a basic structure. The children were encouraged to use headings on the story charts to generate questions before and during the composing-revising process.

- What is the setting in my story?
- Who are the characters?
- How does the story begin?
- What is the problem?
- What happens?
- Why does it happen?
- How is the problem solved?

- How does the story end?
- How is the beginning connected to the ending?

The questions which were introduced initially to facilitate the comprehension of narrative were now being used to facilitate the composition of narrative. These questions, derived from story grammar, served to highlight key elements in a story and their relationship to each other.

The quality of the children's responses to the stories selected for this Focus Unit and the quality of their own stories reflected their growing awareness of story structure and their use of this knowledge to enhance their comprehension and the composition of narrative.

References

Fitzgerald, Jill. "The Relationship between Reading Ability and Expectations for Story Structures." *Discourse Processes*, vol. 7, no. 1, 1984, pp. 21–41.

Gordon, Christine, and Carl Braun. "Using Story Schema as an Aid to Reading and Writing." *The Reading Teacher*, vol. 37, no. 2, Nov. 1983, pp. 116–121.

Hansen, Jane. *When Writers Read*. Portsmouth, N.H.: Heinemann, 1987.

McConaughy, Stephanie. "Using Story Structure in the Classroom." *Language Arts*, vol. 57, no. 2, February 1980, pp. 157–165.

Rand, Muriel K. "Story Schema: Theory, Research and Practice. *The Reading Teacher*, vol. 37, no. 4, January 1984, pp. 377–382.

Ringler, Lenore, and Carol Weber. "Comprehending Narrative Discourse: Implications for Instruction." *Reader Meets Author/Bridging the Gap*. Judith Langer and M. Trika Smith-Burke, eds. Newark, DE: IRA, 1982, pp. 180–195.

Sadow, Marilyn. "The Use of Story Grammar in the Design of Questions." *The Reading Teacher*, vol. 35, no. 5, February 1982, pp. 518–522.

Spiegel, Dixie Lee, and Jill Fitzgerald. "Improving Reading Comprehension through Instruction about Story Parts." *The Reading Teacher*, vol. 39, no. 7, March 1986, pp. 676–682.

Stein, Nancy, and Christine Glenn. "An Analysis of Story Comprehension in Elementary School Children." *New Directions in Discourse Processing*, vol. 2, R. O. Freedle, ed. Norwood, N.J.: Ablex, 1979, pp. 53–120.

Bibliography of Cat Tales

Fiction

Adler, C. S. *The Cat Who Was Left Behind*. N.Y.: Clarion, 1981.

Babbitt, Natalie. *Nellie—A Cat on Her Own*. N.Y.: Farrar, Straus & Giroux, 1989.

Baker, Leslie. *The Third-Story Cat*. Boston: Little, Brown, 1987.

Bayley, Nicola, and William Mayne. *The Patchwork Cat*. Hammondsworth: Puffin, 1984.

Belting, Natalia M. *Cat Tales*. "The Cats of the Mountain—A Tale Told in Tuscany," pp. 73–78; "When the Rooster Was King of the Cats—A Tale Told in West Africa," pp. 11–15. N.Y.: Henry Holt, 1959.

Birnbaum, A. *Green Eyes*. N.Y.: Capitol, 1953.

Bohdal, Susi. *Selina, the Mouse, and the Giant Cat*. Boston: Faber & Faber, 1981.

Briggs, Katharine. *Nine Lives: The Folklore of Cats*. N.Y.: Pantheon, 1980.

Brown, Marcia. *Dick Whittington and His Cat*. N.Y.: Scribner, 1950.

Brown, Ruth. *Our Cat Flossie*. N.Y.: Dutton, 1986.

Bryan, Ashley. *The Cat's Purr*. N.Y.: Atheneum, 1985.

Buck, Pearl. *The Chinese Storyteller*. N.Y.: John Day, 1973.

Calhoun, Mary. *Audubon Cat*. N.Y.: Morrow, 1981.

———. *Cross-Country Cat*. N.Y.: Mulberry, 1979.

———. *The Witch of Hissing Hill*. N.Y.: Morrow, 1964.

———. *The Witch Who Lost Her Shadow*. N.Y.: Harper, 1979.

Carlson, Natalie. *Spooky and the Ghost Cat*. N.Y.: Lothrop, Lee & Shepard, 1985.

———. *Spooky Night*. Andrew Glass, illus. N.Y.: Lothrop, Lee & Shepard, 1982.

———. *Spooky and the Wizard's Bats*. N.Y.: Lothrop, Lee & Shepard, 1986.

———. *The Talking Cat and Other Stories of French Canada*. N.Y.: Harper, 1952.

Carpenter, Frances. *Wonder Tales of Dogs and Cats*. "Shippei Taro and the Monster Cat," pp. 128–135; "The Enchanted Black Cat," pp. 222–234. Garden City, N.Y.: Doubleday, 1955.

Cate, Riki. *A Cat's Tale*. N.Y.: Harcourt Brace Jovanovich, 1982.

Cleary, Beverly. *Socks*. N.Y.: Morrow, 1973.

Clymer, Eleanor. *Horatio*. N.Y.: Atheneum, 1968.

Coats, Laura Jane. *Goodyear the City Cat*. N.Y.: Macmillan, 1987.

Coatsworth, Elizabeth. *The Cat Who Went to Heaven*. N.Y.: Macmillan, 1959 (1930).

Coombs, Patricia. The *Magician and McTree*. N.Y.: Lothrop, Lee & Shepard, 1984.

Corbett, Scott. *The Turnabout Trick*. Paul Galdone, illus. Boston: Little, Brown, 1967.

deRegniers, Beatrice Schenk. *This Big Cat and Other Cats I've Known*. (Poems). N.Y.: Crown, 1985.

Domanska, Janina. *A Scythe, A Rooster and a Cat* (adaptation of a Russian folktale). N.Y.: Greenwillow, 1981.

Eisler, Colin. *Cats Know Best*. N.Y.: Dial, 1988.

Fisher, Aileen. *My Cat Has Eyes of Sapphire Blue* (Poems). N.Y.: Crowell, 1973.

Flory, Jane. *We'll Have a Friend for Lunch*. Boston: Houghton Mifflin, 1974.

Gág, Wanda. *Millions of Cats*. N.Y.: Coward, 1928.

Galdone, Paul, adaptor and illus. *Puss in Boots*. N.Y.: Seabury, 1976.

Graeber, Charlotte. *Mustard*. N.Y.: Macmillan, 1982.

Griffiths, Helen. *Moshie Cat*. N.Y.: Holiday House, 1969.

———. *Russian Blue*. N.Y.: Holiday House, 1973.

Grimm Brothers. *Bremen Town Musicians*. Elizabeth Shub, trans.; Janina Domanska, illus. N.Y.: Greenwillow, 1980.

Hamley, Dennis. *Tigger and Friends*. N.Y.: Lothrop, Lee & Shepard, 1989.

Hearn, Lafcadio. *The Boy Who Drew Cats and Other Tales*. N.Y.: Macmillan, 1963.

Hogrogian, Nonny. *The Cat Who Loved to Sing*. N.Y.: Knopf, 1988.

Holman, Felice. *Silently, the Cat and Miss Theodosia*. N.Y.: Macmillan, 1965.

Hooks, William. *Pioneer Cat*. N.Y.: Random House, 1988.

Hurd, Edith T. *The So-So Cat*. N.Y.: Harper, 1964.

Hurlimann, Ruth. *The Proud White Cat*. Anthea Bell, trans. N.Y.: Morrow, 1977.

Jagendorf, M. A. *The Priceless Cats and Other Italian Folk Stories*. N.Y.: Vanguard, 1956.

Jeschke, Susan. *Lucky's Choice*. N.Y.: Scholastic, 1987.

Jeter, Jacky. *The Cat and the Fiddler*. N.Y.: Parents' Magazine Press, 1968.

Joyce, James. *The Cat and the Devil*. N.Y.: Dodd, Mead, 1964.

Kendall, Carol, adaptor. *The Wedding of the Rat Family*. N.Y.: Macmillan, 1988.

Kent, Jack. *The Fat Cat: A Danish Folktale*. N.Y.: Parents' Magazine Press, 1971.

King-Smith, Dick. *Martin's Mice*. N.Y.: Crown, 1989.

Kipling, Rudyard. *The Cat that Walked by Himself—A Just-So Story*. William Stobbs, illus. N.Y.: Peter Bedrick, 1983.

Knott, Howard. *The Winter Cat*. N.Y.: Harper, 1972.

Larrick, Nancy, compiler. *Cats Are Cats*. Ed Young, illus. N.Y.: Philomel, 1988.

Leach, Maria. *The Lion Sneezed: Folktales and Myths of the Cat*. N.Y.: Crowell, 1977.
LeCain, Errol. *The White Cat*. London: Macmillan, 1973.
LeGuin, Ursula. *Catwings*. N.Y.: Watts, 1988.
Levitin, Sonia. *All the Cats in the World*. N.Y.: Harcourt Brace Jovanovich, 1982.
Livingston, Myra Cohn. *Cat Poems*. N.Y.: Holiday House, 1987.
Mann, Peggy. *William the Watch Cat*. Pleasantville, N.Y.: Reader's Digest, 1972.
Manning-Sanders, Ruth. *A Book of Cats and Creatures*. N.Y.: Dutton, 1981.
McHugh, Elisabet. *Beethoven's Cat*. N.Y.: Atheneum, 1988.
Menuhin, Yehudi, and Christopher Hope. *The King, the Cat and the Fiddle*. N.Y.: Holt, Rinehart and
   Winston, 1983.
Miles, Miska. *Nobody's Cat*. Boston: Little, Brown, 1969.
Ness, Evaline. *Sam, Bangs, and Moonshine*. N.Y.: Holt, Rinehart and Winston, 1966.
Northrup, Mili. *The Watch Cat*. Indianapolis, IN: Bobbs-Merrill, 1968.
Oakley, Graham. *The Church Mouse*. N.Y.: Atheneum, 1972.
Robinson, Tom. *Buttons*. N.Y.: Viking, 1938.
Smith, Susan M. *No One Should Have Six Cats!* Cleveland: Modern Curriculum Press, 1982.
Stanley, Diane. *A Country Tale*. N.Y.: Four Winds, 1985.
Stolz, Mary. *Cat Walk*. N.Y.: Harper, 1983.
Thayer, Jane. *The Cat that Joined the Club*. N.Y.: Morrow, 1962.
Titus, Eve. *Anatole and the Cat*. Paul Galdone, illus. N.Y.: McGraw-Hill, 1957.
Turkle, Brinton. *Do Not Open*. N.Y.: Dutton, 1981.
Whitney, Alma. *Leave Herbert Alone*. Reading, MA: Addison Wesley, 1972.
Wolski, Slawomir. *Tiger Cat*. Elizabeth Crawford, trans. N.Y.: North-South, 1988.
Zaum, Marjorie, reteller. *Catlore: Tales from around the World*. N.Y.: Atheneum, 1985.

Nonfiction

Bridge, Linda. *Cats: Little Tigers in Your House*. Washington, D.C.: National Geographic Society,
   1974.
Feder, Jan. *The Life of a Cat*. Chicago: Children's Press International, 1982.
Grabianski, Janusz. *Cats*. N.Y.: Franklin Watts, 1966.
Kuklin, Susan. *Taking My Cat to the Vet*. N.Y.: Bradbury, 1988.
Stevens, Carla. *The Birth of Sunset's Kittens*. N.Y.: Young Scott Books, 1969.
Towe, Elizabeth, and Christine Metcalf. *All Color Book of Cats*. N.Y.: Crown, 1972.
Winston, Peggy. *Wild Cats*. Washington, D.C.: National Geographic Society, 1981.

Magic Object Tales: Literature, Literacy, and Critical Thinking

THINKING, READING, AND WRITING

If a primary goal of education in a democratic society is to produce individuals who can and do think independently and critically, then our schools need to provide adequate opportunities for students to engage in critical thinking. The Focus Units in this book are based on the premise that literary response, comprehension and composition, and critical thinking are interrelated, and that students develop and use critical-thinking skills as they actively construct meaning through reading and writing literature. Reading is a process of critical thinking when readers activate relevant information from their stored knowledge and use it to make predictions, formulate questions, and relate the information in the text to their own experiences and values. Reading is a critical thinking process when readers/thinkers view reading as a meaning-generating process and interpret texts in light of their prior knowledge and literary history to generate and shape meaning. Readers/thinkers engage in analysis, synthesis, application, and evaluation of the meaning generated from a text (Bloom and Krathwohl, 1956).

The dialogue, a central feature of the Focus Unit, provides opportunities for students to think out loud, to articulate their thinking, and to share their thoughts with others in a supportive environment in which risk-taking, divergent thinking, and exploration are viewed as natural and essential aspects of the learning process. The Focus Unit provides opportunities for students to move beyond the text; to respond to it through writing, art, and drama. They are invited to express their thoughts, feelings, and ideas in writing and to use writing as a vehicle for reflection, problem-solving, and critical and creative thinking.

This chapter highlights the development of critical thinking and literary and literacy skills in the context of a Focus Unit featuring a basic literary motif: magic objects. Since special attention is given to metacognition and questioning, these two strategies will be discussed first.

Metacognition

In the *Handbook of Reading Research* (Pearson, 1984) researchers Linda Baker and Ann Brown define metacognition as "the knowledge and control the child has over his/her own thinking and learning activities, including reading" (p. 353). They discuss two basic aspects of meta-cognition associated with the reading process. Readers who are consciously aware that reading is a meaning-getting/constructive process constantly monitor what they are reading to make sure it makes sense. Awareness of what to do when comprehension breaks down is another aspect of metacognition.

Reading requires metacognitive skills and self-regulatory and autocritical strategies. "Effective readers are those who monitor their own understanding while reading, being constantly alert to comprehension failure" (Brown, 1982, p. 29). Self-monitoring and self-correction differentiate good readers from poor ones. Successful readers are aware that reading is an active process of information-gathering, evaluating, and hypothesis-testing; they monitor their comprehension and evaluate their progress in light of their purposes (Brown, 1982, p. 49).

Writing, like reading, involves metacognitive reflection. Writing . . . "is essentially an exploration into the unknown: we write to discover what we know. The desire to write becomes a need to discern order and make connections" (Glatthorn, 1985, p. 69).

Questioning

Questioning can be used as a teaching tool to facilitate critical thinking in comprehension and composition. The art of teaching entails the art of questioning students so as to stimulate and guide reflection and to form in them the independent habit of inquiry (Dewey, 1910). All learning begins with questions. The teacher demonstrates questioning strategies for students and invites them to formulate questions to direct their inquiries. The quality of readers' interactions with a text depends, in large part, on the quality of the questions they initiate to guide the comprehension process and to generate meaning. To become an independent learner one must learn the art of questioning.

Questions should be invitations to set up possibilities. "Teachers should deliberately encourage and support their pupils in developing an open and hypothetical style of learning" (Barnes, 1975, p. 52). "Hypothesis-demanding questions" would help to develop a "what if . . ." frame of mind and would encourage student-initiated exploratory and hypothetical questions and statements.

THE MAGIC OBJECT FOCUS UNIT

This unit was designed to introduce students in second- and third-grade classrooms to traditional and modern stories with a common literary motif, and to invite them to compare these tales in terms of the motif, as well as the language, patterns, narrative elements, and basic themes found in the tales.

This chapter is structured to point out the nature of the questions used by the teacher to foster critical thinking, and the nature of critical thinking reflected in children's responses to literary selections. As in other Focus Units students were invited to share their comments and questions prior to the introduction of teacher-initiated questions. Students also assumed greater responsibility for the direction and content of the dialogue as they accumulated literary knowledge and gained experience as critical readers/thinkers in the course of the Focus Unit sequence.

Teacher-initiated questions introduced prior to reading a story aloud are listed as *Prequestions*. Questions introduced at significant points during oral presentations are listed as *Insert Questions*. *Postquestions* are used to designate questions introduced after the story has been read aloud and the children have had an opportunity to respond spontaneously with their comments and questions. Examples of teacher-initiated questions and the theoretical rationale (enclosed in brackets) for the questions are included along with excerpts from students' dialogue.

Session One

The Flying Shoes by Cynthia Jameson (1973).

Prequestions

1. Can you name any stories about magic objects that you've heard or read? [This question was designed to introduce the new unit to the children and to set the stage for comprehension by prompting retrieval of relevant information from their memory stores.]

The story titles generated by the children in response to this question were recorded on a chart. For children who had difficulty retrieving relevant titles the teacher assisted with prompts: "I'm thinking of a story about a magic pot . . . or a magic mirror . . . or a magic pipe." Just before reading the first story aloud the teacher told the children she would be sharing with them many different stories about magic objects. "As you listen to each story look for the magic object or objects. Then we will compare these with the magic objects in the stories listed on the chart."

Insert Questions

1. What do you think will happen next? [This type of question encourages children to make predictions, a basic reading strategy. By asking them to predict what might happen next, the teacher helps them develop an anticipatory attitude toward print.]
2. What is the meaning of:
   The shoes had a will of their own.
   The shoes were almost as old as his feet.
   These shoes are cursed!
   [Key words or phrases which contribute significantly to the meaning of the text may need to be clarified or translated. This focus on new words, unfamiliar phrases, or figurative language helped students make sense of the text. They were encouraged to figure out the meaning from the context.]

Postquestions

1. How did you figure out what was going to happen? [This question was directed toward children who made accurate predictions during the story. Their responses demonstrated metacognitive reflection. For example, one child used the context within the narrative; another used knowledge of patterns found in similar stories.]
2. What was the magic object? [Literal comprehension was required.]
3. What magic powers did it have? [This required inferential thinking because the information is only implied in the text, not stated explicitly.]
4. Which character owned the magic object?
5. How did each character get the object? [Literal comprehension of narrative sequence was required.]
6. Did it work the same for each character? Explain.
7. What are the important differences between the characters using the magic object?

   [The last two questions helped the children to see the role of the magic object in the story and the way it is used to highlight different qualities of the characters. The true owner wove the shoes and cared for them. Of the three who took the shoes, one stole them because of need and envy; one took them to inspire envy in his friends; the third took them out of greed. Previous questions requiring literal comprehension were used to build up to the questions which required higher-level thinking.]
8. What do you think the storyteller wants you to learn? [This question focussed on the theme as well as the didactic nature of many folktales intended to transmit values to each new generation.]

Session Two

Strega Nona, retold by Tomie dePaola (1975).

Prequestions

1. Look at the cover. Have you ever heard of Tomie dePaola?
2. Do you know of other stories written by this person? What kind of story do you think this one will be?
3. What do you think this story will be about? [These questions set the stage for enjoying the story. Many children were familiar with this popular author/artist. One child predicted that this would be a "funny story with make believe in it, and the pot will be magic."]
4. The cover tells us that this is "an old tale retold and illustrated by Tomie dePaola." What does this mean? [This question drew attention to the difference between traditional and modern tales. Since traditional tales are from the oral tradition they have no identified authors. Words such as "told," "retold," "adapted by" are clues that the story has been handed down from early storytellers.]

Insert Questions

1. Do any of you want to change your prediction about the old lady with the pot on the book cover?
2. After the scene in which Big Anthony first discovers the magic pot: What do you think Big Anthony will do next? How do you know? [This last question invited metacognitive reflection about predictions.]

Postquestions

This time the children were invited to formulate questions to get the discussion started. The first five questions below were introduced by children; the rest were initiated by the teacher.

1. What did Strega Nona do to help people?
2. What magic objects did she have?
3. How come the magic pot didn't work for Big Anthony the way it worked for Strega Nona? [This question prompted responses which emphasized the misuse of magical objects obtained by deception.
   "He didn't know the magic formula because it wasn't *his*."
   "It only works for the one who owns it."
   "He didn't know about the three kisses!"]
4. What did Strega Nona tell Big Anthony before she went out? [This question focussed attention on the "warning," a common pattern found in magic object tales.]
5. What happened when Big Anthony *didn't pay attention*!? [This question required the children to infer a cause-effect relationship between Big Anthony's personality traits and the problem with the pasta pot.]
6. How was Strega Nona similar to the old man in *The Flying Shoes*?
7. Which character was Big Anthony similar to in *The Flying Shoes*? Or, How was he similar to the merchant?
   [Questions 6 and 7 encouraged the children to compare two texts and to see connections between two different tales, one from Italy, the other from Russia. In this case they were asked to find parallels between characters in two separate stories, requiring them to think *beyond* the information in a given text. In response to Question 6 one child noted, "In *both* stories the magic object only worked for the *true* owner." One response to Question 7 was, "Big Anthony and the merchant both just wanted to show off to all the people!"]
8. What other stories on our chart are about magic pots? In what ways are the pots different?
9. How would you explain these differences? [This question was intended to focus attention on the way the setting produces different details in otherwise similar stories. One child reasoned, "Strega Nona's pot made pasta because it's Italy!" Another child exclaimed, "Oh, I get it! The pot from India made rice because they like to eat rice in India. So . . . I guess they must eat porridge in England! (the setting of the third magic pot tale)." In addition to stimulating critical thinking, this question contributed to the literary background of these children by giving them a glimpse of the way folktales are shaped by the cultures from which they evolve.]

10. What did Big Anthony learn? [This required interpretation of the theme.]

11. What did Strega Nona mean when she said, "The punishment must fit the crime" before she made him eat all that pasta? [This required elaboration, translating text language into one's own words.]

Session Three

Tattercoats: An Old English Tale told by Flora Annie Steel (1976).

Prequestions

1. Look at the title. What is the meaning of the word *tatters*? What do you think *Tattercoats* means?

2. What do you think this story could be about?

3. Look at the picture on the cover. What kind of story do you think it is? [This question invited the children to classify stories. One child said, "I think it'll be one of those 'long ago, far away' stories." Another child predicted, "It will be fantasy—not real life." Later, they were asked to evaluate these initial predictions as the story unfolded.]

4. The title page tells us that this story was "*told* by Flora Annie Steel." What does this suggest? [This question stimulated the children to draw from their prior knowledge, gained from the previous discussion of *Strega Nona*, and to apply it to this new text. One child replied, "It means that Mrs. Steel didn't make up the story herself. It's an old, old one that she decided to put in a book." Another speculated, "She's a lot like Tomie dePaola. They both like old stories, and they like to tell them in their own words."]

Insert Question

1. Who do you think the stranger really is? Why? [This question invited the children to make predictions based on their store of literary knowledge.]

Postquestions

1. Why didn't the rich old man want to *look* at his granddaughter? [This question was intended to help clarify the meaning of the introductory paragraph which presents the major setting of the tale.]

2. After several responses to this first postquestion, one child asked, "I have a question about something confusing. How come those servants were so mean to Tattercoats? [This question required inferential thinking to fill significant gaps in the narrative. The discussion helped to clarify the notion that the servants modeled their behavior after their master's.]

3. How do you think the servants would have behaved toward her if the grandfather had loved her? [They were asked to seek alternatives in response to a hypothetical question (Barnes, 1975). This question, asked by the teacher to expand on the second question, reinforced

their understanding of the motivation behind the servants' behavior which is never stated in the text.]

4. Why wasn't Tattercoats given a real name? [The children were asked to infer the significance of this omission.]

5. Who was kind to Tattercoats? How did they help her? [These were literal questions about information which is explicitly stated in the text. It was important for pointing to a common motif in folklore: the role of the "helper" character.]

At this point the children were encouraged to ask questions about the story.

6. What was the magic object?

7. What was *magic* about it? [This student-initiated question prompted a number of different interpretations about the pipe which helped several children grasp the logical relationships between significant events in the narrative sequence.]

8. What other story is like this? [Most of the children had recognized the similarity between Tattercoats and Cinderella early in the story reading. This student's question initiated a thoughtful comparative analysis. "The gooseherd is like the fairy godmother in Cinderella because he helped Tattercoats get to the party."
"The grandfather is like the stepmother. He was mean to Tattercoats and she was mean to Cinderella."
"The servants treated Tattercoats just like the grandfather; and the stepsisters treated Cinderella just like the stepmother."
"Both girls lost their moms."
"The pipe is like the wand. The pipe changed the geese to pages; and the wand changed the mice to horses."
"The gooseherd disappears at the end. So does the fairy godmother."
"The grandfather refused to take Tattercoats to the ball. The stepmother refused to take Cinderella to the ball."
"But then it got different. Tattercoats *came* to the ball at midnight—in rags! Then *after* twelve she got changed and was beautiful. Cinderella came in nice clothes but at midnight they changed to rags."
"And the prince saw Tattercoats in rags first! The other prince saw Cinderella in her beautiful dress first!"
"Maybe *that* prince would never have paid attention to Cinderella if he saw her in rags instead of that fancy gown!"]

9. How would these stories have been different if the grandfather and stepmother had been nice to Tattercoats and Cinderella? [This question required the assumption of a hypothetical stance. It was introduced by the teacher to call attention to the key role of the antagonist in a narrative. One child responded, "The story would be sort of boring!" Another added, "You wouldn't feel sorry for them (the heroines) and want to get even with the *mean* characters!"]

At the end of the third session the teacher pointed to a display table which held a collection of many magic object stories (*see* bibliography at the end of this chapter). She invited the children to select stories they'd like to read independently. A regular quiet reading time was scheduled for this purpose. In subsequent group story sessions discussions covered not only those stories which had been read aloud but those which the children had read independently. In addition, small groups were established so that children who had selected the same stories for independent reading could enter into a dialogue about the stories and could work together to transform written texts into art, drama, or dance. The children also enjoyed creating questions about each story. These questions were printed on a card and clipped to the back of the book for the next reader to try to answer. One group began to evaluate these questions to determine "which ones are the most interesting." They concluded that the most interesting questions were:

. . . the ones where the author doesn't give you the answer in the story; and the ones where you have to look for clues; and the ones that make you think about another story.

Session Four

The Magic Stove adapted by Mirra Ginsburg (1983).

This session opened with the children's spontaneous comments. They made predictions based on the title and book cover illustration. Their comments suggested that they had begun to internalize the questioning strategies modeled by the teacher in the first three sessions, and were learning new ways to interact with texts and become critical readers.

The children noted that the couple on the front cover looked poor; and they predicted that the magic stove would give them food. They couldn't decide what role the rooster (also on the cover) would play in the story. One child said, "I guess that's a question we'll be able to answer after we hear the story!" Thus, they had a question and several predictions to set the stage for their interaction with this narrative.

As the story was read aloud the children were very anxious to express their thoughts. They were invited to interrupt the story with new predictions or relevant comments. The children's contributions demonstrated their ability to apply new reading/thinking strategies. They were actively interacting with the text to generate meaning. For example, at the point in the story when the old man shared his last piece of bread with the rooster, one child exclaimed, "It's the rooster who's going to get them the magic stove. I just know it!" When asked to explain this prediction he replied, "Because in a lot of those old stories someone gets rewarded for being kind and sharing with someone who has magic powers hidden away!" The story was interrupted again when the king arrives on the scene and sees the magic stove: "I bet he's going to steal it." Again the child was asked to explain. "Well, it's just like *The Flying Shoes* and *Strega Nona*. People want the magic things because they're greedy or jealous." These children modeled their metacognitive strategies for their classmates and their use of prior literary experiences to make sense of current texts.

The third interruption occurred when the king is trying to get rid of the rooster who's demanding the return of the stove. The king throws the rooster in the pond, but he swallows all the water. Then the king throws him into the fire. The children immediately responded with a logical conclusion: "The rooster's going to put out the fire with the water!"

As the story unfolded, the children engaged in an ongoing dialogue which was remarkably similar to the internal dialogue the critical reader generates in interacting with a text.

Postquestions

1. Think about the predictions you made before and during the story. Did you change anything? Add anything? What new information made you revise or change your predictions? [These questions provide opportunities for students to articulate their thinking and to engage in metacognitive strategies.]

2. Why did the old man get the magic stove? [This question was introduced by one of the children. It focussed attention on the basic folktale pattern in which magic objects are given as rewards for kindness. At this point the children spontaneously compared this story with others they had heard or read independently. They had begun to make connections between texts on their own, and to identify recurring patterns in traditional literature. This discussion prompted another child to ask a question which reflected his ability to use the language of literary analysis.]

3. Who was the helper in this story? [By this time the children were ready to identify this specific character type, "the helper." They grasped the idea that the rooster (in *The Magic Stove*) served the same function as the gooseherd in *Tattercoats*, and the shoes in *The Flying Shoes*.]

4. We've been using the word "prediction." What does it mean? [This question was introduced by the teacher to check the children's understanding of the word which had been used in context but not specifically defined. Some of their responses were:
   "It's like a guess—but not a wild guess."
   "It's like when you predict the weather; you tell how it is going to be tomorrow."
   It's when you figure out what could happen later on or in the future—like who will win a race."]

5. How do you make predictions about a particular story? [This question was used to help children become aware of thinking strategies behind their predictions:
   "I use the title first—and make a guess from that."
   "I guess from what happened in other stories I know."
   "I figured out that the rooster would save himself with the pond water—because I know that you use water to put out a fire."]

Session Five

The Little Jewel Box by Marianna Mayer (1986).

The children looked at the cover of the book and made these comments:

"Well, the magic object is probably the jewel box."
"And that girl on the cover is probably the main character."

"I wonder why she's dressed like a boy?"

"We'll have to answer that later!"

"I think those animals—that bird and frog and mouse—help her."

"They're probably the 'helper characters,' like the rooster and the gooseherd."

"I wonder what kind of trouble she gets into?"

Their comments suggest that they're making spontaneous predictions, using their prior knowledge about narrative structure and character types, and asking questions which will guide their listening comprehension.

Insert Questions and Comments

1. Explain this picture in which Isabel is gazing into the fire. What does she see? [The children must use their schema for abstract representations to figure out that the dragon in the flames was "in her imagination." That is, they had to read beyond the surface structure of the picture to interpret the meaning intended by the illustrator.]

2. Where the text reads, "Isabel decided to go out in the world to seek adventure," a child said, "*Now* I know why she's dressed like a boy. She's doing just what the *boys* usually do in old stories. You know—the prince or the third son goes off to seek his fortune or do something brave."

3. Other brief interruptions in the story occurred as children made predictions, revised or confirmed earlier predictions, and noted similarities with other stories.

Postquestions

1. What was Isabel's dream? What does this tell you about her? [Inferences about implied meanings are derived from explicit information.]

2. What were the first two tasks she had to perform? Why did John's father set up these tasks for her? [These questions required detection of the logical relationships between events.]

3. What is the meaning of this sentence? "Then my dear," the master said calmly, "you must forfeit your life; that is *if* you are still here tomorrow." [This question required detection of implied meanings behind words. The children figured out the meaning of the unfamiliar word, *forfeit*, from the context as well as what the master was probably thinking: "He thought she would run away as soon as he said that! And that's just what he really wanted—to just get rid of her!"]

4. Can you think of other stories in which the main character had to pass tests or do special tasks? [This question required retrieval of relevant stories from their literary backgrounds and was introduced to focus on another recurring pattern in folktales.]

5. What was the third task, and who helped her? [At this point the children recalled their earlier predictions.]

6. Why did the animals help? [This focussed attention on a recurring theme: rewards for kindness.]

7. This kind of story is called a "quest tale." It is a story in which the main character searches

for something. What was Isabel's quest? [A new word was introduced in context so children could add it to their growing store of language for literary analysis.]

8. Do you have any comments or questions for the author if she were to visit us or if you were to write to her?

9. What would you have added or changed if *you* were the author?

[The last two questions invited the children to engage in creative thinking, to explore possibilities and alternatives. Here are a few of the responses: "I'd ask her what happened to the servant girl who stole the magic jewel box. I think she should have gotten punished for what she did." "I'd ask Mrs. Mayer about Isabel's parents. I think they should have been invited to the wedding and to live in the castle! It didn't seem right that she just forgot about her parents." "I would like to ask her why she made the animals so big sometimes and then *normal* size at other times."]

Session Six

Aladdin and the Wonderful Lamp retold by Andrew Lang (1981).

Again the session opened with the spontaneous comments of the children. They assumed that the wonderful lamp must be the magic object and predicted that someone magic would emerge from it as in *The Little Jewel Box*. Several children noticed the "retold by Andrew Lang" on the cover and commented that he wasn't the "real" (*i.e.*, original) author and that the story "must be one of those very, very old ones."

Postquestions

1. How did Aladdin get the magic lamp? [This required the ability to grasp the complex language of this retelling, and to reconstruct the sequence of events leading up to this point in the story.]

2. Why did the magician send Aladdin into the cave to get the lamp? [This information was given briefly *after* the event, so they had to restructure the sequence to make sense of the narrative.]

3. When did Aladdin first discover the lamp's power? How do you know he was not aware of this when he first found the lamp? [This required the use of subtle clues to draw conclusions.]

4. What other story is like this one? [This question was introduced by one of the children.]

5. In what ways are the two stories similar? [Most of the children recognized the similarity between *Aladdin* and *The Little Jewel Box*. As they looked for more specific connections they examined the structure. Here is an excerpt from their comparative analysis:
"Men came out of the magic objects to serve the owner."
"Both Isabel and Aladdin found someone to marry—but just because they are poor, they have to do impossible tasks."
"After the weddings in the stories the magic object is stolen and their house disappears!"
"So does Isabel's husband and Aladdin's wife."
"Then they have to go search for it or they'll die. It's like a quest!"]

6. How is this story similar to, or different from, the other stories with magic objects? [In the following dialogue excerpt the children argued a point and found supportive evidence in the text. The teacher only intervened once: "In the other stories, the main character got the magic object as a reward for kindness or for a gift of love. But Aladdin just *took* the lamp. It wasn't his really."

   "Yes it was!"

   "Why do you say that? Did the storyteller give this information?" (Teacher's questions.)

   "Well not exactly. But the magician said he could only get the lamp from the hand of Aladdin—so maybe it belonged to his family like the little jewel box."]

7. Why do you think the storyteller decided not to let the magician keep the lamp? [This led the children beyond the text to consider the nature of the fairytale. One seven-year-old responded, "Because he was going to rule the world and he's evil—but this is like a regular fairytale—so the good guy gets to be king!"]

Session Seven

"The Tinder Box" by Hans Christian Andersen (1970).

Prequestions

1. Do you know this author?
2. Can you name any stories he's written? [These questions were followed by a brief explanation about the difference between the folk- and fairytales read prior to this and Andersen's *original* stories—the difference between traditional and modern stories.]

Postquestions

1. How did the soldier get the magic object? [The children noted how similar this was to the Aladdin story. They expressed their opinions about this story:

   "But I didn't like it when the soldier killed the witch for no good reason. I mean—she wasn't going to *hurt* him!"

   "It was different in Aladdin! That magician was going to let him die in the cave."

   "I know! It didn't seem right when the soldier did that. The heroes in other fairytales never do that."

   "But he *was* kind to the poor people and gave them money. So he wasn't *all* bad."

   "Maybe he *knew* the witch would do evil with it like the magician, so he had to get rid of her."

   "But then Mr. Andersen should have *said* that. That way it would be okay."

   "But he [the soldier] didn't even know it was *magic* until later."

   "Yeah—but he probably *guessed* it was."

   "Well, I still think Mr. Andersen should have *told* us why the soldier killed the witch."]

2. What was meant by ". . . and none of his friends came to see him, because there were so

many stairs to climb"? [This required a translation of the denotative meaning to interpret the hidden, connotative meaning. The children responded: "They only like him when he's rich—not when he has to live in an *attic*!"

"They're not *real* friends!"

"I didn't like *that* part either!"]

3. How else is this story like *Aladdin*? [The children noted that the soldier ended up marrying the princess and ruling the kingdom, just as in Aladdin. Then the teacher gave a little background information about Andersen and his childhood. He especially enjoyed listening to *The Arabian Nights* as a child. The children were not at all surprised to learn that the Aladdin story had been one of his favorites.]

Session Eight

The Water of Life retold by Barbara Rogasky (1986).

Spontaneous comments guided by internalized questions set the stage for this story. Here is an excerpt from the opening dialogue:

"I bet the water of life is something that can cure sick people."

". . . or bring dead people back to life!"

"Maybe the story's about someone who goes off to find it for someone who is sick or dead."

"Then it would be a *quest* tale!"

"And then he would get the magic from a weird stranger because he's so nice to him."

"The pictures look so real."

"And look at all the details. This is a very good artist."

"I know her! She came here once. She signed a book for me!"

"Would you bring it to school?"

The teacher showed the children a picture of the artist. After looking at some of the beautiful illustrations in the book one child exclaimed, "Look! The princess looks just like Mrs. Hyman!" [the illustrator].

As they listened to the story the children became very emotionally involved in this complex tale of quest and intrigue. They expressed anger against the treacherous brothers; horror when the king ordered their innocent victim, the youngest son, to be killed; and relief when the huntsman decided not to kill the boy. ("Just like in 'Snow White,'" exclaimed one child.)

But the emotional response was intertwined with cognitive and metacognitive responses: The children engaged in the process of confirming or revising original predictions; and they made new predictions as the story unfolded. For example, after the first two brothers were punished by the dwarf, they predicted that the youngest brother would be nice to the dwarf and get rewarded.

Postquestions

1. What folktale patterns did you find in this story? [At first they were puzzled by this challenging question. Then one child asked about the meaning of the word *pattern*. Other

children responded with various examples until eventually a child said, "Oh I see. A pattern in a folktale is the part that's a *repeat*! Like when someone gets rewarded for kindness, it's like a *repeat* of a lot of the other stories."

"And when the main character uses the magic thing to help others . . . like when the youngest son helped those three kings who had war and famine."]

2. How did the king discover his son's innocence? [This question helped the children see the logical connection between two different episodes in the narrative.]

3. What test did the princess use to discover which brother was the true savior? [This question focussed attention on the role of greed in this and other folktales.]

Session Nine

"Grandfather Pavel and the Priceless Pebble," *A Book of Heroes and Heroines* by Ruth Manning-Sanders (1982).

Since this was the first story included in a collection, instead of a single illustrated edition, the teacher took some time with the children to look closely at the anthology, the table of contents, and the illustrations. Several of the children were disappointed that there were so few pictures; and some were concerned that "all those words would be hard to understand!" One child replied, "You just have to *listen* better—like when the picture on the T.V. gets like . . . lines." Another child added, "It's like in the olden days when they only had stuff on radio and you had to *pretend* the picture." The teacher suggested that they try to make pictures in their minds as they listened to the story.

Prequestions

1. What is the meaning of the word "priceless"? [The children made a number of attempts to figure it out before the teacher said, "It's something too valuable to be given a price. Can you give me an example?" One child said, "It's like my mom would never sell me because she loves me too much!"]

2. Can you name some other stories about magic pebbles? [The children named *Sylvester and the Magic Pebble* by William Steig and *Alexander and the Wind-Up Mouse* by Leo Lionni which they had read independently. Some of the children predicted that a character would be transformed as in the Steig and Lionni stories.]

As the story was read aloud it became apparent to the children that this original prediction was inaccurate. In fact, as soon as they came to the scene where the grandfather helps the lizard escape the fire, one child cried, "Oh—it's going to be *that* kind of story—where someone does a good deed and then gets rewarded!" Another child noted, "But there *was* a lizard in the Alexander story; and it had the magic pebble. So that's the same." When they came to the description of the priceless pebble from the crown of the Emperor Lizard, another child said, "This story has a lot more details than the other pebble stories."

Postquestions

1. What was the grandfather's first wish? What does this tell you about him? [The second question required inferential thinking and the ability to draw conclusions.]
2. Why did the grandfather hand the priceless pebble to Ivan? What did this tell you about him? [Character traits often have to be inferred from behavior.]
3. What did Ivan wish for? [This question was the starting point for a comparison with *The Little Jewel Box*. The children observed:

   "When Ivan uses the pebble, the palace is whisked away just like when the maid got the little jewel box."
   "The helpers were the same too. The cat and dog helped grandfather get the pebble back; and the animals helped Isabel get her jewel box back."
   "And both dropped it in the water because they started arguing."
   "When that fisherman catches the fish it's the one that swallowed the pebble! It made me think of a story about a tin soldier that got swallowed by a fish."
   "Oh, I read that! When the cook opened the fish there's the toy soldier!"]

4. What is the grandfather's last wish? [This question was intended to focus on a basic theme of the story.

   "He wished he could just be back in his little hut with his dog and cat."
   "He felt more at home and happy in the hut than in that big palace."
   "It's like the ending in *Sylvester and the Magic Pebble*. The mom and dad said that the *best* wish had come true, because they got their son back. So they didn't need any more wishes either."
   "It's like in *The Wizard of Oz* when she [Dorothy] said, 'There's no place like home.'"]

Session Ten

The Magic Horse retold by Sally Scott (1985).

This was the last story read aloud in the magic object Unit. By this time the children used their own questions to generate discussion before, during, and after the reading of the story. They noticed the "retold by" and saw it as a clue for classifying this story as a traditional tale. They noticed that the pictures had much in common with those in *Aladdin and the Wonderful Lamp*; and they were delighted to discover that both tales were set in Persia. They noticed that the magic ebony horse was the cause of several problems, which in turn set the plot in motion—and it was the cause of happiness as well.

At the conclusion of this last session the teacher helped the children move toward synthesis by asking them to think about *all* the stories of magic objects and how they are connected. In the process they would be focussing on some of the important characteristics and patterns of folklore. The children's responses included:

"The stories mostly start with 'long ago and far away' or 'once upon a time.'"
"But each story is from a specific country. But not now—long ago in that country. Like Persia doesn't even have the same *name* anymore!"
"And they end happily ever after."

"And there's magic. The magic objects are usually given as rewards for kindness."

"Sometimes the magic object helps a poor person get rich. Or it helps find someone to marry."

"And the magic objects get stolen a lot of times. But usually the greedy people get punished."

"And sometimes the magic thing gives a lot of wishes but the person realizes he's happy with what he already *has*."

"Like in *Sylvester* and the story about the priceless pebble."

"Most of the stories have helpers like a dwarf or an old man or an animal."

"And when there were three brothers you know the youngest is going to win in the end."

"Because he's usually kind and clever."

The children gradually pulled together information from many tales which they had heard or read independently. They developed generalizations about the nature of these traditional tales. In the process they were building up a "folktale schema," as well as their "narrative schema." For example, they were becoming familiar with specific character types—such as the helper, villain, and hero/heroine—and their roles and functions in a narrative sequence. The children could see the connection between the rooster in *The Magic Stove*, the dwarf in *The Water of Life*, the gooseherd in *Tattercoats*, and the shoes in *The Flying Shoes*. As one child put it, "They were all helpers; but they could punish greedy or bad people too."

The question "How did the magic objects change the lives of the main characters?" was introduced to focus attention on the role of the magic object in plot development. Another question—"What were the basic themes of these stories?"—helped to highlight key themes in traditional literature, such as the rewarding of honesty, kindness, and generosity; and the punishment of deceit, cruelty, and greed.

The discussion generated by these two questions set the stage for the final question: "Who told these old tales and why did they tell them?"

This required divergent thinking and creative reasoning. The children's responses included:

"A lot of the main characters are poor, so probably the first storytellers were poor people too. They told stories about their own lives."

"And a lot of times they [the poor characters] got rich because they were kind or good. When you don't have things, you *wish* you did—and so they (the storytellers) told stories about getting magic things so their wishes could come true!"

"Some of the stories are about rich people—like kings and queens in big palaces. . . ."

"Well—the regular people probably like to tell stories about kings and queens. It's like when you watch *Dallas* and all those rich people—you think about what it would be like to be so rich and important."

"So—those old stories are sort of like wishing tales!"

"But the *real* reason they told stories is because they didn't have T.V.!"

"They didn't even have radio!"

"Or books!"

"So—at night they probably all sat around telling stories until it was time for bed!"

"But I think the stories weren't just for *fun*. They all seem to teach a lesson sort of. Like—you shouldn't be greedy, and you shouldn't lie."

"Because the kind people got rewarded, and the greedy ones got punished."

"So the stories show it's better to be kind and friendly!"

The excerpts from this ongoing dialogue about magic object tales demonstrate that the children gradually moved from analysis to synthesis. As they participated in this sequential, cumulative literary experience they were learning ways of interacting thoughtfully with texts and using various critical reading strategies to generate meaning. More specifically, they discovered a great deal about the folktale as a traditional literary genre; and they acquired background knowledge which enabled them to respond critically and creatively in subsequent reading experiences.

WRITING

The magic object Focus Unit culminated in a writing project in which the children composed and illustrated their own magic object tales. The exploration of magic object tales from different countries, the nature of the folktale as a literary genre, and the structure of narrative served as preparation for this creative experience. The writing experience, in turn, served to reinforce the children's new knowledge and understandings.

The final products of the writing project were delightful, original tales which the children proudly shared with their classmates in the next group story sessions. They were asked the same kinds of thoughtful questions and were given the same sort of comments from their peers and teacher as those professional writers had received earlier.

LITERATURE, LITERACY, AND CRITICAL THINKING

The magic object Focus Unit provided a context for students for learning to use critical thinking skills to explore, study, and enjoy literature. In this context they were building the knowledge background necessary to make sense of and respond critically to literary texts. They were learning to activate relevant knowledge from their background store to interact with new texts, to make predictions and formulate questions, and to consider new information in light of prior knowledge and new texts in light of earlier texts. They articulated and shared their thinking with others in the social context of the classroom, as they engaged in the process of becoming critical and creative readers and writers.

References

Baker, Linda, and Ann L. Brown. "Metacognitive Skills and Reading." *Handbook of Reading Research*. P. David Pearson, ed. N.Y.: Longman, 1984, pp. 353–394.

Barnes, Douglas. *From Communication to Curriculum*. N.Y.: Penguin, 1975, pp. 35–78.

Bloom, Benjamin, and David Krathwohl, eds. *Taxonomy of Educational Objectives*. N.Y.: David McKay, 1956.

Brown, Ann. "Learning How to Learn from Reading." *Reader Meets Author/Bridging the Gap*. Langer, Judith A., and M. Trika Smith-Burke, eds. Newark, DE: IRA, 1982, pp. 26–54.

Dewey, John. *How We Think*. Boston: Heath, 1910.

Glatthorn, Allan A. "Thinking and Writing." *Essays on the Intellect*. Frances R. Link, ed. Alexandria, VA: ASCD, 1985, pp. 67–88.

Bibliography: Magic Object Tales

Andersen, Hans Christian. *The Flying Chest and Other Tales*. Friedrich Hechelmann, illus. Bridgeport, CT: Burke, 1983.
———. *The Tinderbox*. Otto S. Svend, illus. N.Y.: Van Nostrand Reinhold, 1970.
Buffet, Jimmy, and Savannah Jane. *The Jolly Mon*. N.Y.: Harcourt Brace Jovanovich, 1988.
Coombs, Patricia. *The Magic Pot*. N.Y.: Lothrop, Lee & Shepard, 1977.
Demi. *Chen Ping and His Magic Axe*. N.Y.: Dodd Mead, 1987.
dePaola, Tomie, reteller. *Strega Nona*. Englewood Cliffs, N.J.: Prentice-Hall, 1975.
Galdone, Paul. *The Magic Porridge Pot*. Boston: Houghton Mifflin, 1976.
Ginsburg, Mirra. *The Magic Stove*. N.Y.: Coward-McCann, 1983.
Haviland, Virginia, reteller. "The Page Boy and the Silver Goblet." *Favorite Fairy Tales Told in Scotland*. Boston: Little, Brown, 1963.
Haviland, Virginia, reteller. "The Wonderful Pot" and "The Knapsack." *Favorite Fairy Tales Told in Denmark*. Boston: Little, Brown, 1971.
Hutchins, Hazel. *Casey Webber the Great*. N.Y.: Annick/Firefly, 1988.
Hutton, Warwick, reteller. *The Nose Tree* (German tale). N.Y.: Atheneum, 1981.
Jameson, Cynthia. *The Flying Shoes*. N.Y.: Parents' Magazine Press, 1973.
Kennedy, Richard. *The Blue Stone*. N.Y.: Holiday House, 1976.
Kimishima, Hisako. *Ma Lien and the Magic Brush*. N.Y.: Parents' Magazine Press, 1968.
Kimmel, Eric A. *Anansi and the Moss-Covered Rock*. N.Y.: Holiday House, 1988.
Lang, Andrew, reteller. *Aladdin and the Wonderful Lamp*. Errol Le Cain, illus. N.Y.: Viking, 1981.
Lionni, Leo. *Alexander and the Wind-Up Mouse*. N.Y.: Pantheon, 1969.
Luenn, Nancy. *The Dragon Kite*. N.Y.: Harcourt Brace Jovanovich, 1982.
Manning-Sanders, Ruth. "Grandfather Pavel and the Priceless Pebble." *A Book of Heroes and Heroines*. London: Methuen, 1982.
Matsutami, Miyoko. *The Witch's Magic Cloth*. N.Y.: Parents' Magazine Press, 1969.
Marshak, Samuel, reteller. *The Month-Brothers: A Slavic Tale*. Diane Stanley, illus.; Thomas Whitney, trans. N.Y.: Morrow, 1983.
Mayer, Marianna. *The Little Jewel Box*. N.Y.: Dial, 1986.
Meyers, Odette. *The Enchanted Umbrella*. Margot Zemach, illus. N.Y.: Harcourt Brace Jovanovich, 1988.
Mosel, Arlene, reteller. *The Funny Little Woman*. N.Y.: Dutton, 1972.
Porazínska, Janina. *The Enchanted Book—A Tale from Krakow*. Jan Brett, illus.; Bozena Smith, trans. N.Y.: Harcourt Brace Jovanovich, 1987.
Riordan, James. *The Three Magic Gifts*. N.Y.: Oxford University Press, 1980.
Rogasky, Barbara, reteller. *The Water of Life*. Trina Schart Hyman, illus. N.Y.: Holiday House, 1986.
San Souci, Robert D., reteller. *The Enchanted Tapestry—A Chinese Tale*. Laszlo Gal, illus. N.Y.: Dial, 1987.
Scott, Sally, reteller. *The Magic Horse*. N.Y.: Greenwillow, 1985.
Steel, Flora Annie, reteller. *Tattercoats: An Old English Tale*. Diane Goode, illus. Scarsdale, N.Y.: Bradbury, 1976.
Steig, William. *Sylvester and the Magic Pebble*. N.Y.: Simon and Schuster, 1969.
Towle, Faith M., reteller. *The Magic Cooking Pot—A Folktale of India*. Boston: Houghton Mifflin, 1975.

Werth, Kurt, adaptor. *The Cobbler's Dilemma—An Italian Folktale.* N.Y.: McGraw-Hill, 1967.
Willard, Nancy. *Firebrat.* N.Y.: Knopf, 1988.
Winter, Jeannette, reteller. *The Magic Ring—A Tale by the Brothers Grimm.* N.Y.: Knopf, 1987.
Williams, Jay. *The Silver Whistle.* N.Y.: Parents' Magazine Press, 1971.
Zemach, Harve, adaptor. *Too Much Nose: An Italian Tale.* N.Y.: Holt, Rinehart and Winston, 1967.

EIGHT

Bird Tales:
Fact and Fiction

LITERATURE AND LITERACY LEARNING ACROSS THE CURRICULUM

Literacy learning is not confined to the language arts program but is an integral part of all areas of the curriculum. Children build concepts as they read and write many kinds of discourse. In the process they build their literacy skills. Literacy learning and content learning are complementary and interrelated. Reading and writing are processes in which meaning is generated and shaped. According to Jerome Harste "meaning generation is the essence of learning [and] learners must actively construct knowledge for themselves. . . ." (1988, p. 5).

Literacy across the curriculum means that students will move from one form of discourse to another as they engage in the process of constructing meaning. Content learning is facilitated by the use of both fiction and nonfiction. The exploration of a particular topic—in science, math, social studies, or the arts—can begin with stories and poetry and then move into informational books and first-hand observation and experience. Literature can serve as a springboard for inquiry and exploration, and reading and writing serve as the core. In this chapter a Focus Unit on birds illustrates the integration of fact and fiction and comprehension and composition in the exploration of a topic.

THE STUDY OF BIRDS

Birds were choosen as a topic for many reasons. First, most children are fascinated by these creatures. Whether feeding pigeons in a park, observing a family of sparrows in a window-ledge nest, chatting with exotic birds at the zoo, or listening to the songs of the birds at dawn or dusk, children have discovered that birds can be a source of wonder and delight. Generations of poets, artists, and musicians have been inspired by birds' graceful flight, their lovely colors, and their sweet songs. The bird evoked dreams of flight centuries before such dreams could be realized for humans with the invention of the first gliders and airplanes.

Since ancient times birds have been part of legend and superstition: The ibis of Egypt was sacred; in Europe many believe that a stork nest on a roof means good luck; in Japan the crane symbolizes peace, good will, and longevity; sailors believe that harming an albatross will bring bad luck; the dove is often used as a symbol of peace; and the owl is a symbol of wisdom—associated with Minerva, the goddess of wisdom. The phoenix, a fabulous bird in Greek mythology, had a life of 500 years or more. After each life cycle the phoenix burned itself on a funeral pyre, and another phoenix rose from the ashes with fresh youth and beauty. Because of this long life and rebirth, it is used as a symbol of immortality and spiritual rebirth.

Birds have been immortalized in great literary works over the centuries. These include the biblical story of Noah and the dove; and the poems of both English and American writers such as Shelley's "To a Skylark," Keats' "Ode to a Nightingale," Coleridge's albatross in "The Rime of the Ancient Mariner," and Edgar Allan Poe's "The Raven." The crows, storks, and cranes in the fables of Aesop; the Grimm Brothers' "The Seven Ravens" and "The Golden Goose"; and Hans Christian Andersen's tales of "The Ugly Duckling" and "The Nightingale" are just some of the bird characters in literature.

Although particular birds have been used to symbolize evil or misfortune, in general the bird since earliest times has been viewed as the symbol of the soul (Rowland, 1978, p. xiii). Their association with heaven and paradise have empowered these winged creatures with a spiritual significance and has given them an aura of joy and aspiration. In her remarkable book, *Birds with Human Souls* (1978) Beryl Rowland demonstrates that "the study of birds is a study in human culture" (p. xv).

In an introduction to *Fairy Tales of the Orient* (1965), Pearl Buck comments:

The significance of birds in fairy tales, or simply their usefulness as a device, I find especially interesting. It harks back, I imagine, to very early days when birds were thought to be messengers from the gods, particularly from the Sun God. Especially in spring, when life bursts forth from field and forest, it was easy to associate the new creativity with birds returning from some sun-warmed winter haunt. The divine mission of birds, for good or ill, still lingers in legends of the stork bringing babies, of doves descending with olive branches of peace, even of angels whose bodies, cast in human frame, are borne upon the wings of birds (pp. 16–17).

A survey of folk- and fairytales from cultures around the world reveals that the bird is a remarkably popular literary device. The dove and other gentle birds representing love and peace assist the hero or heroine on his or her quest. Eagles, hawks, owls, and other birds of prey, with their powerful feet and claws and heavy beaks for killing their victims, are often used to represent the forces of evil and to serve as the villains or adversaries who threaten the lives of protagonists. Many birds in literature are associated with specific human traits, such as the proud peacock, the graceful swan, the silly goose, the clever crow, and the mischievous and thieving bluejay. Like humans, a bird's appearance is often deceptive. The nightingale is plain and small but has a beautiful voice. The bluejay has beautiful blue-and-white plumage and a crested head, but its voice is loud and harsh; and it eats the eggs and young from the nests of other birds. Such distinguishing characteristics have provided a rich resource for storytellers.

In this context it seemed natural to integrate the study of birds in nature and birds in literature and to explore the relationship between fact and fiction in the process. The end result of this integrated unit was a literary, literacy, and content learning experience in which exposure to literature enhanced the study of birds; and the growing knowledge of birds enhanced the enjoyment of literature.

THE BIRD FOCUS UNIT

The bird Focus Unit was introduced in the Spring when children appreciate the arrival of birds, buds, and warm breezes. The search for bird literature proved to be a never-ending process. The extensive bibliography at the end of this chapter is not complete, but suggests the wealth of material available for developing such a unit for many age groups.

The study of birds began with narratives and poetry. As selections were read aloud in group sessions or independently during quiet reading periods, questions were raised about bird habits, habitats, and the distinguishing features of different species. These questions served as the catalyst for consulting informational books and using first-hand experiences. Gradually, individual children began to identify special areas of interest, and eventually defined a topic for a research project. Some of the projects were carried out in small groups; others were done independently. The stories and poems were not used to gather facts or literal information about birds but they did set the stage for data-gathering. They motivated and stimulated intellectual curiosity which initiated a movement from fiction to fact and back to fiction.

As the children recognized that many bird tales and poems are grounded in fact, they began to speculate about what information or observations the author or poet used in the creation of a particular literary piece. In turn, as they gained new knowledge about the world of birds, children drew from this to interact with literary selections.

This natural movement between fact and fiction can enrich the learning experiences in various areas of the curriculum. According to Professor Charlotte Huck (1987):

Fiction gives a perspective that allows us to know facts in another way. It is especially important for children to confirm what they are learning from informational sources by meeting similar ideas in the more human frame of literature (p. 618).

As children move between fiction and nonfiction they are exposed to different forms of discourse. Given opportunities to read and write in these forms, children develop an awareness of the distinguishing features and functions of each and practice using appropriate strategies for making meaning.

Session One

The bird unit was introduced with the question: "What is a bird?" If children were unable to define birds as animals with feathers, a book such as *What Makes a Bird a Bird* (Garelick, 1969) was read aloud to help them distinguish the bird from other animals that fly, have wings, sing, build nests, and lay eggs. The brief text in this lovely picture book leads the reader to discover the distinctive feature of birds: Only birds have feathers.

The second question: "What else do you know about birds?" was designed to invite children to share their background knowledge and personal experiences. As interesting facts about birds were contributed, they were recorded on a large chart under the heading: BIRD FACTS. Additional information was added to this chart throughout the unit of study as the children's knowledge of birds expanded. As the chart filled with a great array of isolated facts and figures the children recognized a need to put them in order. They selected major headings, and then sorted and organized items accordingly. One child noted, "It's like taking a junk drawer and organizing it into neat compartments so you can *find* things!"

After establishing a context for the bird unit the teacher read aloud the story *Birdsong* (Haley, 1984) about old Jorinella the birdcatcher and an orphan girl, Birdsong, who loved all feathered creatures. The children quickly recognized the significant difference between these two characters, and inferred Jorinella's motive for befriending this homeless girl whose pipe-playing attracted wild birds. At the end of the story one child observed: "Jorinella used Birdsong as *bait* to get the birds to come into her traps." At this point the teacher asked, "Why didn't the birds fly away when Birdsong unlocked the cages that night after Jorinella went home?" One child replied: "It was because it was night and the birds said they couldn't see to fly." This prompted another child to ask the teacher, "Is that really true? Don't real birds ever fly at night?" The teacher responded by pointing to a group of nonfiction books about birds on a display table. She invited the children to consult these books and search for an answer. Several children volunteered and the first "research committee" was established. Then the teacher went back to the story, asking the children to discuss the way the problem in the story was solved.

- When Birdsong finally helped all those birds escape, I thought the old lady was going to kill her. I was so scared!
- But it all worked out perfect. The birds helped Birdsong escape, and Jorinella ended up with *nothing*.
- So Birdsong helped the birds and they helped her. I like it when it works out that way.

After discussing the story the children were given an opportunity to examine the beautiful illustrations more carefully. They were able to identify many of the kinds of birds portrayed, although quite a few were unfamiliar to them. Several children volunteered to consult bird books in order to figure out the names of the unknown birds. So a second "research committee" was formed. This group became very interested in discovering the many different kinds of birds, and eventually decided to make an illustrated dictionary of birds around the world.

At the conclusion of this first session the teacher pointed out two display tables and explained that one held a collection of literature and the other a collection of nonfiction about birds. Special times during the day were to be set aside for independent browsing and reading. The teacher also handed a notebook to each child for keeping a learning log, an ongoing record of his or her involvement in the study of birds in story and birds in nature.

The learning log is a vehicle for recording learning experiences and new knowledge, understandings, and skills which have resulted from these experiences.

For the bird Unit the children were asked to write in their learning logs about something they had learned or discovered, a connection they had made, or a question they wanted to answer. Entries could be in the form of prose, outlines, charts, diagrams, or sketches. The children were encouraged to experiment with different ways of making meaning by using a variety of communication systems.

This first session was designed to set the stage for the study of birds through the integration of fact and fiction, and to develop an atmosphere of inquiry and discovery. Within this context the children would be encouraged to make connections: between literary selections, between literary selections and nonfiction, between fantasy and realism.

Session Two

The Five Sparrows (Newton, 1982), adapted from an old Japanese tale, was read aloud in the second group session. After discussing this tale of kindness rewarded and greed punished, the children were asked to compare it to *Birdsong*.

- They both had a character who really loved the birds.
- And they both had a character who just wanted to get rich.
- The mean neighbor [in *The Five Sparrows*] and the birdcatcher were mean to the birds.
- The birds *knew* who their real friends were, and they rewarded them for being so kind.

When asked what the theme or message of these two tales might be, one eight-year-old boy responded: "If you're mean or greedy, somehow it will catch you up."

The children were especially interested in a phrase used in the Japanese tale, "to lose face." They tried to figure out the meaning of this phrase from the context.

- It's like feeling embarrassed.
- It's like if you don't want to show your face.
- Like when you're ashamed and you cover your face.

The story of *The Five Sparrows* prompted one boy to write in his learning log: "Are there really sparrows in Japan? Do sparrows live *every*where?" After reading his log the teacher suggested that he join the research committee which was studying the different species of birds, and their distinctive features, habits, and habitats. Eventually he was able to record an answer to his questions in his log. In the process he discovered a new area of interest, as well as new questions.

Session Three

Before reading *Anna and the Seven Swans* (Silverman, 1984) in the third group session the teacher asked the children to look at the pictures on the front and back covers. "As you listen to the story, think about why the artist chose these two pictures to put on the book's covers." By the end of the story the children were able to see that these pictures were selected to highlight the beginning and ending of the plot.

- On the front cover it shows Ivan when the swans carried him off. That's the *real* beginning of the story.

- It shows the *problem*. That's when it [the story] really starts.
- And the *back* cover is the ending. It shows that the problem got solved because Ivan is home safe and sound with Anna and their mom and dad.

After this the children were asked to compare or contrast *Anna and the Seven Swans* with the two tales read previously.

- All of them are about someone who gets rewarded for doing something nice. The old lady [in *The Five Sparrows*] helped the hurt sparrow, and she got the magic gourds. Birdsong helped the birds, and they helped her escape. And Anna helped the stove and the apple tree and the river of milk, and they helped *her* escape from Baba Yaga.
- And the little mouse helped Anna, too, because she fed it.
- I think the birdcatcher lady was sort of like Baba Yaga. She captured innocent birds for people to eat, and Baba Yaga captured innocent children to eat.
- But the birds were different! In *Birdsong* the birds were nice and they helped a good person, but in *Anna* the birds worked for an evil person.
- That didn't seem right. Swans are so pretty and graceful. It didn't seem right for them to be with the witch. Like in *Birdsong*—remember that mean lady had a black crow. Baba Yaga should have had black crows or a hawk, maybe.
- I think I know. See, the swans were under a spell. They used to be people—remember that story about the seven brothers that got changed into swans? Well, Baba Yaga *changed* them and makes them do what she wants.
- I think they used to be *children*, and the witch changed them and made them into her slaves.
- And it's the same with that little frog. Remember in the very beginning, it shows the little brother going after that frog? See, it's under the witch's power and she *uses* it to attract a kid into the forest.
- Maybe she even put that trail of flowers to get children into her forest.

The teacher commented that these interesting ideas could be used to start a new story. The children who had generated the ideas decided to work together to create a story about "Baba Yaga and the Seven Swans and How the Spell Was Broken."

The child who raised the question of the appropriateness of swans as witch's helpers had apparently already begun to develop a schema for literary devices in which certain animals are associated with the forces of good and others with the forces of evil. To her, the graceful white swan did not seem to be a valid symbol for evil because it violated the schema she had developed. She was quite satisfied with the explanation that these swans were the victims of a transformation enchantment. Her personal schema remained intact.

In their learning logs several children posed the question: "Can swans really fly?" The teacher suggested that these children work together to answer this question. Initially, they looked up information about swans, but then they raised new questions about *how* birds fly and the focus of the research committee expanded. Two boys, known for their special interest in airplanes, joined the group, and were delighted to discover that birds can fly for the same basic reason that an airplane can. Again, we have an example of the way a story served as a springboard for further study and for identifying special interests—in this case, aerodynamics.

Session Four

Tattercoats (Steel, 1976) elicited a number of interesting comparisons.

- It's just like Cinderella!
- But the one who helps her is the gooseherd with the magical pipe instead of the fairy godmother.
- It's also like *Birdsong*. She played on those pipes and all the birds came.
- And when the gooseherd played a special tune, Tattercoats' rags changed to a beautiful dress and the geese changed into pages!
- Maybe that's just what *did* happen in *Anna and the Seven Swans* but instead of changing geese into people, Baba Yaga changed people into swans!

The children expressed an interest in this transformation motif and several children told about transformation tales they had selected from the bird tale collection for independent reading: *The Glass Mountain* (Hogrogian, 1985), a Grimm Brothers tale about a princess who is changed into a raven and is finally released from her enchantment by the man who is able to climb up the glass mountain; *The Crane Wife* (Yagawa, 1981), an old Japanese tale about a wounded crane who becomes a beautiful woman and marries the poor farmer who has rescued her from death; *Jorinda and Joringel* (Gág, 1975), a Grimm Brothers tale about an old enchantress who turns young girls into singing birds and Joringel, the lad who manages to break the spell and free his friend Jorinda and seven thousand other enchanted maidens; and *The Six Swans* (Grimm Brothers, 1973) about the transformation of the king's six sons into swans by their jealous stepmother and the long and difficult trial endured by their sister to save them.

Session Five

When *Perfect Crane* (Laurin, 1981) was read aloud in the fifth session the children immediately recognized this as another type of transformation tale.

- This time it's a paper crane, an origami bird, that's changed into a *real* crane!

They also noted that *The Crane Wife*, mentioned in the previous session, was from Japan, also the setting for *Perfect Crane*. This prompted several children to tell about other Japanese crane stories they had found in the collection. One girl decided to do some research on the crane and try to find out why it is such a popular bird among the storytellers of Japan.

The teacher now guided their attention back to the text of *Perfect Crane*. She asked the children to listen to the author's dedication and think about its connection to the story: "For my mother, who gave me life. I return still."

- It's just like when the magician gave life to the paper crane. The crane said, "You are my father. You gave me life."
- But he had to let the crane go so the crane could go where it was warm.
- He was sad. He didn't want him to go. My mom cried when I went to camp. I think the author's mom was sad, too, when she went away.

- But it says, 'I return still.' And so did the crane. He said he would always return.
- This story reminds me of a story I just read about a witch named Agatha [*The Witch's Egg*, Edmondson, 1974]. She lives in this empty eagle's nest on top of a mountain. Well, one day she finds this egg. She keeps it warm, and it hatches; and she takes care of it and feeds it. But *then* it has to fly away when winter comes.
- Was it a cowbird? *They* lay their eggs in other birds nests! I just read that. I wrote it in my log.
- No. The book said it was a baby cuckoo bird. But she called it her Witchbird. She was so sad when he had to go south. But he always came back from Florida in the spring so they stayed good friends.

Several children told of another migration tale, Leo Politi's *Song of the Swallows* (1949), in which the swallows return each spring on Saint Joseph's Day to Capistrano, a town in California.

These tales elicited a number of questions about bird migration:

- Why do they have to fly south?
- How do they know the way?
- How can you tell that it's the *same* birds coming back?
- Do they always fly in groups?
- Which birds stay here?
- How do they know when it's time to go and come back?

These questions served as the starting point for a research committee on bird migration.

Session Six

The Fisherman and the Bird (Levitin, 1982) is a realistic tale of a lonely fisherman, Rico, and the large, beautiful birds who build a nest on the mast of his boat. Rico plans to destroy the nest until he learns that this rare bird is threatened with extinction. When he finds two eggs "the color of pale gold" in the nest Rico decides to become their guardian. The villagers join him as he waits for the eggs to hatch; and he discovers the reciprocal nature and pleasure of friendship.

The discussion of this story focussed on the change in the central character, Rico, and the issue of endangered species. The children immediately recognized this as a realistic tale, but saw the thematic connections between it and other tales they had heard in previous group sessions or had read independently.

- It's like *Perfect Crane*. The crane helps the magician make friends so he's not lonely any more.
- It's like *The Witch's Egg* because Agatha changed too. She started to *care* about Witchbird. She got more human.
- I read a really funny one, and it's sort of like this. It's called *We'll Have a Friend for Lunch* (Flory, 1974), and it's about these cats who decide to become birdwatchers, and they watch

this robin family because they plan to *eat* them, but then they get to *know* them and to *like* them. So they change their minds!

- I read a funny one too. It's called *The Wolf's Chicken Stew* (Kasza, 1987), and it's about this wolf who plans to eat this chicken and first he decides to fatten her up. But then he finds out she has all these cute baby chicks and they hug him and call him Uncle Wolf so he *can't* eat their mother!

After discussing the basic theme of *The Fisherman and the Bird* and similar stories the children turned their attention to the threat of extinction. They discussed the meaning of the word *extinct* and shared their knowledge of endangered species. Several of the children had some interesting stories to tell about their families' involvement in local and national efforts to protect birds and other wildlife. By the end of this session another committee was formed to study endangered species and bird protection.

Session Seven

Eli (Peet, 1978) was introduced in the seventh session as an example of a modern, humorous tale. Eli is an elderly lion who no longer has the strength or energy to maintain his image as the King of Beasts. He manages to survive by eating the meat of dead animals along with vultures whom he despises. When Eli rescues one of the vultures from the jaws of a jackal one day he suddenly becomes a hero among the vultures, who are anxious to show their gratitude. Later, when they manage to save Eli from lion hunters, he, too, is filled with gratitude and accepts the vultures' offer of friendship. The story ends on a happy note. "The old lion discovered that life was not nearly so dreary and lonely with a tree full of friends for company. And even if they were a bunch of old bone-pickers, Eli was ever so proud of them" (p. 38).

Before reading the story aloud the teacher asked, "What is a vulture?" Several children were able to explain that this is a bird of prey which eats dead animals or carrion. The information was important for comprehending the story.

After hearing the story and enjoying the delightful cartoonlike illustrations the children made a number of observations.

- In this story the important characters are animals like in that story about the cats and the robins [*We'll Have a Friend for Lunch*], but in most of the other stories there are people and birds together.
- A lot of them were magical birds, but in the stories about Eli and the cats they acted more like animals, but they could talk—at least to each other.
- And those are funny tales—more like cartoons.
- It's because they're modern instead of being old, old tales. But I liked the one about the fisherman and the birds because it seemed so real—like maybe it's really true.

At the conclusion of this session the teacher asked the children to think about all the books they had discussed so far and to search for a common thread which seemed to run through most, if not all, of them.

- The birds helped people. Like getting riches or friends.
- And sometimes they helped someone escape danger like in *Birdsong*.
- And the birds helped Eli. They saved him from the lion hunters.
- And sometimes the birds didn't even *know* they were causing someone to change, like in *The Fisherman and the Bird*.
- But in *Perfect Crane* I think the crane *knew* he was helping the magician be a better friend.
- The only one that was different was *Anna and the Seven Swans*. But *they* were probably under a spell.
- In real life birds can be helpful too. Like if you have a pet parrot, it can make you feel happy.
- And it's nice to hear their songs. It's like a free concert.
- And they help farmers and gardeners. Birds eat insects that are bad for crops.
- And the rooster is like an alarm clock. He wakes up the farmer.
- That could be another committee—to find out all the ways birds can be helpful.

THE RESEARCH COMMITTEES AND PROJECTS

Each research committee used the classroom or school library to search for answers to the questions they had formulated when the committee was established. Each group decided how to record and share the information they gathered. Some created booklets with narrative and illustrations; some made charts or diagrams; one group traced a large map of the United States and put in the names of state birds; another compiled a biographical sketch of naturalist and painter John J. Audubon and framed the prose with drawings of birds. Several children worked individually. One painted a series of large posters about endangered species; another printed directions for building various kinds of bird feeders and accompanied the handouts with a number of completed samples. These and other results of the ongoing research associated with the bird unit were put on display.

Many of the children became interested in making bird feeders to put in their backyards. The teacher suggested that several could be hung in the trees outside the big classroom windows. This set the stage for first-hand observation of birds at home and at school. The children learned to identify the birds who came to the feeders and discovered fascinating patterns of behavior as they watched these winged creatures day after day. Several children were fortunate in having nests outside their windows, which enabled them to observe a bird family in the process of hatching and caring for its young. These children recorded their observations in their logs and shared the logs with their classmates. The excitement and curiosity in the class often meant that these "birdwatchers" were met at the classroom door in the morning with questions such as, "Did they hatch yet?" "What did the babies look like?" "Did they learn to fly?" "How does the mother feed them" One of these "birdwatchers" wrote: "I worry about my birds—especially when it gets real cold at night. My mom says they'll be ok. but how will they keep warm?" When he read his log to several friends, one said, "It sounds like you've *adopted* that family!" Another said that he had read about how birds keep warm and would show him the book which contained this information.

A fourth-grade research committee interested in bird-watching contacted some local birdwatchers in order to learn more about ways to observe and study birds. Later, the birdwatchers joined the class on a field trip to a nearby nature center, planned as the culminating event for the bird Unit. By this time the children had acquired a rich background to bring to this experience, which also enhanced their ability to enjoy it.

The projects and activities which grew out of the study of birds were integral parts of the total learning experience. The children used different communication systems to generate meanings, and experimented with different ways of expressing these meanings. They applied the concepts and information acquired through their research to solve problems and to construct meanings in new contexts. The collaborative nature of these activities provided opportunities for social learning, an important dimension of participation in a community of learners.

Session Eight

When Hans Christian Andersen's *The Nightingale* (1965) was read in the eighth session the children responded with rapt attention as they "lived through" this story. After the closing lines there were several moments of complete silence before they expressed their appreciation for the beauty of the story and Nancy Burkert's illustrations. Several children observed that the Russian firebird served the Tsar in much the same way that the nightingale proposed to serve the Chinese Emperor, by bringing news of the people in all parts of their kingdoms. The Nightingale said to the Emperor:

I'll sing of happy people and of those who suffer; I'll sing of the good and evil all around which is kept hidden from you; for the little songbird flies far and wide—to the poor fisherman, and the peasant in his hut, to all those who are far away from you and from your Court (p. 32).

One child noted, "This story made me think of what my mom says when I ask her how she found out about something secret, and she says, 'Oh, a little bird told me.'"

Others added to the list of common threads which served to bind many of these bird tales together:

- The nightingale helped the Emperor. She made him happy.
- Like those birds changed the fisherman's life. He wasn't lonely and unhappy anymore.
- The nightingale *saved* the Emperor's life!
- So did the vultures. They saved Eli's life.
- But that was a funny story and this is a serious one. That part when the Emperor almost died was sort of scary. But I *knew* the nightingale would come back.

Finally, the teacher asked about the theme of this tale. "What did the Emperor learn?"

- He learned that the *real thing*, a living creature, is better than an artificial one.
- He learned that you shouldn't be so impressed with jewels and gold.
- Like when you say "beauty is only skin deep." It's like that. The real nightingale was plain on the outside but beautiful on the inside, and the other one was only beautiful on the outside.
- I think the lesson of the story is you shouldn't judge people by how they *look*.

Session Nine

The Boy Who Had Wings (Yolen, 1974) is about a Greek boy born with wings, who spends his days alone and unhappy and hiding his wings until the time he uses them to fly over the mountains in order to rescue his father. This unusual tale by a master storyteller prompted a great deal of discussion. Initially the children compared it to other bird tales, such as *Tico and the Golden Wings* (Lionni, 1964), *Borka, The Adventures of a Goose with No Feathers* (Burningham, 1963), *The Magic Wings* (Wolkstein, 1983), *The Plaid Peacock* (Alan, 1965), and *The Little Wood Duck* (Wildsmith, 1972).

- The boy with wings was exactly the opposite of Tico. Tico was a bird born *without* wings; and the boy was a human born *with* wings.
- But all those stories are alike because all the characters were born different. That peacock had a plaid tail, and the wood duck could only swim in circles because he was born with one foot bigger.
- The other animals were mean to the peacock and the wood duck just because they were different. And the same thing with the boy with the wings. His father didn't want to even *look* at him, and he didn't have any friends.
- But in all three of those stories they save someone and then everyone likes them. The boy saved his dad; the peacock saved the soldiers from the fire; and the duck saved his brothers and sisters from the fox.
- I liked the part in the peacock story when he was a hero and all the mothers wanted their babies to have plaid tails.
- It was the same in the one about the boy with wings. At the end all the kids prayed they could have wings—a *long* time after he became a hero.
- I read *The Magic Wings*. It's about this goose girl who wishes she could grow wings, and then *all* the girls copy her. They want to fly, too. But this Spirit that grants wishes for wings comes down and chooses the goose girl to get the wings because she loves nature and wasn't just always thinking about herself like the others.
- In *Tico*, his friends took care of him when he had *no* wings, but when he got the *gold* ones he was different, so they left. They only came back when he got the black wings like theirs.
- The same thing happened in this story [*The Boy Who Had Wings*]. When his wings fell off his family started to like him.
- I think the lesson in these stories is that you shouldn't be mean to someone just because he's different.
- That's right. My mom says that *everyone* is different and *special*!

The teacher expanded on this idea of the uniqueness of each individual and the gifts and qualities which make each person special. She read aloud the author's words printed on the back flap of the book's dust jacket:

. . . the story is really very autobiographical. It might also serve as biography for anyone who has ever been blessed with a gift—whether of writing, painting, or the like. For to be different . . . is not an easy thing when, as a child, you are longing to be like everyone else. I think I have been much luckier than Aetos . . . I never lost my wings or gave them away. And now that I know that my writing can bring pleasure to others . . . I am grateful and proud of my wings.

These words helped several of the children move toward an understanding of the author's use of wings as a literary device. One girl responded to the last lines of the author's commentary in this way:

- The characters who were different, like Tico and the plaid peacock, *also* brought pleasure to others. Tico gave his gold feathers to make others happy. The plaid peacock made the soldiers happy—and even saved their lives. So being different can be good if you *use* the gift in a good way.

Other children preferred to interpret the story in a more literal way. They puzzled over the notion of wings on a human child and struggled to come up with an explanation which would satisfy them.

- I think Aetos is really an angel.
- But aren't they supposed to live up in heaven instead of on earth?
- I think the author was thinking about Icarus in that Greek myth. Remember, his dad made wings so they could escape from that tower.
- I remember that one. Maybe she [author Yolen] just made up a story about what it would be like to be able to fly—to have your own wings!
- But it wasn't so great. He was so unhappy.
- But he did fly that one time. He loved it. I wish I could do it just once—but not have wings *growing* on me.
- It's a strange story. Why would a boy be born with wings?
- It doesn't make much sense if he can't fly around and *enjoy* them!
- I think the gods gave the boy wings so he could use them that *one* time to save his father. I think that was the *purpose*. So then they fell off when his dad was safe!

A number of the children were very pleased with this last explanation. It seemed to satisfy their need for an orderly tale in which everything has a purpose. But not all the children were comfortable with this interpretation. Those who had begun to see the wings as a literary device or metaphor reentered the discussion. One boy pointed to the dedication as an important clue for interpreting the story. After reading the words aloud, "For Adam: dare to try your wings," he commented:

See—the author talks about wings like they're a special gift that you should use even if it's hard or if you feel different. Aetos *hid* his wings, and then he lost them. I bet Adam is her son, and she's telling him to *use* the gifts he has and not to be afraid to be different.

This was not the end of the discussion. The children continued to express their thoughts about this tale long after the group session had drawn to a close. Because the teacher supported these divergent responses the children discovered that different readers can read the same story and generate very different interpretations or viewpoints. In the process they learned to value each other's responses and began to entertain the possibility that a literary piece can be interpreted in diverse ways and at many different levels. According to Rosenblatt, ". . . every aesthetic reading of a text is a unique creation, woven out of the inner life and thought of the reader . . ." (1982, p. 277).

Session Ten

Throughout this unit of study the children had been reading bird poems which they found in various collections of poetry or single editions. They learned to use the table of contents and index in each collection or anthology, and enjoyed the process of searching for and discovering a bird poem and sharing it with a friend. They were asked to select their favorites to copy and illustrate. These were read aloud in the tenth group session and then bound together into a book of favorite bird poems. Many of the children chose poems which related to the area of research in which they were engaged. For example, a member of the migration committee selected Rachel Field's "Something Told the Wild Geese" and Tsumori Kunimoto's "The Wild Geese Returning" (Larrick, 1968, p. 135).

Some children chose poems about their favorite birds; others decided on poems which seemed to capture the essence of a particular bird such as Alfred Lord Tennyson's "The Eagle" (Arbuthnot, 1961, p. 54), Emily Dickinson's "A bird came down the walk" (Larrick, 1968, p. 128), and Issa's "The Wren" (Merrill and Solbert, 1969, p. 25).

CREATING A BOOK OF FACT AND FICTION

In preparation for the final project for this unit the children were introduced to *Someone Saw a Spider* (Climo, 1985). This collection of folktales, beliefs, and facts about spiders served as a model for the creation of individual books about a favorite bird. Each book was to include factual information as well as an original story inspired by the bird.

Once the children had selected particular birds, they recorded the name of the bird along with their names on a large chart. Since a great deal of information had already been gathered by individuals and committees, the children could serve as resources for each other. A child who had some information about eagles would consult the chart to discover who would be interested in this information or the names of the books used to gather it. Again, social interaction was the context for learning.

The next step was to make use of the classroom, school, or local libraries to search for additional information. The children were encouraged to include sketches or colored drawings of the bird and its habitat to illustrate the informational aspects of their books.

Most children found that a review of their learning logs was very helpful. For example, one boy had written about a new skill: "Today I learned how to use the index to look up things in the *Wildlife Encyclopedia*" [Burton, 1969]. When he reread his log this reminded him of a wonderful resource he could use.

Another child discovered that he had started each entry with a question and then had recorded the answers he was able to find. When he shared this discovery with his classmates, many decided it was a fine idea to use as the format for their "bird fact and fiction" books. This was a significant discovery: That questions can be used to generate and guide learning not only to check comprehension.

This background information provided a starting point for creating original narratives. Before beginning the composing process the children met as a group to review some of the themes and patterns which threaded through the tales they had read independently or heard in group sessions. These connecting threads were recorded on an easel to help them write their stories. The list included such items as:

• Helpful birds
• Birds that change someone's life
• Birds that are *different*
• Magic spells that change people into birds.

They also reviewed these stories in terms of the information about birds individual authors had used in creating their tales. As they recorded some of the facts which authors had apparently used in the creation of fiction one child observed: "I think what an author does is get really good ideas from reading about *real* birds. Like, if you didn't know about migration, you wouldn't write about a bird friend having to *leave*—like in *Perfect Crane!*"

The stories which were eventually produced by these young authors reflected their involvement with both fact and fiction. Yet the language and form of each narrative distinguished it as a literary piece. For example, one six-year-old started her story this way:

• Thar was a pelican long ago. A friendle pelican was he. Now one sunne morning . . .

Another six-year-old opened his story with:

• Once there was a very selfish bluejay. He stole berries from all the other birds. So one day a robin decided to call a meeting of the birds. . . .

It is interesting to note that this writer used the dove as the "peacemaker" in his story.

The children drew from and blended their literary background of traditional and modern stories and their factual knowledge from nonfiction and first-hand observations to create delightful tales. These were then bound into their individual fact-fiction books. Many of the children found poems about their favorite birds and placed copies of these poems in their books. Others, using *Someone Saw a Spider* as a model, decided to include a bibliography of the reference books they had used, as well as stories which featured their birds.

For example, a seven-year-old whose book was about pelicans included such titles as *Come Again, Pelican* (Freeman, 1961), *Pelican* (Wildsmith, 1982), *The Pelican Chorus* (Lear, 1967), and *The Reason for the Pelican* (Ciardi, 1959).

An older student who had selected cranes as her focus began to read the many lovely crane tales from Japanese folklore. The teacher recommended *Sadako and the Thousand Paper Cranes* (Coerr, 1977) to her. After recording the titles and authors or retellers of these crane stories in her bibliography, the student decided to copy a poem from Coerr's moving story and use it as an introduction to her *Book of Cranes: Fact and Fantasy*.

Out of colored paper, cranes come flying into our house (p. 39).

A nine-year-old boy whose book was about crows included a discussion of *Crow Boy* (Yashima, 1955) and *The Cry of the Crow* (George, 1980). He developed a keen interest in the language of crows after reading these stories. Many children searched for legends about their particular birds and included a retelling of the tales in their fact-fiction books.

During one of the group sessions the children shared the legends they had found, and were surprised to discover some interesting similarities. For example, the child who had selected the peacock as the focus of her book retold the story of "Brother Anansi and Sir Peacock" (McNeill, 1964). Upon hearing this tale the girl who had chosen to focus on the bluejay responded:

- The legend about my bird is just like that! The bluejay used to be brown but when it gave his beautiful voice to a princess, he was given beautiful blue feathers in return. It was the same with that peacock. It *used* to be ugly, but it had a beautiful voice. Then Anansi tricked it into giving his voice to a prince. But the King rewarded him with fine clothes so that's why peacocks are so fancy! [This child had read "The Beautiful Blue Jay" (Spellman, 1967)].

Each book was unique, reflecting the interests, imagination, and style of its creator. Every child had become an expert about a particular bird and shared his or her book with pride.

FACT AND FICTION

The study of birds began with stories and poetry and then moved into nonfiction as the children formulated questions to initiate research activity. Moving between fact and fiction the children discovered interesting connections between the story world and the real one. Reading, writing, and content-learning evolved naturally in a social context. For these children the development of literacy and literary skills was an integral part of the process of content-learning as they expanded their knowledge base and learned how to learn.

References

Arbuthnot, May Hill. *The Arbuthnot Anthology of Children's Literature*. Glenview, IL: Scott, Foresman, 1961.

Burton, Maurice, and Robert Burton. *The International Wildlife Encyclopedia*. N.Y.: Marshall Cavendish, 1969.

Ciardi, John. *The Reason for the Pelican*. Philadelphia: Lippincott, 1959.

Climo, Shirley. *Someone Saw a Spider: Spider Facts and Folktales*. N.Y.: Crowell, 1985.

Edmondson, Madeleine. *The Witch's Egg*. N.Y.: Seabury, 1974.

Harste, Jerome, Kathy Short, and Carolyn Burke. *Creating Classrooms for Authors: The Reading-Writing Connection*. Portsmouth, N.H.: Heinemann, 1988, p. 5.

Huck, Charlotte S., Susan Hepler, and Janet Hickman. *Children's Literature in the Elementary School*, 4th ed. N.Y.: Holt, Rinehart and Winston, 1987.

Rosenblatt, Louise. "The Literary Transaction: Evocation and Response." *Theory into Practice*, vol. 21, no. 4, Autumn 1982, pp. 268–277.

Bibliography of Bird Tales

Traditional Tales—Collections

Baker, Augusta, selector. *The Golden Lynx and Other Tales*. "Queen Crane" (Sweden), pp. 46–53; "The Rooster, Handmill and Hornets" (Sweden), pp. 54–57. Philadelphia: Lippincott, 1960.

Barbeau, Marius, and Michael Hornyansky. *The Golden Phoenix and Other Fairy Tales from Quebec*. Toronto: Oxford University Press (1958), 1980.

Berger, Terry. *Black Fairy Tales*. "The Fairy Bird" (Swazi), pp. 106–123. N.Y.: Atheneum, 1975.

Bierhorst, John, ed. *The Fire Plume—Legends of the American Indians*. "The Broken Wing," pp. 58–65. N.Y.: Dial, 1969.

Brown, Dee, reteller. *Teepee Tales of the American Indian: Retold for Our Times*. "The Rooster, the Mockingbird, and the Maiden" (Hopi), pp. 14–18; "The Bluebird and the Coyote" (Pima), p. 146. N.Y.: Holt, Rinehart and Winston, 1979.

Buck, Pearl S., ed. *Fairy Tales of the Orient*. N.Y.: Simon and Schuster, 1965.

Carey, Bonnie. *Baba Yaga's Geese and Other Russian Stories*. Bloomington, IN: Indiana University Press, 1973.

Cheney, Cora. *Tales from a Taiwan Kitchen*, "The Lantern Baby," pp. 25–34; "The Man Who Loved Tiny Creatures," pp. 37–52; "Good Neighbors Come in All Sizes," pp. 53–55; "The Mud-Baked Hen," pp. 143–149; "Lin Tachian," pp. 150–156. N.Y.: Dodd, Mead, 1976.

Cole, Joanna. *Best Loved Folktales of the World*. "Ashenputtel" (Germany), 68–75. Garden City, N.Y.: Doubleday, 1982.

DeRoin, Nancy, ed. *Jataka Tales: Fables from the Buddha*. "Cooperation," pp. 78–81. Boston: Houghton Mifflin, 1975.

Fenner, Phyllis R. *Giants and Witches and a Dragon or Two*. "King Stork," pp. 3–17. N.Y.: Knopf, 1943.

Fuja, Abayomi, collector. *Fourteen Hundred Cowries and Other African Tales*. "Oni and the Great Bird," pp. 48–59; "The Hen and the Hawk," pp. 113–115; "Concerning the Egas and Their Young," pp. 116–119; "The Elephant and the Cock," pp. 120–125; "Why the Hawk Never Steals," pp. 203–209. N.Y.: Lothrop, Lee & Shepard, 1962.

Gillham, Charles E. *Beyond the Clapping Mountains—Eskimo Stories from Alaska*. "How the Black Turnstone Came to Nest Near the Sea," pp. 127–134; "The Mountains that Clapped Together," pp. 1–16; "How the Sea Gulls Learned to Fly," pp. 17–30; "Mr. Crow Takes a Wife," pp. 31–43; "How the Little Owl's Name Was Changed," pp. 44–50; "How Mr. Crane's Eyes Became Blue," pp. 76–85; "How the Ptarmigans Learned to Fly," pp. 86–98. N.Y.: Macmillan, 1943.

Ginsburg, Mirra. *The Kaha Bird: Tales from the Steppes of Central Asia*. N.Y.: Crown, 1971.

Grimm, Brothers. *Favorite Folktales from Around the World*. Jane Yolen, ed. "The Goose Girl." N.Y.: Pantheon, 1986.

Hardendorff, Jeanne B., selector. *The Frog's Saddle Horse and Other Tales*. "Waukewa's Eagle," pp. 17–24. Philadelphia: Lippincott, 1968.

Hatch, Mary C., reteller. *13 Danish Tales*. "The Three Tailors and the White Goose," pp. 58–72. N.Y.: Harcourt, Brace, 1947.

Haviland, Virginia, reteller. *Favorite Fairy Tales Told in Norway*. "Boots and the Troll," pp. 75–88. Boston: Little, Brown, 1961.

———, reteller. *Favorite Fairy Tales Told in Poland*. "About Jan the Prince, Princess Wonderface, and the Flamebird," pp. 55–81; "The Lark, the Wolf, and the Fox," pp. 39–54. Boston: Little, Brown, 1963.

Heady, Eleanor B. *When the Stones Were Soft: East African Fireside Tales*, "The Little Crow," pp. 47–51. N.Y.: Funk and Wagnalls, 1968.

Jagendorf, M. A., and Virginia Weng. *The Magic Boat and Other Chinese Folk Stories*. "Why the Sun Rises When the Rooster Crows," pp. 87–91. N.Y.: Vanguard, 1980.

Leach, Maria. *How the People Sang the Mountains Up—How and Why Stories*. "Why the Birds Are Different Colors" (North Carolina), pp. 89–90; "How Rooster Got His Comb" (China), pp. 92–93; "Why Robin Has a Red Breast" (Congo), p. 95. N.Y.: Viking, 1967.

Leodhas, Sorche Nic. *Thistle and Thyme: Tales and Legends from Scotland*. "St. Cuddy and the Gray Geese," pp. 39–45. N.Y.: Holt, Rinehart and Winston, 1962.

Lurie, Allison, reteller. *Clever Gretchen and Other Forgotten Folktales.* "The Black Geese," pp. 17–22. N.Y.: Crowell, 1980.

Manning-Sanders, Ruth. *A Book of Ghosts and Goblins.* "The Kindly Ghost," pp. 103–110. London: Methuen, 1968.

———. *A Book of Mermaids.* "The Geese and the Golden Chain" (Portugal), pp. 98–107. N.Y.: Dutton, 1967.

———. *A Book of Ogres and Trolls.* "Tritil, Litil, and the Birds" (Iceland), pp. 20–31. N.Y.: Dutton, 1972.

———. *A Book of Witches.* "Lazy Hans," pp. 27–37. London: Methuen, 1965.

Masey, Mary Lou, reteller. *Stories of the Steppes: Kazakh Folktales.* "The Fox and the Quail," pp. 113–115. N.Y.: David McKay, 1968.

McNeill, James. *The Double Knights—More Tales from Around the World.* "Brother Anansi and Sir Peacock" (Trinidad), pp. 30–35. N.Y.: Henry Z. Walck, 1964.

Parker, Arthur C. *Skunny Wundy Seneca Indian Tales.* "Weasel and Old Snowy Owl," pp. 204–212; "How the Wood Duck Got His Red Eyes and Sojy Had His Coat Spoiled," pp. 43–51; "The Owl's Big Eyes," pp. 72–74; "The Mink and the Eagle," pp. 124–131; "How the Bluebird Gained the Color of the Sky and the Gray Wolf Gained and Lost It," pp. 139–145. Chicago: Albert Whitman, 1970.

Ransome, Arthur. *The War of the Birds and the Beasts and other Russian Tales.* "The War of the Birds and the Beasts," pp. 13–25; "The Swan Princess," pp. 26–34. London: Jonathan Cape, 1984.

Segal, Lore, and Maurice Sendak, selectors. *The Juniper Tree and Other Tales from Grimm.* "The Golden Bird," pp. 201–216. Vol. II. N.Y.: Farrar, Straus & Giroux, 1973.

Sewadda, W. Moses. *Songs and Stories from Uganda.* "Tweriire," pp. 21–25. N.Y.: Crowell, 1974.

Spellman, John W., collector and ed. *The Beautiful Blue Jay and Other Tales of India.* "The Beautiful Blue Jay," pp. 3–7; "The Little Bird's Rice," pp. 44–48; "The Crow and the Sparrow," pp. 12–14. Boston: Little, Brown, 1967.

Toor, Frances. *The Golden Carnation and Other Stories Told in Italy.* "The Youth Who Became an Ant, a Lion, and an Eagle," pp. 67–79. N.Y.: Lothrop, Lee & Shepard, 1960.

Vo-Dinh. *The Toad Is the Emperor's Uncle: Animal Folktales from Vietnam.* "The Ravens Build a Bridge," pp. 35–39; "The Crow's Pearl," pp. 115–122. Garden City, N.Y.: Doubleday, 1970.

Weinstein, Krystyna, compiler. *Owls, Owls—Fantastical Fowls.* N.Y.: Arco, 1985.

Wiggin, Kate Douglas, and Nora A. Smith, eds. *The Fairy Ring.* "The Golden Bird" (Scandinavian), pp. 42–51; "The Wild Swans" (Scandinavian), pp. 80–96; "The Goose Girl" (German), pp. 236–243; "Drakesbill and His Friends" (French), pp. 304–312; "The Bird-Cage Maker" (Spanish), pp. 343–348; "The Storks and the Night Owl" (Arabic), pp. 355–366. Garden City, N.Y.: Doubleday, 1967.

———, eds. *Tales of Laughter.* "King Wren," pp. 172–175; "Reynard and Chanticleer," pp. 287–288; "The Golden Goose," pp. 124–128. Garden City, N.Y.: Doubleday, Page, 1927.

———, eds. *Tales of Wonder.* "What the Birds Said," pp. 8–9; "The Storks and the Night Owl," pp. 30–40; "The Bird of Truth," pp. 189–199. Garden City, N.Y.: Doubleday, Page, 1927.

Traditional Tales—Single Editions

Aardema, Verna, reteller. *Why Mosquitoes Buzz in People's Ears: A West African Tale.* Leo and Diane Dillon, illus. N.Y.: Dial, 1975.

Cauley, Lorinda Bryan, reteller. *The Goose and the Golden Coins.* N.Y.: Harcourt Brace Jovanovich, 1981.

Climo, Shirley. *King of the Birds.* N.Y.: Crowell, 1988.

Denman, Cherry. *The Little Peacock's Gift: A Folktale from China.* N.Y.: Peter Bedrick, 1988.

Gág, Wanda. *Jorinda and Joringel.* N.Y.: Coward, McCann & Geoghegan, 1975.

Grimm, Brothers. *The Seven Ravens.* Felix Hoffman, illus. N.Y.: Harcourt, Brace and World, 1962.

————. *The Six Swans*. Adrie Hospes, illus. N.Y.: McGraw-Hill, 1973.

Hogrogian, Nonny, reteller and illus. *The Glass Mountain*. N.Y.: Knopf, 1985.

Ishii, Momoko, reteller. *The Tongue-Cut Sparrow*. Katherine Paterson, trans. N.Y.: Dutton, 1982.

Kamen, Gloria, reteller. *The Ringdoves* (retold from the Fables of Bidpai). N.Y.: Atheneum, 1988.

Kirn, Ann. *The Peacock and the Crow* (Chinese fable). N.Y.: Four Winds, 1969.

Matsutani, Miyoko. *The Crane's Reward*. London: Adam and Charles Black, 1983.

McDermott, Gerald. *Papagayo, the Mischief Maker*. N.Y.: Windmill/Wanderer, 1980.

Newton, Patricia, adaptor. *The Five Sparrows: A Japanese Folktale*. N.Y.: Atheneum, 1982.

Pyle, Howard. *King Stork*. Trina Schart Hyman, illus. Boston: Little, Brown, 1973.

Silverman, Maida. *Anna and the Seven Swans*. N.Y.: Morrow, 1984.

Steel, Flora, reteller. *Tattercoats: An Old English Tale*. Scarsdale, N.Y.: Bradbury, 1976.

Toye, William, reteller. *The Loon's Necklace*. N.Y.: Oxford University Press, 1977.

Wahl, Jan. *Drakestail* (French folktale for beginning readers). N.Y.: Greenwillow, 1978.

Wolkstein, Diane, adaptor. *The Magic Wings—A Tale of China*. Robert Andrew Parker, illus. N.Y.: Dutton, 1983.

Yagawa, Sumiko, reteller. *The Crane Wife*. Katherine Paterson, trans. N.Y.: Morrow, 1981.

Modern Tales—Picture Books

Alan, Sandy. *The Plaid Peacock*. N.Y.: Pantheon, 1965.

Alexander, Sue. *Peacocks Are Very Special*. Garden City, N.Y.: Doubleday, 1976.

Andersen, Hans Christian. *The Nightingale*. Nancy Elkholm Burkert, illus. N.Y.: Harper and Row, 1965.

————. *The Ugly Duckling*. Marianna Mayer, illus. N.Y.: Macmillan, 1987.

————. *The Wild Swans*. Susan Jeffers, illus. N.Y.: Dial, 1981.

Bartholic, Edward. *Cricket and Sparrow*. N.Y.: Collins, 1979.

Baumann, Kurt. *The Prince and the Lute*. N.Y.: North-South Books, 1977.

Brighton, Catherine. *Hope's Gift*. N.Y.: Doubleday, 1988.

Bunting, Eve. *The Man Who Could Call Down Owls*. Charles Mikolaycak, illus. N.Y.: Macmillan, 1984.

Burningham, John. *Borka, The Adventures of a Goose with No Feathers*. N.Y.: Random House, 1963.

Coerr, Eleanor. *The Josefina Story Quilt* (for beginning readers). N.Y.: Harper and Row, 1986.

Cole, Brock. *The Winter Wren*. N.Y.: Farrar, Straus & Giroux, 1984.

Delafield, Clelia. *Mrs. Mallard's Ducklings*. N.Y.: Lothrop, Lee & Shepard, 1946.

Demuth, Patricia. *Max, the Bad-Talking Parrot*. N.Y.: Dodd, Mead, 1986.

Duvoisin, Roger. *Day and Night*. N.Y.: Knopf, 1960.

Edmondson, Madeleine. *The Witch's Egg*. N.Y.: Seabury, 1974.

Elkin, Benjamin. *Why the Sun Was Late*. N.Y.: Parents' Magazine Press, 1966.

Flack, Marjorie. *The Story about Ping*. N.Y.: Viking, 1933.

Flory, Jane. *We'll Have a Friend for Lunch*. Boston: Houghton Mifflin, 1974.

Freeman, Don. *Come Again, Pelican*. N.Y.: Viking, 1961.

————. *Fly High, Fly Low*. N.Y.: Viking, 1957.

Gerstein, Mordicai. *Prince Sparrow*. N.Y.: Four Winds, 1984.

Haley, Gail E. *Birdsong*. N.Y.: Crown, 1984.

Hamburger, John. *The Wish*. N.Y.: Norton, 1967.

Haugaard, Erik Christian. *Prince Boghole*. N.Y.: Macmillan, 1987.

Kasza, Keiko. *The Wolf's Chicken Stew*. N.Y.: Putnam, 1987.

Laurin, Anne. *Perfect Crane*. N.Y.: Harper and Row, 1981.

Levitin, Sonia. *The Fisherman and the Bird*. Boston: Houghton Mifflin, 1982.

Lionni, Leo. *Tico and the Golden Wings*. N.Y.: Pantheon, 1964.

Lobel, Arnold. *How the Rooster Saved the Day*. N.Y.: Greenwillow, 1977.
Lobel, Anita. *King Rooster, Queen Hen* (for beginning readers). N.Y.: Morrow, 1975.
Mathers, Petra. *Maria Theresa*. N.Y.: Harper and Row, 1985.
McCloskey, Robert. *Make Way for Ducklings*. N.Y.: Viking, 1979.
McLerran, Alice. *The Mountain Who Loved a Bird*. Eric Carle, illus. Natick, MA: Picture Book Studio USA, 1985.
Peet, Bill. *Eli*. Boston: Houghton Mifflin, 1978.
Politi, Leo. *Song of the Swallows*. N.Y.: Scribner's, 1949.
Polushkin, Maria. *The Little Hen and the Giant*. N.Y.: Harper and Row, 1977.
Rabinowitz, Sandy. *The Red Horse and the Bluebird*. N.Y.: Harper and Row, 1975.
Singer, Isaac Bashevis. *Why Noah Chose the Dove*. N.Y.: Farrar, Straus & Giroux, 1973.
Sis, Peter. *Rainbow Rhino*. N.Y.: Knopf, 1987.
Stevenson, James. *Howard*. N.Y.: Greenwillow, 1980.
Surany, Anico. *Lora, Lorita*. N.Y.: Putnam, 1969.
Wiest, Robert, and Claire Wiest. *There's One In Every Bunch*. Chicago: Children's Press, 1971.
Wildsmith, Brian. *Hunter and His Dog*. N.Y.: Oxford University Press, 1979.
———. *The Little Wood Duck*. London: Oxford University Press, 1972.
———. *Maurice Maeterlink's Blue Bird*. N.Y.: Franklin Watts, 1976.
———. *The Owl and the Woodpecker*. N.Y.: Franklin Watts, 1971.
———. *Pelican*. N.Y.: Pantheon, 1982.
Wittman, Sally. *Pelly and Peak* (for beginning readers). N.Y.: Harper and Row, 1978.
Yashima, Taro. *Crow Boy*. N.Y.: Viking, 1955.
Yolen, Jane. *The Boy Who Had Wings*. N.Y.: Crowell, 1974.
———. *Owl Moon*. N.Y.: Philomel, 1987.

Modern Fiction—Novels

Adler, C. S. *Fly Free*. N.Y.: Coward-McCann, 1984.
Aiken, Joan. *Arabel's Raven*. Garden City, N.Y.: Doubleday, 1974.
Anderson, Mary. *F-T-C Superstar*. N.Y.: Atheneum, 1977.
Bunting, Eve. *One More Flight*. N.Y.: Frederick Warne, 1976.
Byars, Betsy. *The House of Wings*. N.Y.: Viking, 1972.
Coerr, Eleanor. *Sadako and the Thousand Paper Cranes*. N.Y.: Putnam, 1977.
Erickson, Russell. *Toad for Tuesday*. N.Y.: Lothrop, Lee & Shepard, 1974.
———. *Warton and the Contest*. N.Y.: Lothrop, Lee & Shepard, 1986.
George, Jean C. *The Cry of the Crow*. N.Y.: Crown, 1980.
King-Smith, Dick. *Harry's Mad*. N.Y.: Crown, 1987.
Kushner, Donn. *The Violin-Maker's Gift*. N.Y.: Farrar, Straus & Giroux, 1981.
Langton, Jane. *The Fledgling*. N.Y.: Harper and Row, 1980.
Mattingley, Christobel. *Duck Boy*. N.Y.: Atheneum, 1986.
Mowat, Farley. *Owls in the Family*. Boston: Little, Brown, 1961.
Robertson, Keith. *In Search of the Sandhill Crane*. N.Y.: Viking, 1973.
Tolan, Stephanie. *A Time to Fly Free*. N.Y.: Scribner's, 1983.
White, E. B. *The Trumpet of the Swan*. Harper and Row, 1970.

Poetry

Adoff, Arnold. *Birds*. Harper and Row, 1982.
Arbuthnot, May Hill. *The Arbuthnot Anthology of Children's Literature*. "The Secret," author unknown,

p. 51; "What Robin Told," George Cooper, p. 51; "Crows," David McCord, p. 52; "Chickadee," Hilda Conkling, p. 52; "The Blackbird," Humbert Wolfe, p. 53; "The Snowbird," Frank D. Sherman, p. 53; "The Sandhill Crane," Mary Austin, p. 53; "Wild Geese," Eleanor Chipp, p. 53; "Gull," William Jay Smith, p. 54; "The Eagle," Alfred, Lord Tennyson, p. 54. N.Y.: Scott, Foresman, 1961.

Ciardi, John. *The Reason for the Pelican*. Philadelphia: Lippincott, 1959.

Cole, Joanna. *A New Treasury of Children's Poetry: Old Favorites and New Discoveries*. "Duck," Valerie Worth, p. 78; "Mrs. Peck-Pigeon," Eleanor Farjeon, p. 78; "The Toucan," Pyke Johnson, Jr., p. 79. Garden City, N.Y.: Doubleday, 1984.

Fisher, Aileen. *Up the Windy Hill*. "Bird Talk." N.Y.: Abelard-Schuman, 1953.

Larrick, Nancy, ed. *Piping Down the Valleys Wild*. "A bird came down the walk," Emily Dickinson, p. 128; "Seagulls," Patricia Hubbell, p. 136; "The Heron," Theodore Roethke, p. 137; "The Eagle," Alfred, Lord Tennyson, p. 134; "The Owl," William Jay Smith, p. 134; "The Wild Geese Returning," Tsumori Kunimoto, p. 135; "Something Told the Wild Geese," Rachel Field, p. 135. N.Y.: Dell, 1968.

Lear, Edward. *The Owl and the Pussycat*. Janet Stevens, illus. N.Y.: Holiday House, 1983.

———. *The Pelican Chorus*. N.Y.: Parents' Magazine Press, 1967.

Merrill, Jean, and Ronni Solbert, selectors. *A Few Flies and I—Haiku by Issa*. N.Y.: Pantheon, 1969.

Prelutsky, Jack. *The Random House Book of Poetry for Children*. "The Sparrow Hawk," Russell Hoban, p. 87; "Night Heron," Frances Frost, p. 86; "The Vulture," Hilaire Belloc, p. 86; "Sea Gull," Elizabeth Coatsworth, p. 84; "The Sandpiper," Frances Frost, p. 84; "The Sandpiper," Witter Brynner, p. 84; "The Canary," Ogden Nash, p. 83; "The Duck," Richard Digance, p. 83; "The Hen," Lord Alfred Douglas, p. 85. N.Y.: Random House, 1983.

Roberts, Elizabeth Madox. *Under the Tree*. "The Woodpecker." N.Y.: Viking, 1922, 1930.

Sherman, Nancy. *Gwendolyn the Miracle Hen*. N.Y.: Golden Press, 1961.

Wise, William. *Nanette the Hungry Pelican*. Chicago: Rand McNally, 1969.

Nonfiction

Austin, Elizabeth. *A Random House Book of Birds*. N.Y.: Random House, 1970.

Ayars, James Sterling. *John James Audubon*. Champaign, IL: Garrard, 1966.

Brenner, Barbara. *Baltimore Orioles* (for beginning readers). N.Y.: Harper and Row, 1979.

———. *On the Frontier with Mr. Audubon*. N.Y.: Coward, McCann, 1977.

Bonners, Susan. *A Penguin Year*. N.Y.: Delacorte, 1981.

Buff, Mary, and Conrad Buff. *Elf Owl*. N.Y.: Viking, 1958.

Burton, Maurice, and Robert Burton. *The International Wildlife Encyclopedia*. N.Y.: Marshall Cavendish, 1969.

Cole, Joanna. *A Bird's Body*. N.Y.: Morrow, 1982.

Earle, Olive L. *White Patch—A City Sparrow*. N.Y.: Morrow, 1958.

Featherly, Jay. *Ko-hoh: The Call of the Trumpeter Swan*. Minneapolis: Carolrhoda, 1986.

Fisher, Clyde. *The Life of Audubon*. N.Y.: Harper and Bros., 1949.

Freschet, Bernice. *The Flight of the Snow Goose*. N.Y.: Crown, 1970.

Gans, Roma. *When Birds Change Their Feathers*. N.Y.: Crowell, 1980.

Garelick, May. *What Makes a Bird a Bird?* Chicago: Follett, 1969.

Goudey, Alice. *Graywings*. Scribner's, 1964.

Greenberg, Polly. *Birds of the World*. N.Y.: Platt and Munk, 1983.

Hamberger, John. *The Call of the Loon*. N.Y.: Four Winds, 1969.

Henry, Marguerite. *Birds at Home*. Chicago: Donahue, 1942.

Hirschi, Ron. *City Geese*, color photographs by Galen Burrell. N.Y.: Dodd, Mead, 1987.

———. *What Is a Bird?* N.Y.: Walker, 1987.

———. *Where Do Birds Live?* N.Y.: Walker, 1987.

Hornblow, Leonora, and Arthur Hornblow. *Birds Do the Strangest Things*. N.Y.: Random House, 1965.

Hurd, Edith. *The Mother Owl*. Boston: Little, Brown, 1974.

Jerr, William. *The Question and Answer Book about Birds*. N.Y.: Golden Press, 1957.

Kaufmann, John. *Robins Fly North, Robins Fly South*. N.Y.: Crowell, 1970.

Lavine, Sigmund. *Wonders of the Eagle World*. N.Y.: Dodd, 1974.

Lewis, Naomi. *Puffin*. N.Y.: Lothrop, Lee & Shepard, 1984.

Martin, Bernard. *How Birds Keep Warm in Winter*. N.Y.: Holt, Rinehart and Winston, 1964.

McGowan, Tom. *Album of Birds*. Chicago: Rand McNally, 1982.

National Audubon Society. *The Audubon Nature Encyclopedia*. N.Y.: Curtis, 1971.

Oram, Sandie. *Birds and Migration* (MacDonald First Library). London: MacDonald, 1971.

Patent, Dorothy Hinshaw. *Where the Bald Eagles Gather*. N.Y.: Clarion, 1984.

Peterson, Roger Tory. *Birds* (Life Nature Library). N.Y.: Time-Life, 1963, 1968.

————. *A Field Guide to the Birds*. Boston: Houghton Mifflin, 1947.

Rowland, Beryl. *Birds with Human Souls: A Guide to Bird Symbolism*. Knoxville: University of Tennessee Press, 1978.

Selsam, Millicent. *Tony's Birds* (for beginning readers). N.Y.: Harper and Bros., 1961.

Selsam, Millicent, and Joyce Hunt. *A First Look at Birds Nests*. N.Y.: Walker, 1984.

————. *A First Look at Owls, Eagles and Other Hunters of the Sky*. N.Y.: Walker, 1986.

Shackleford, Nina. *When Birds Migrate*. Austin, Texas: Steck-Vaughn, 1968.

Stoutenburg, Adrien. *A Vanishing Thunder: Extinct and Threatened American Birds*. Natural History Press, 1967.

Stuart, Marjorie. *Birds Around Us*. Racine, WI: Whitman, 1961.

Vessel, Matthew F., and Herbert Wong. *Introducing Our Eastern Birds*. Palo Alto, CA: Fearon, 1970.

Webb, Addison. *Birds in Their Homes*. Garden City, N.Y.: Doubleday, 1947.

Williamson, Margaret. *The First Book of Birds*. N.Y.: Franklin Watts, 1951.

Wolff, Ashley. *A Year of Birds*. N.Y.: Dodd, Mead, 1984.

Zim, Herbert. *Birds: A Guide to the Most Familiar American Birds*. N.Y.: Simon and Schuster, 1956.

NINE

Wish Tales:
The Literary Dialogue-Journal

THE DIALOGUE-JOURNAL

The dialogues described in Chapter 2 are a significant part of the social context in which natural language learning occurs in the classroom. In both oral and written dialogues the teacher and children encounter each other as unique individuals. They exchange ideas and make an effort to understand and respect the viewpoint of others. Dialogue-journals are used as vehicles to establish ongoing written conversations between teachers and students.

According to Jana Staton, who initiated the first research on the dialogue-journal (Staton, 1980), this personalized written form serves three major purposes:

1. It provides an opportunity to give individual attention to each student.
2. It motivates students to write, and to see writing as a meaningful and useful experience.
3. It provides a format for responding to children's writing and to help them improve as writers (p. 514).

The children are invited to write about their experiences, feelings, and thoughts, and to ask questions which they prefer not to air in public. In responding to each entry the teacher focusses on the writer's message, not the mechanical aspects of writing. Teachers encourage more written expression by answering children's questions; by introducing questions and comments which support and extend children's topics; by introducing new or related topics; by expressing appreciation, empathy, understanding, admiration, and other appropriate human responses; and by sharing their own personal thoughts, feelings and experiences. By responding to the children teachers show their acceptance of children's ideas and at the same time model accepted conventions of written language in a meaningful context.

Sumitra Unia, a fifth-grade teacher, distinguishes between the personal writing associated with dialogue-journals and public writing:

Students came to see journals as a vehicle of expression not requiring any correcting. Revising and editing were done in other contexts: book reports, stories, and projects were often taken beyond the first draft. It was at this time that we attended more closely to the conventions of writing, giving them their proper place (1985, p. 66).

Unia observed that journal writing was the least threatening of all writing activities and "the spontaneity encouraged in journal writing lends itself particularly well to fostering confidence and increasing written fluency" (p. 66).

The dialogue-journal provides a context in which reading and writing can be taught as complementary processes of meaning-making. As the children become active participants in the written dialogue as readers and writers they develop an awareness of the purpose of reading and writing as vehicles for communication. At the same time they gain practical experience with the use of language in a natural context with a real audience.

The dialogue-journal provides teachers with valuable information about their students as unique individuals and as learners. Leslie Reed, a sixth-grade teacher, comments that the dialogue-journal allows her "to personalize her teaching and keep up with the rapid changes in each student" (Staton, 1980, p. 515). She plans her lessons based on their responses and feedback and creates individual assignments for those who need extra help.

THE LITERARY DIALOGUE-JOURNAL

In the Focus Unit featuring wish tales, to be described in this chapter, the dialogue-journal was introduced to the children as "a place to share your thoughts about stories with your teacher" and was described as "a written conversation about stories between you and your teacher." The children decided to call it their "Story Journal," and used it throughout the school year to write about their encounters with literature and to share their responses, insights, and interpretations.

Each of the Focus Units described in this book is designed to create a literate environment in which children hear and read literature, talk about literature, write about literature, and compose their own literary pieces. Oral discussions during the group story sessions set the stage for written conversations about literature in the literary dialogue-journals (or "story journal") between the teacher and individual students. The dialogue writing is used to "extend kid's thinking about books—to go inside other's written language in written conferences" about books (Atwell, 1984, p. 242).

WISH TALES

Wish tales were selected as the focus of a literature unit designed for six-, seven-, and eight-year-old children because wishing is as important in the lives of young children as it is in the lives of storybook characters. Indeed, the granting of a wish is a typical motif or pattern found in traditional literature. In some of these stories a wish is granted and then used foolishly or in anger. Rash wishing has undesirable consequences. In other stories a wish is granted and used wisely, often to help others. In many stories wishes are granted in return for a kind and generous deed. In most, main characters learn something from their experiences, and the reader/listener learns something about human nature.

Session One

To introduce the motif in the tales selected for this Focus Unit the teacher asked, "Did you ever make a wish? Tell us about it."

Every child in every age group had something to share. They told about making wishes on the first star of evening, before blowing out birthday candles, in their bedtime prayers, and by throwing pennies into fountains and wishing wells. They recited poems and special formulae and rules which were part of the wishing process. Many told personal stories of "a wish that came true." While for some these experiences served to confirm their belief in the powers of magic, Santa Claus, the tooth fairy, or wishing wells; for others, these experiences had logical and rational explanations. One child observed, "When you wish for a special toy or something your mom and dad can usually grant the wish, but if you wish you didn't have allergies or freckles—well they can't do that." Another child added, "Or if you wish you can fly—*that* kind of wish is only granted in stories." A third child argued, "But I wished for a baby sister, and that's just what we got!" The first child responded, "But your wish didn't *make* it a girl. That's from the genes or something. But in a *story*, you can wish for a baby even if you're not pregnant! That's what happened in 'Tom Thumb.'"

At the end of this discussion, during which none of the children seemed to change their personal beliefs about wishing, the teacher brought out *The Three Wishes* (Zemach, 1986). After looking at the title and the picture on the front cover the children offered some preliminary observations:

- I bet our story unit is going to be on wish tales this time!
- The man and lady on the cover look sort of poor. So I think they're going to wish for riches.
- They're nice. You can tell by their faces and the way they're petting the dog.
- But who's going to *give* them the three wishes?
- Maybe the dog is magic.

These predictions and questions set the stage for reading aloud this new edition of a very old traditional tale. At the end of the tale the teacher asked, "Why were the poor woodcutter and his wife given three wishes?" Some of the children's responses were:

- Because they helped someone who could give wishes.
- But they didn't *know* the imp could give wishes.
- See—I *told* you they were nice!
- They got rewarded for being kind and helpful.

A second question, "What did you think about the couple in this story?" elicited these ideas:

- I think they should've wished for food because they didn't have enough to eat!
- They really should've paid attention to the imp. Remember he *warned* them to be real careful with their wishes.
- He said, "There are only three—so wish wisely my friends." [This child had turned to the text to get the exact words.]
- Well, they certainly didn't wish very wisely. They were pretty foolish!
- But in the end they weren't too upset. At least they had the sausage to eat for dinner.
- And they had each other.
- And their dog.

After this discussion the children were invited to select books for independent reading from the display shelf which held a collection of wish tales (*see* bibliography of wish tales at the end of this chapter). The children were asked to search for connections between the books read independently and the ones read aloud in the group story sessions, and to share their discoveries in group discussions. In addition they were encouraged to write regularly about these wish tales in their "story journals."

Session Two

The Fisherman and His Wife (Brothers Grimm, 1978) was introduced in the second session. A look at the cover prompted the children to compare it with the previous story.

- This time it's a *fisherman* and his wife.
- They probably got three wishes, too.
- But they don't look as nice. He looks sad. And she looks sort of bossy—the way she's standing.
- And *they* have a dog, too. But he looks sort of weird.
- And look at that thing in the back. Is that their *house*?

Not long after they had settled down to listen to the story the children interrupted with a number of spontaneous comments.

- See, she really *is* bossy!
- Oh no! She's asking for *too* much now.
- She should be happy with that cute cottage.
- Look how mad that fish is getting. I don't blame him.
- That fisherman is such a wimp. He keeps doing everything she says!
- I bet she's going to lose everything if she makes more wishes!
- She's so greedy!

When the tale came to an end they continued their spontaneous commentary.

- I just knew they'd end up back in that night pot house.
- It's because she was so greedy.
- I really liked that cottage. Who'd want to live in that big castle anyway?
- I think the fish punished her because she's so greedy.
- I think the fisherman should have wished for the flounder to turn back into a prince.

- They [the fisherman and his wife] didn't seem very happy. They probably should've got a divorce.
- But this is an old, old story. Maybe they didn't have divorces then.

One child volunteered to ask his dad, a lawyer, about this; and the teacher guided the discussion back to the text by asking students to compare it with *The Three Wishes*. These observations were recorded on a chart:

How Are They Alike?

1. Both had magic.
2. Both were about people who got rewarded for being kind.
3. The fish and the imp both granted wishes.
4. Both stories ended the same. The people were back where they started.
5. The wishes didn't do much good.

How Are They Different?

1. The woodcutter and his wife weren't greedy. They didn't want much.
2. They were foolish. The fisherman's wife was selfish and greedy.
3. The fisherman's wife made *all* the wishes. The woodcutter and his wife took turns.

When asked to comment on the illustrations several children observed that the pictures in *The Three Wishes* were more humorous than those in *The Fisherman and His Wife*. When someone noted the central role played by the fish throughout the second story, in contrast to the relatively minor role played by the imp who disappeared after granting the wishes, one child suggested: "I think it was the artist who made the fish so important in that story. He was so *huge* and glittery! And then when the fish got mad, the sea *looked* mad, too!"

The teacher asked, "Why do you think these stories were created by storytellers long ago?" The children responded by identifying the central themes or messages.

- The storyteller wanted to teach you a lesson—to show what happens if you get too greedy.
- . . . or if you act foolish and don't think.
- To show that you should be satisfied with what you have.

The last question was designed to call attention to the structure of these narratives. "Why could these stories be called circle tales?"

- They just went around in a circle and didn't *get* anywhere.
- They both *ended* where they *started*!
- The woodcutter and his wife thought of all the things they could wish for—a big house, a mountain of gold coins. But in the end, they were sitting at the *same* table in their little house.
- And the fisherman and *his* wife started out in the night pot on the first page and ended up in the night pot on the *last* page!

Several of the children wanted to construct graphic representations of these circle tales. They were given drawing paper cut into the shape of circles. The children divided their circles into four or six equal wedges, like a pie, and drew the key events in one of the tales so that the picture in the first wedge represented the beginning as well as the ending of the story. They moved freely between writing and art in their attempts to generate meaning, and, in the process, they gained new perspectives on knowing.

Session Three

While listening to *The Old Woman Who Lived in a Vinegar Bottle* (Godden, 1972) in the third session the children made and confirmed predictions as the story unfolded.

- I bet she's going to throw that little fish back.
- It's going to be a *magic* fish.
- She'll get a reward.
- Oh no—I bet *she's* going to get too greedy and then the fish is going to get mad.

At the end of the story they were asked to compare it with *The Fisherman and His Wife*. First, they considered the similarities.

- The fisherman's wife and the old woman both wanted more and more.
- They got greedier and greedier.
- There's a magic fish in both stories who can give wishes.
- Both lived in weird houses—the night pot and the vinegar bottle.
- And in both stories they all ended up back in their weird houses.
- They're both circle tales!
- It's like *The Three Wishes*, too! They're all three circle tales; and they *all* get wishes because of helping someone.

The next step was to focus on the differences.

- The old woman said, "I'm sorry."
- She changed at the end. She's not greedy anymore.
- She *learned* something. Remember that part when she said, "I'm a greedy old woman and I didn't even know it."
- But the fisherman's wife was greedy to start with; and the old woman was *nice* at first—and ended up nice.
- In the vinegar bottle story the old woman got a meal at the end because the fish was *pleased* with her.
- In both stories the fish got so mad because they got greedy. But in *that* one [*The Old Woman Who Lived in a Vinegar Bottle*] he stopped being mad because *she* stopped being greedy.
- I liked the part where he said he thought it was going to be a *sad* story, but it wasn't.

Session Four

As soon as the teacher had finished reading the fourth story, *Do Not Open* (Turkle, 1981), the children began to compare it with the first three tales. First, they identified the similarities.

- They all had wishes.
- The wishes came true.
- This lady [in *Do Not Open*] lived by the sea just like the fisherman and his wife.
- And the vinegar bottle lady lived by a lake.
- And she had a cat just like Miss Moody [*Do Not Open*].
- And the woodcutter had a dog and so did the fisherman. They all had pets—but no kids.
- She got her wish granted because she did a nice thing just like the others.

Then they focussed on the differences.

- Miss Moody didn't say the wish out loud like the others did.
- That's the way you're *supposed* to make a wish. You blow out the candles, and in your head you say the wish. If you tell, it won't come true.
- She didn't wish for too much like the others. She just wanted her clock to work.
- She wasn't greedy.
- And when she made a wish she really didn't know anyone would grant it.
- It was really a different kind of wish tale.
- It's because the wish isn't the *main* part of the story like the others.

After this spontaneous comparative analysis the teacher introduced a few questions to focus on the story characters. The first, "Why was the cat afraid of storms?" required inferential thinking, the ability to make connections between isolated events in the story, and to draw from relevant experiential knowledge.

- It reminded the cat of the night he almost drowned when Miss Moody rescued him.
- It's like when I got bitten by that dog down the street, and I *never* go near dogs now.
- So it's like you're reminded of something scary that happened, and then you feel scared again.

The second question, "Why did Miss Moody *say* to the monster that she was afraid of mice?" was intended to assist comprehension of a rather subtle interaction. Those who had grasped the implied meaning shared their insights.

- She wasn't *really* afraid of mice. She wasn't afraid of anything. Not the storm! Not the monster!
- She just said that to trick him like he tricked her!
- Yeah—he said he was a little kid stuck in the bottle so she felt sorry for the crying kid.
- Like she felt sorry for the cat.
- But she figured the monster would show off and want to *prove* his powers to change into things.
- That was so neat when the monster changed into a mouse and the cat ate him.
- It reminds me of the end in "Puss in Boots."

A follow-up question reinforced the notion that information provided by the author early in a narrative can become the basis for comprehending subsequent events: "How did the author let you know that she was not telling the monster the truth about being afraid of mice?"

- Because you already *know* she's just not that kind of lady. She's brave! She reads ghost stories even when there's a big loud storm!
- She lives alone. She's *very* independent.
- And it just wouldn't make any sense if she's afraid of mice and not that horrible monster!
- I think you sort of get to know somebody at the beginning of a story, and then you can kind of figure out what they'll do next.
- Maybe that's why the author told all that stuff at first so then you'd *know* it was just a trick on the monster.

By this time the children had had time to make a number of entries in their story-journals. It was interesting to note that most of them were beginning to make comparisons between these four stories and those they had selected to read independently. They had apparently internalized some of the questions that had been introduced in group sessions to generate discussion and to guide interaction with texts. The content of the story-journals suggested that group discussions had served to demonstrate ways to respond to literature and that the children were *using* these demonstrations to build their own strategies for responding to literary texts. These written comments often helped children organize their thoughts prior to sharing them publicly in group sessions. This proved to be especially useful for children who were hesitant about expressing their ideas in a group setting. The teacher used the dialogue-journal to encourage these children to become more active participants with such comments as: "I enjoyed reading your ideas about the story you just read. I hope you will share this in our next group meeting! I think you could help some of the others think about the books *they* are reading."

Session Five

Tye May and the Magic Brush (Bang, 1981), adapted from an ancient Chinese folktale for beginning readers, and *Liang and the Magic Paintbrush* (Demi, 1980), another retelling of this tale, were read aloud in the fifth group session. The children were very interested in the exquisitely detailed illustrations for these two brief stories. Most preferred the colorful water-color pictures in the Liang story to the primarily black-and-white line drawings in the Tye May story. Several children expressed appreciation of Molly Bang's effective use of a single color, red, to draw attention to Tye May and the other key characters in the story. They recognized immediately that these two tales were essentially the same with a few interesting exceptions.

- One was about a boy and one was about a girl.
- They both loved to paint but they were too poor to buy a brush.
- Both wished for a brush.
- The wish people both came at night when they were asleep.
- But one was an old woman and one was an old man on a phoenix.
- They both gave a magic brush and said, "Use it carefully!"
- Just like in *The Three Wishes*!
- And the paint brushes were magic. Everything they painted became real.
- They both used their magic brushes to make things for poor people.

- They weren't greedy.
- Both stories have greedy people though. And the magic doesn't work for *them*.
- And they both outsmarted that mean Emperor.
- But the stories didn't really *end* the same even though the Emperors got punished in both.
- One Emperor got drowned and the other got left on the island and had to work.

The children were asked to try to explain the essential similarity and significant differences between these two tales. They were guided toward an understanding of the way old tales have been handed down through the years and shaped by generations of storytellers. When they grasped the notion that each author/artist had selected the same Chinese tale of the magic brush to retell and illustrate in book form, they became intrigued with the differences between these two interpretations. They wondered which tale was "closer to the one told by the first storyteller." One child suggested that Molly Bang's version was probably changed the most "because it was written like an 'easy reader' and so she expected younger kids to read it and so she didn't have the Emperor die at the end because that would be too sad."

In her story-journal one eight-year-old girl wrote: "I liked Tye May better because of the end. Because the Emperor did not drown." The teacher replied, "I liked the way the Tye May story ended, too. In the other story about Liang it bothered me to see the Emperor and his whole family drown in the sea. It seemed to me that in the Tye May story this cruel and selfish Emperor was taught a lesson." The child replied, "He learned not to be so greedy and mean. And he learned what it feels like to work all day like the poor people. That's a better ending. It's happier."

Another child wrote: "I told my mom and dad about the stories. We went to the library after dinner and we found a book with all Chinese stories. It had *our* story in it. The Emperor died. Also the kid was a boy, *not* a girl!"

Session Six

After *Tico and the Golden Wings* (Lionni, 1964), a story about a bird born without wings, was read aloud the children were asked to compare it with the magic paint brush stories.

- They all *needed* something. Tye May and Liang needed a brush and Tico needed wings.
- So they wished for the one thing they needed.
- And they all had dreams about the wishes and someone came in the night and granted the wish.
- Tico got wings from the wishingbird.
- The wishingbird is just like in all the other stories. There's a wish-giver in *all* the stories.
- So their dreams came true. It's like when you daydream about something you want. A dream is like wishing.
- Wish dreams are the good ones; and nightmares are the bad ones.
- Tico was like Tye May and Liang because he gave his gold feathers to other people just like they did. I mean they painted things for other people. Things they needed. They helped people.
- So—it *is* like the other stories. Everyone who got a wish did something nice. But in the

first stories, they got wishes after they did something nice. In these three stories they did nice things *after* they got the wish.

To conclude this session the teacher reread the last lines of *Tico and the Golden Wings*. "We are *all* different. Each for his own memories, and his own invisible golden dreams." Then she asked them to explain what Tico meant.

- Well, a memory is something that happened a long time ago. Then later it comes back to your brain and you remember it. Everybody has different memories, so inside their brain they're different.
- Tico has memories of all those people he helped and the other birds don't. So he's different. He's special.
- Even though he *looks* like the other birds now, he's different inside.
- He probably dreams about those people . . . the bride and the basket maker and the fisherman. He probably wants to go see them again. But those other birds don't care. So he's different. They don't know what he has in his mind.

Finally the teacher asked, "And what makes *you* special?" Each child shared a special memory or golden dream—what they had done which gave them a feeling of pride; what they wanted to do or be when they were older. The teacher shared her memories and dreams in this thoughtful and personal interchange.

Tico and the Golden Wings prompted several children to write in their journals about secret wishes for wings. For example, one seven-year-old wrote:

It was a good story. I wish i had wings. The pichers were so good. The wings looked reel! If i had those wings I cold [could] fly south with all the birds. I wold go to Florida to see Disney World!!!

One child who had read *The Wish* (Hamberger, 1967) wrote that the penguin in this story was like Tico because they are both birds who wished they could fly. He was especially interested in the contrast between these two kinds of birds.

Session Seven

When *Sidney Rella and the Glass Sneaker* (Myers, 1985) was introduced in the seventh session the children immediately caught on to the humor of the title and the picture on the front cover. They couldn't wait to make predictions about this story based on their prior knowledge of "Cinderella, or the Little Glass Slipper."

- That boy with the broom must be Sidney Rella. He has to work all day like Cinderella.
- And that little man with the wand—he's the fairy godmother.
- It's a god*father*!
- And that clock in the back looks like it's pointing to twelve, so there's probably going to be a warning about midnight.
- But the pictures are like cartoons. It's going to be a funny story. It's like a mixed up Cinderella story.

As the story was read aloud the children confirmed or revised their original predictions and added new ones as more information was revealed. And they giggled all the way through.

At the end of the story the children were asked to explain what the author had done.

- She took an old, old story and made it *modern*. Like the boy wishes he could play on the football team instead of going to a party at the palace.
- And when the little fairy godfather warns Sidney to get home by 6 o'clock instead of midnight, that's when you're *supposed* to be home after playing ball. So it made sense.
- And it's the football coach who goes around looking for the one who fits the glass sneaker—instead of the prince. So *that* makes sense, too.
- But the author made some things the same. Like it was the two brothers who wouldn't let him go to the football practice just like the stepsisters wouldn't let Cinderella go to the *ball*. And the brothers never believed he was the mysterious player. They laughed at Sidney just like the stepsisters.
- So the author made some things the same so you could *recognize* what story it was—but she changed things to make it funny.

One child who had read Jane Yolen's *Sleeping Ugly* (1981) exclaimed, "My book is just like this but the author used Sleeping Beauty and changed it around to make it funny. And it's *also* like those other wish tales because Plain Jane—she's the one the prince wakes up with a *kiss*—she gets three wishes from the fairy for being so nice and generous!"

Session Eight

To introduce *Yeh-Shen* (Louie, 1982) the teacher explained that this story is at least 1000 years older than the familiar European version of the Cinderella fairytale. This led to another discussion of the way traditional tales travel over time and space, and the way they are shaped and polished as they pass from one storyteller to the next. The children were encouraged to speculate about how this tale might have been carried all the way from Asia to Europe before air travel.

After reading this beautiful tale aloud the teacher asked the children to consider similarities and differences between this tale and the Cinderella tale they had known for a long time. They were also invited to suggest possible reasons for changes made by various storytellers over time and across cultures. They easily identified the similarities: the stepmother, the stepsister, the wish, the wishgiver, the warning, the flight, the loss of the slipper, the discovery of the true owner, the marriage to the king. They were especially intrigued with the differences between the wishgivers in these stories.

- In *Yeh-Shen* it's the bones of her pet fish that help her instead of the fairy godmother.
- I think in places like China they used to believe in spirits—like a ghost of a dead animal can help living people. Remember that story we read about the little white dog that got killed and he punished the guy who killed him? [He was referring to a Japanese tale "The Old Man of the Flowers." The comparison was a valid one.[1]]

[1]Uchida, Yoshiko, reteller. "The Old Man of the Flowers." *The Dancing Kettle and Other Japanese Folk Tales*. N.Y.: Harcourt Brace, 1949, pp. 147–156.

- Maybe they hadn't invented the fairy godmother yet so the storyteller in the old, old story didn't use it.
- Or maybe different countries just have different magic people. Like in Japan they have those big Oni and in Russia they have Baba Yaga. So maybe the fairy godmother is only in certain places.

They also discussed the nature of the slipper.

- Those slippers that Yeh-Shen wore are probably what ladies used to wear in China. But Cinderella had to wear high heels because that's what you're supposed to wear with a ball gown.
- My uncle went to China. He said in the olden days a lady was supposed to have little tiny feet so they used to put straps around a baby's feet to keep them small. So maybe that's why the king thought it was so great that Yeh-Shen had such little feet!

Many of the children included comments about Yeh-Shen in their story-journals. For example, one seven-year-old wrote:

I liked the prat when Ya-Shen tok the shoes and the king thot that she *stoll* the shoes. But we *knew* she diden't.

The teacher responded:

Yes, I liked that part, too. I couldn't wait until he found out the truth! As readers, we often know things about one character that the *other* characters don't know. Why do you think the king thought she was stealing the shoes?

The child answered:

Beacuse she took them and she had alredy turned bak into her rags. So she didn't look rich enuf to have sutch nice shoes. The *best* part was when she tried on the sleper.

Session Nine

"The Wind Cap" is one of the tales included in *The Hundredth Dove and Other Tales* created in the tradition of the classical folktale by Jane Yolen (1976, 1977). Many of the children recognized Yolen as the author of *Sleeping Ugly* and predicted that this would be another funny tale. They soon revised their prediction as this thoughtful and somewhat disturbing tale unfolded. They recognized the now familiar themes: a wish is granted as a reward for kindness to a wishgiver (in this tale, a tiny green fairy man who takes the form of a turtle), and the discovery that "a fairy gift is not altogether a blessing" (Yolen, p. 21). One child suggested that "Ms. Yolen probably read a lot of fairytales when she was young so she knows all about them." Another child explained that he had heard the story of "Jonah and the Whale" at his Temple and that "one part of 'The Wind Cap' reminded me of the time when Jonah was thrown into the sea!" He concluded, "I bet the author had heard the Jonah story, too!" When the teacher pointed out that the main character's name was spelled "J-o-n," he exclaimed, "See—she [Yolen] even named him after Jonah!"

At the end of this session, the teacher asked, "What lesson do you think Jon learned?"

- He should've listened to his mom's warning about fairy gifts.
- He learned to appreciate what he had.
- He learned that it's not good to wish for *too* much of something . . . that it's better to live *partly* on land and *partly* on sea.
- He learned that the sea is not the only thing in the world.
- It reminds me of the story I read about King Midas. He wanted *everything* to be gold. But he learned that this was a stupid wish.
- I read that, too. He found out that some things are more precious than gold.
- And Jon found out that he really liked being with his mom and working on the farm.

Session Ten

"Bridget's Hat" is another story in a collection of originals: *Tale of a One-Way Street and Other Stories* by Joan Aiken (1978). The children were intrigued with the silhouettes created to illustrate each story; and they contrasted them with the more realistic charcoal drawings used to illustrate Jane Yolen's tales. One child predicted: "I think this story is going to be funnier—not as serious as *The Wind Cap*." As the story unfolded, this prediction was confirmed. The children thoroughly enjoyed the lighthearted tale and the delightful descriptions of the characters. They easily recognized Bridget as the hardworking "good character" who is rewarded for her kindness to the King of the Grasshoppers, and her twin brother Solomon as the lazy "greedy character" who gets punished for his selfishness. They observed that the nature of their wishes fit their personalities. Bridget made a modest wish which would make her job a bit easier; and Solomon wished for gold. They also noted the specific directions and warning given to Bridget about the magic wishing boots. Several children commented that they had anticipated that Solomon would try to steal the boots, but would not use them the right way and get himself into trouble.

- He *did* get into trouble, but he just got what he deserved and so did Bridget.
- It ended just like a fairytale except she married the mayor's son instead of a prince.

Many of the children wrote about "Bridget's Hat" in their story-journals.

Bridget was so kind and nice just like Tye May. And she was so nice to her brother and she worked so hard. I thought it was a grate story. I liked the part when the grasshopper fell in the porridge. That was so funny. And I liked the snoring part when Solomons snores put the dragon to sleep.

Another child wrote:

Solomon learned he shouldn't go fooling around with other people's things. My cousin is just like Solomon because he lays around and plays with his car and doesn't do his jobs or help. So I better tell him about Solomon and what happened to him!

A third child wrote:

I liked the part when that grasshopper hopped in the soup and gave her the wish. I liked the way the story ended. Everything worked out right. Bridget really deserved to get that job at the palace and Solomon really deserved to get that job with the dragon. He was good at snoring and she was good at sewing.

Session Eleven

When "Lie-A-Stove" in *The Talking Tree and Other Stories* (Baker, 1955) was introduced, the children expressed curiosity about the meaning of the title. The teacher had brought along a copy of *The Fool of the World and the Flying Ship*[2] which the children had heard several months prior to this unit. As soon as she held up the picture of the fool lying on the big stove the children were able to make the appropriate connection.

- Oh—it's *that* kind of stove!
- So it's about someone who likes to lie on the stove all day!
- It could be another Russian story.

And after the first lines were read aloud several children interrupted with, "He's just like that boy Solomon!" A second interruption occurred at the point in the narrative when Lie-A-Stove encounters a fish who asks for his freedom and says:

I can serve you better whole and free than if sliced upon your dinner table. . . . You only have to say
  "Grant my wish
Golden Fish" (p. 211).

The children recognized the magic fish who grants wishes.

- It's just like in *The Fisherman and His Wife* and *The Old Woman Who Lived in the Vinegar Bottle.*
- And they have the same little jingles to call the fish when they want to make a wish.

At the conclusion of the story the teacher referred to the original comparison that had been made between Lie-A-Stove and Solomon in "Bridget's Hat" and asked, "In what way were these two lazy characters different?"

- Lie-A-Stove *did* try to help his mom when he got the magic even though he was still lazy. But Solomon *never* helped his sister.
- Lie-A-Stove changed at the end of the story. When he got married and had his own house and kids, he started working and took care of his mom and his family and his garden. But Solomon *never* changed.
- Lie-A-Stove was really nice to people and he forgave his father-in-law. Solomon never did anything nice for anybody. He only thought of himself.
- He started out lazy and ended up lazy.

[2]Arthur Ransome, reteller. *The Fool of the World and the Flying Ship—A Russian Tale.* N.Y.: Farrar, Straus & Giroux, 1968.

After this session several children noted that one of the stories they had selected for independent reading was quite similar to "Lie-A-Stove." One nine-year-old boy wrote:

Guess what! I found another story almost like Lie-A-Stove. It's called The Fool and the Magic Fish and it's in a book of stories from Russia. [Riordan, 1976] Did you read it? You should. It's really funny. He just had to say—By will of the fish do as I wish—And remember the part when Lie-A-Stove goes to the palace right on the stove? Well, it's the same thing in this story. That was so funny. And he's nice too. He invited everyone to the wedding when he married the princess—even all the poor people.

Session Twelve

Juma and the Magic Jinn (Anderson, 1986) was the last story read aloud in group sessions for the unit on wish tales. The title prompted several children to guess that the Jinn could be a kind of genie who grants wishes. When the book was opened to reveal the title page and the large picture of the unusual blue jar they were convinced that the Jinn was, indeed, a genie who lived in a jar—"just like in *Do Not Open!*"

After listening to this fantasy adventure of a young boy who lives on the island of Lamu in Kenya the children had a number of questions about this exotic island and the Muslim culture as portrayed in the magnificent and detailed illustrations of Charles Mikolaycak. Following a discussion in which these questions were addressed, the teacher asked, "What words would you use to describe Juma?" The children's responses included: an artist, a poet, imaginative, curious, bored, impatient, a daydreamer, stubborn, friendly.

Another question, "Why did Juma's mother warn him not to touch the Jinn jar?" elicited responses such as:

- It's like in *Do Not Open*—that was a *bad one*—but she didn't *know* it would be.
- It's also like when Jon's mother said, "you can't always be sure that fairy magic will be good for you."

A third question focussed on Juma's three wishes and the consequences of each. The comments generated by this question led to a discussion of what Juma learned from his experiences, what his magic Jinn had taught him.

- He learned to appreciate the life he had and his home.
- Like in *The Wizard of Oz*. Dorothy said, "There's no place like home."
- He realized it was important to go to school and *learn* things.
- It was like 'The Wind Cap.' They both learned that it's better not to have everything all one way.
- In the woodcutter story they had three wishes, too. And they learned how happy they were even without all the stuff they thought of wishing for.
- The vinegar bottle lady learned the same thing. She realized she liked her life the way it was and she didn't need all that fancy stuff.

The journal entries about this story were generally quite thoughtful. For example, one boy wrote:

It was lucky for Juma that his jinn was a good one. Juma was afraid the jinn would be evil and he was brave to open the jar, but the jinn was good. She said, 'I'll do whatever you desire—Just make a wish.' So *then* he felt better and he wasn't scared anymore. That was a good part in the story. I thought it was going to be an awful monster like in *Do Not Open*. So I felt better, too!

Another child decided to reread the story and found some interesting clues which led him to interpret the wish-adventures as part of a dream sequence.

At first the jar was empty but then when he closed his eyes he saw her. She had *cat-like* eyes—like Paka his cat, and when she [the jinn] talked she *purred*! And she looked like his mom too. And he had a really big imagination too. Remember? He imagined that Paka could talk to him. And he was a poet. So I think he *dreamed* it. When you dream—people you know are in it but doing weird things. I just think he dreamed it all—but it was a good story.

A third child made connections with her own experience.

My MOM is just like Juma's MOM. She says don't tuch that!!!! It's a speshal doll. It's vary delicat. I know something bad wold happen if I tuched it—cause it wold brake. I thot the jinn jar wold brake. Juma was so lucky that he didnt get in truble.

COMPOSING NEW WISH TALES

After listening to, reading, discussing, and writing about the stories in the wish tale collection the children were invited to compose their own tales. In preparation for the composing process the teacher met with them to review the twelve stories introduced in the group sessions and to help them focus on the central characters, the wish givers, the nature of the wishes, and the consequences, as well as the implied lessons and themes.

The children's grasp of the recurring patterns and themes found in this group of tales was reflected in their narratives. Almost every child clearly identified the main character and his or her problem, described an encounter with a wish-giver character, the granting of a wish or wishes, and the consequences. And most of these stories were developed around a central theme, such as kindness rewarded and greed punished, or the undesirable consequences of rash or foolish wishing.

The influence of the language of literature on children's writing was also in evidence; various phrases embedded in their stories echoed the language of the fairytale world. For example, a six-year-old wrote:

Once up pon a time there wusz a dragin. He wudz hunormus! But he wuz so nise. Wun dae he suo [saw] a man stuk in a bush. The dragin helpt the man out of the bush. The man wusz magik. The man gave the dragin a wish. He wisht for gold becuz he had not wun coin. So he got his wish. He got as mutch gold as he wantd. He kep it in his castle.

When his story was finished, this young author read it aloud to himself and then wrote this title on top of his paper: "Gold to a Dragin Is Like Cande to a Child."

A seven-year-old wrote this story:

The Broken Wing

Once upon a time there was a man. He lived with his wife. They wanted a child. Now one day the woman went out to pick blackberries. On the way she found a small bird that had hurt his wing. She picked him up and took him home. When she got home she fixed his wing. When he was better he said to her, I am the king of all the birds. You have saved my life. In return I will grant you one wish. The woman said, My wish is a child! The bird said, Look behind you. And the woman looked and there was a beautiful little baby. And the bird stayed with the man and his wife and their child for the rest of their lives. And they all lived happily ever after.

Another seven-year-old wrote:

The Horse and What his Wish Was

Once upon a time there was a horse. He did not have a tail. He wished he did. One day he went out to go grazing. He found a rabbit. The rabbit was bleeding. The horse licked the rabbit until he stopped bleeding. The rabbit said, Thank you my friend for that. I will give you a wish! The horse thought. Then he said, Are you a magic rabbit? Yes, said the rabbit. Well then, said the horse, I would really like to have a tail. Very well said the magic rabbit. You shall have your tail! Then he disappeared! And the horse had a lovely new tail! And that is how the horse got his wish.

While the children were composing these narratives several of them discussed the writing process with the teacher in their story-journals. A seven-year-old's story-journal included this interaction:

Teacher: I like the story you are writing about the woman who helps a bird and gets a wish. Where did you get your ideas for this story?
Child: I thout of the king of the birds from Bridget's Hat. Remember the king of the grasshoppers in that story who fell in the soup? And she helped him. I thout maybe birds could have a king too. A nice bird. Like a dove. Then I thout about The Wind Cap and how the boy helped the turtle. But it was really a fairy and he granted his wish. But I wanted my bird to stay with them so he didn't change into a fairy. But he could talk.
Teacher: It is interesting the way you have used ideas from different stories to create your *own* story. This is what authors have done for years and years. The more writers read, the more they learn about how to create a story. They get ideas and inspiration from what they read and from their own experiences, too!

Here is an excerpt from a dialogue in another seven-year-old's journal:

Teacher: The wish story you are writing is very interesting. I can't wait to find out what is going to happen next! It sounds like you are writing about some of your own experiences with your brothers. Where did you get the idea for that magic cup?
Child: Well, one day I was at a store and I wanted a magnin [magnet] and my mom siad get a cup because every night I go upstairs—I sleep in the basement—and get a cup and go downstairs and get water. So she siad now you will not have to go upstairs and get a cup. My cup is about 5 inchs tall and has pichurs of flowrs all around and a funny handel.
Teacher: You must have had a very clear picture of your special cup as you were writing your wish

tale. You certainly used your imagination to think up that part about the water rising and turning into a woman who asks you what you want! Most authors use ideas from their own experiences, from their imagination, and from things they read just as you did!

Child: I am writing another story at home now. It's about me and my baby brother. We have lots of adventures. It's like a dream. We can fly over montins.

Teacher: I liked the way you ended your wish-tale. Wouldn't it be nice if these wishes could come true in real life! [In her story, the child had written: "all I want is my brothers to stop teasing me and I wish my baby brother could talk and me and my baby brother could fly over montins."] I liked that part when you began to list more wishes and the cup-woman said, "Hold it! Too many wishes." Also, I would love to read the story you are writing at home! It sounds like it could be a *sequel* to your wish-tale.

These journal entries reveal the kinds of connections children were making as they moved from reading literature to writing it. The teacher's responses were intended to help children see that making connections between reading and writing is valued and to become aware that what an author composes is like a tapestry woven with many strands drawn from a literary background; personal experiences, feelings, and opinions; and imagination. Like Tico, each writer is unique, bringing to the page his or her "own memories, and invisible golden dreams."

THE STORY-JOURNAL AND LITERACY LEARNING

The dialogue-journal offers a context for social interaction usually associated with natural oral conversation, and creates a dialogic partnership between student and teacher (Shuy, 1987). The fundamental purpose of the journal is meaningful communication. Children begin with what they already know, and share and explore ideas that are personally meaningful and relevant. Children practice using language in a natural context with a real audience. Writing with a particular reader in mind helps to reinforce the concept of reading and writing as vehicles of communication. As children begin to think about the effect of their writing on their readers, they learn to read their writing critically and to take the perspective of their potential audiences. In the process children become aware of the relationship between reading and writing and that the goal of both processes is to make sense, to construct meaning.

The story-journal dialogues described in this chapter fostered confidence and increased written fluency, and helped children see themselves as writers. For those children who had rarely contributed to group discussions, these private written conversations in the story-journals seemed to pave the way for more active participation in the public arena. The teacher's supportive responses encouraged these children to take the leap and to share their ideas and opinions with the larger community.

All learning involves risk. Every learner must be prepared to explore the unfamiliar. In the whole language classroom learners are encouraged to take risks: to make predictions as they try to make sense of texts, to engage in divergent thinking, to create new connections, to use language for their purposes. "Developing writers must be encouraged to think about what they want to say, to explore genre, to invent spellings, and to experiment with punctuation. Learners need to appreciate that miscues, spelling inventions, and other imperfections are part of learning" (K. Goodman, 1986, pp. 39–40).

The focus of the story-journal is on the writer's message, not the mechanical aspects of writing. The child is invited to take risks necessary to engage in authentic exploration and communication of meaning.

Authenticity is a distinguishing feature of a whole language classroom. Children are encouraged to engage in authentic writing, to construct texts which have meaning and purpose, and which are intended for a real audience.

In the Focus Unit described in this chapter the children were introduced to authentic literary texts and then invited to respond to these texts in a social context, as well as in a private written conversation with the teacher. The story-journal set the stage for extensive authentic writing, a natural activity in the literate environment of the whole language classroom.

References

Atwell, Nancie. "Writing and Reading Literature from the Inside Out." *Language Arts*, vol. 61, no. 3, March 1984, pp. 240–252.

Goodman, Kenneth. *What's Whole in Whole Language?* Portsmouth, N.H.: Heinemann, 1986.

Shuy, Roger W. "Research Currents—Dialogue as the Heart of Learning." *Language Arts*, vol. 64, no. 8, December 1987, pp. 890–897.

Staton, Jana. "Writing and Counseling: Using a Dialogue Journal." *Language Arts*, vol. 57, no. 5, May 1980, pp. 514–518.

Unia, Sumitra. "From Sunny Days to Green Onions: On Journal Writing." *Whole Language—Theory in Use*, Judith Newman, ed. Portsmouth, N.H.: Heinemann, 1985, pp. 65–72.

Bibliography of Wish Tales

Adoff, Arnold. *Flamboyan*. N.Y.: Harcourt Brace Jovanovich, 1988.

Aiken, Joan. *Tale of a One-Way Street and Other Stories*. "Bridget's Hat," pp. 41–56. Hammondsworth, Middlesex, England: Puffin Books, 1978.

Anderson, Joy. *Juma and the Magic Jinn*. Charles Mikolaycak, illus. N.Y.: Lothrop, Lee & Shepard, 1986.

Baker, Augusta. *The Talking Tree and Other Stories—Fairy Tales from 15 Lands*. "Lie-A-Stove" (Poland), pp. 210–217. N.Y.: Lippincott, 1955.

Bang, Molly Garrett, adaptor. *Tye May and the Magic Brush* (a Chinese tale). N.Y.: Greenwillow, 1981.

Brittain, Bill. *The Wish Giver*. N.Y.: Harper and Row, 1983.

Colwell, Eileen. *A Second Storyteller's Choice*. "Volkh's Journey to the East" (Russian), pp. 46–56. N.Y.: Henry Z. Walck, 1965.

DeLeeuw, Adele, reteller. *Legends and Folk-Tales of Holland*. "The Two Wishes," pp. 152–157. N.Y.: Thomas Nelson, 1963.

Demi. *Liang and the Magic Paint Brush*. N.Y.: Holt, Rinehart and Winston, 1980.

Elkin, Benjamin. *Al and the Magic Lamp* (beginning reader). N.Y.: Harper and Row, 1963.

———. *The King's Wish* (beginning reader). N.Y.: Random House, 1960.

Fillmore, Parker, reteller. *The Laughing Prince—Jugoslav Folk and Fairy Tales*. "The Best Wish," pp. 231–240. N.Y.: Harcourt Brace and World, 1921.

Galdone, Paul, illus. *The Three Wishes*. (This retelling is from *More English Fairy Tales*, Joseph Jacobs, ed.) N.Y.: McGraw-Hill, 1961.

Gardner, John. *The King of the Hummingbirds and Other Tales.* "The Witch's Wish," pp. 23–42. N.Y.: Knopf, 1977.

Glass, Andrew. *Chickpea and the Talking Cow.* N.Y.: Lothrop, Lee & Shepard, 1987.

Godden, Rumer. *The Old Woman Who Lived in a Vinegar Bottle.* N.Y.: Macmillan, 1972.

Grimm, Brothers. *The Fisherman and His Wife.* Monika Laimgruber, illus. N.Y.: Greenwillow, 1978.

Hamberger, John. *The Wish.* N.Y.: Norton, 1967.

Haviland, Virginia, reteller. *Favorite Fairy Tales Told in Denmark.* "A Legend of Christmas Eve," pp. 77–90. Boston: Little, Brown, 1971.

———. *Favorite Fairy Tales Told in Sweden.* "The Old Woman and the Fish," pp. 50–58. Boston: Little, Brown, 1966.

Hutchins, Hazel. *The Three and Many Wishes of Jason Reid.* N.Y.: Viking Kestrel (1983), 1988.

Jacobs, Joseph, ed. *Indian Fairy Tales.* "The Farmer and the Money-Lender." N.Y.: Putnam, pp. 184–187.

Jagendorf, M. A., collector. *The Priceless Cats and Other Italian Folk Stories.* "Red Flowers in White Snow," pp. 125–130. N.Y.: Vanguard, 1956.

Jeschke, Susan. *Perfect the Pig.* N.Y.: Holt, Rinehart and Winston, 1980.

Lionni, Leo. *Alexander and the Wind-Up Mouse.* N.Y.: Pantheon, 1969.

———. *Tico and the Golden Wings.* N.Y.: Pantheon, 1964.

Louie, Ai-ling, reteller. *Yeh-Shen: A Cinderella Story from China.* Ed Young, illus. N.Y.: Philomel, 1982.

Manning-Sanders, Ruth. *A Book of Wizards.* N.Y.: Dutton, 1966.

Myers, Bernice. *Sidney Rella and the Glass Sneaker.* N.Y.: Macmillan, 1985.

Newman, Shirlee, adaptor. *Folktales of Latin America.* "Pedro—A Tale of Chile," pp. 31–37. N.Y.: Bobbs, Merrill, 1962.

Price, Margaret, adaptor. *Myths and Enchantment Tales.* "The Golden Touch," pp. 139–145. N.Y.: Rand McNally, 1980.

Riordan, James, reteller. *Tales from Central Russia, Russian Tales: Book One.* "The Fool and the Magic Fish," pp. 165–174. Middlesex: Kestrel Books, 1976.

Singer, Isaac Bashevis. *A Tale of Three Wishes.* N.Y.: Farrar, Straus & Giroux, 1975.

Steig, William. *Sylvester and the Magic Pebble.* N.Y.: Simon and Schuster, 1969.

Titus, Eve, adaptor. *The Two Stonecutters.* Garden City, N.Y.: Doubleday, 1967.

Turkle, Brinton. *Do Not Open.* N.Y.: Dutton, 1981.

Williams, Jay. *One Big Wish.* N.Y.: Macmillan, 1980.

Yolen, Jane. *Greyling.* Cleveland, OH: Collins and World, 1968.

———. *The Hundredth Dove and Other Tales.* "The Wind Cap," pp. 19–27. N.Y.: Crowell, 1976, 1977.

———. *Sleeping Ugly* (for beginning readers). N.Y.: Coward-McCann, 1981.

Zemach, Margot. *The Three Wishes: An Old Story.* N.Y.: Farrar, Straus & Giroux, 1986.

Horse Tales:
Responding to Student Interests

RESPONDING TO STUDENT INTERESTS

The translation of theory into practice is informed by observation of children as they engage in the process of learning to read and write (Yetta Goodman, 1980). The curriculum is shaped by theoretical considerations together with student input. According to recent reviews of research examining connections between literature and literacy, empirical evidence points to the significant contribution of literature to literacy development (Sawyer, 1987; Tunnell, 1989). Translated into practice, these findings support the integration of literature into the literacy-learning curriculum. The reconceptualization of reading as a transaction between a reader and a text in which the reader actively generates meaning by relating prior knowledge and experience and personal feelings, ideas, and attitudes to the text suggest that students should be provided with meaningful and relevant reading material. Every reading experience should reinforce the notion that reading is a meaning-generating process. Meaningful and relevant reading experiences serve as powerful motivational factors in encouraging children to become readers. The challenge for teachers is to find age-appropriate materials which will be meaningful to their students.

By listening to and observing students, teachers can gather important information about their current interests and concerns. Input from children informs the process of selecting meaningful and relevant reading materials and planning literary experiences for them. This chapter describes a Focus Unit which responds to a third grade's widespread interest in horses and horse stories. This horse tale Focus Unit was later adapted for use in other third- and fourth-grade classrooms by "kid-watching"[1] teachers who had discovered a similar interest among their students.

[1]"Kidwatching" was coined by Yetta Goodman in a 1980 article (*see* reference section).

THE HORSE TALE FOCUS UNIT

"Stories about animals provide children with the vicarious experience of giving love to and receiving devotion and loyalty from an animal" (Huck, 1987, p. 515). Children's interest in and affection for animals seems to be universal. Animal stories arouse their desire to nurture and protect and foster compassion and a sense of kinship with animals. Realistic stories about horses and their owners generally portray loyal and devoted relationships. The popularity of such stories is not surprising when one considers the basic human desire to love and be loved, to establish bonds of love and loyalty.

Most of the children in a third-grade classroom had heard or viewed films of *Black Beauty* (Sewell, 1877) and *The Black Stallion* (Farley, 1944). Some were familiar with Marguerite Henry, one of our best writers of horse stories; others had read one or more books by C. W. Anderson or Glen Rounds. Few, if any of the children, had heard or read the traditional horse stories which are part of our literary heritage. So, various folk- and fairytales about horses were selected for the first segment of this unit.

Horses in contemporary realistic fiction are quite different from those found in traditional literature. In realistic stories animals behave like animals and are true to their species. In folktales animals talk and have magical powers. The differences are quite clear. But what similarities or common features connect these modern and traditional tales? This question was presented to the children as they began to explore traditional horse tales.

Session One

During the first group session in which the horse tale Focus Unit was introduced to the class, the children were invited to share their personal experiences and knowledge. What did they know about horses? Had any of them had experience with horseback riding? What horse stories did they know? Most of the children had had some sort of first-hand experience with horses: at a circus, a farm, a ranch, or summer camp. Two of the children lived on farms and were used to caring for and riding horses. One had been to a racetrack; others had watched horse races on television. Several had taken riding lessons; and one child had participated in a local horse show. A list of titles of horse stories the children had heard, read, or viewed on film was recorded on a chart. One child was familiar with Pegasus, the great winged horse of Greek mythology. This was added to the list and would later serve to enrich the discussion of traditional horse tales.

The children were then asked to generate a list of words or phrases associated with horses. This second list was the beginning of a factual study of horses: types and breeds; parts; riding equipment; the art of riding; care and training. Since this list was rather short it was suggested that the children do some research on horses in the school library and share with the class whatever information they could find. This factual study would be used to complement and enhance their literary study of horses. The children were also encouraged to select one or more horse stories to read independently. A collection of modern and traditional stories about horses had been placed on a display table in a corner of the classroom.

Small "special interest" groups were formed to allow children to share their independent reading experiences and to collaborate on research about horses. A variety of projects grew out of these small groups—murals, poems, dioramas, and dramatizations.

Session Two

At the second group session the children were introduced to a Russian fairytale, *The Magic Horse* (Reesink, 1974). Before reading the story aloud the teacher asked them to look at the book cover and make some predictions about this story. The children responded with these comments:

- It's not going to be a *true* story because it's about a magic horse.
- It looks like the horse on the cover is flying. This is a fantasy!
- And flames are coming out of the horse's nostrils, so it's going to be some kind of *super* horse!
- The boy on the horse is wearing old-fashioned clothes, and they're from a different country. So it's an *old* story!
- But what country is it?
- I wonder where they're going in such a hurry?
- Maybe someone is chasing them.

These observations, predictions, and questions set the stage for listening to the tale about Ivan, the miller's youngest son, who solved the mystery of the trampled wheat, and with the help of Greytail, the beautiful grey-tailed white horse, won the Czar's daughter for his bride. As the story unfolded, the children were encouraged to interrupt with brief comments related to their original predictions and questions and to become active participants in the process of meaning construction. The dialogue which began prior to the reading of the story continued, and was taken up again after the story came to its satisfying ending. Spontaneous comments reflected the children's personal reactions to the story.

Several questions introduced by the teacher extended the dialogue and invited the children to consider other perspectives. The question, "Does this story remind you of any others?" invited them to connect this tale and others they had heard or read earlier.

- It's like Cinderella but it's about a boy winning a princess instead of a girl getting a prince.
- The horse is like the fairy godmother. He helped Ivan get the princess.
- And instead of a glass shoe, it's the ring that tells who the mystery prince is!
- It's like the story of "The Princess on the Glass Hill" [Haviland, 1961]. It had the same kind of contest. One had to climb to the top of the hill, and the other had to jump to the top of the palace.
- I just read a book about a rainbow horse that's the *same* story! Except the contest is to ride past this balcony where the girl is sitting.
- I read that, too. It's from Puerto Rico. That was a good story [*The Rainbow-Colored Horse*, Belpré, 1978].

This question was designed to encourage children to "read each new text in light of previous texts" (Harste, 1984), and to focus their attention on recurring patterns and motifs found in traditional literature.

A second question, "Who are the main characters in this story?" stimulated discussion about narrative structure.

- I think the princess is the main character.
- Yes—because she's the Czar's daughter so she's real important.
- But she didn't do anything really. She was just sort of the prize for the contest.
- I think Ivan was the main character, because the story was really about him and how he won the contest and *got* the princess.
- And he was the only brother with a name. So maybe the author wants us to pay attention to him.
- The other main character is Greytail. He has a name, too! And they're both on the cover. I guess the artist is showing us who the *main* characters are.
- But he's a *horse*! Can a horse be a main character?
- Sure—like in *The Black Stallion* [Farley, 1944] . . . the horse and Alec Ramsay are the main characters. They have adventures together.
- And they're good friends.
- Ivan and Greytail are like friends. They have a secret together. They do the contest together.
- And they keep their promises to each other like friends do.

Session Three

The Fire Bird (Bogdanovic, 1972) was read aloud in the third group session. This time the children looked at the book cover and made spontaneous comments and predictions before the story was read aloud. One student pointed to the picture on the front and commented, "There's another magical flying horse and rider. But I think the Fire Bird will be the main character because that's the title!" By the end of the story he had reevaluated his position.

- The archer and the horse *do* everything in the story so *they* must be the main characters. The Fire Bird is important in the story—but not really a main character.

Other comments about this story reflected children's use of their literary backgrounds.

- The king is the villain-character because he's so cruel.
- And he gets punished in the end just like villains usually do in fairytales.
- The horse talks and flies like the one in *The Magic Horse* [Reesink, 1974].
- And he helps the boy get the princess.
- And it's also the same because the boy and the horse are friends . . . like in real life stories about humans and horses.
- So even though it's a fantasy, it shows that the horse is loyal to its owner. That's why I like horses so much. They're really good friends!

The dialogue moved them toward an exploration of the connections between horses in fantasy and in realistic stories, as well as the role of horses in their own lives. One student shared some relevant information he had gathered from his library research about the history of horses. He explained that over 5000 years ago horses were tamed and trained for riding and that they have been used for hunting, wars, and sports ever since. But he was especially interested in a list of famous horses he had found in an encyclopedia: Bucephalus, the beloved horse of Alexander the Great; Cincinnati, the black horse ridden by General Ulysses S. Grant in the Civil War; Marengo, a white stallion ridden by the French Emperor Napoleon; Traveller, the grey gelding of General Robert E. Lee. After hearing some of the names of famous horses in history several children added horse names from stories, such as Pegasus; Greytail; and Silver, the Lone Ranger's horse. One student noted: "All these horses are like *partners* with their owners. They do all their adventures together."

A girl who lives on a farm responded, "My horse is my special friend. He's not like a pet. When we ride together, I feel like he talks to me. . . . I mean . . . well, I can't really explain it."

In response to this child's attempt to explain an intense emotional relationship with her horse, the teacher read Richard Kennedy's *Song of the Horse* (1981), which captures in text and pictures the magical relationship between a girl and her horse. In the poetic text the girl reveals that she knows what her horse says to her. As the children listened to the beautiful language used to describe this powerful relationship between girl and horse, they could begin to understand what their classmate had tried to express about her own special bond with her horse.

Session Four

For the fourth group session the teacher selected Paul Goble's *The Girl Who Loved Wild Horses* (1978), a fairytale about a Native American girl's love of horses, and her special relationship with a beautiful stallion, the leader of the wild horses. At the end of the tale she becomes one of the Horse People, as a beautiful mare who takes her place beside the stallion. The children were ready to grasp the meaning of this unusual tale because of their growing understanding of the powerful bonds which can develop between humans and horses.

The dialogue which started in the initial group sessions came out of literary and personal experiences and a few key questions posed by the teacher. The dialogue continued as a cumulative process from one story session to the next. Gradually the students became more active participants, assuming greater responsibility for the direction and content of the ongoing dialogue.

Session Five

During the fifth session two traditional tales from Canada were read aloud: "Jean-Pierre and the Old Witch" and its sequel, "Goldenhair" (Martin, 1986). Jean-Pierre is an abused child who runs away from home, encounters a witch, and escapes from her with the help of an enchanted white horse. In the second tale Jean-Pierre and his white horse have become traveling companions who come to the castle of a king where the boy enters service as a gardener. When war breaks out Jean-Pierre and the horse manage to defeat the enemy in three consecutive battles. Eventually, he wins the youngest princess' hand in marriage. The horse now asks Jean-Pierre to cut him in two with an ax. When Jean-Pierre sadly agrees to honor his dear friend's request, a handsome prince emerges from the two segments of the white horse. This prince marries the older princess; and they all live happily ever after.

After reading these two stories the teacher asked, "What familiar patterns did you notice in these stories?" The children identified the pattern of the neglected or poor child who accomplishes significant tasks and marries a princess; the use of magic objects to escape a witch; the helpful horse; the close bond between horse and hero; and the discovery of the identity of a mysterious stranger. Several children found connecting links between these Canadian tales; the Russian tale, *The Magic Horse* (Reesink, 1974); the Puerto Rican tale, *The Rainbow-Colored Horse* (Belpré, 1978); and "Cinderella." A boy who had independently read *The Black Horse* (Mayer, 1984) commented:

• I read a story from Ireland about a boy and a magical black horse who have all kinds of adventures after they get mixed up with this evil Sea King. In the end the boy breaks the spell of the Sea King and marries the princess—typical!—and then the horse, who's like his best friend, asks him to kill him with his sword just like in the story of Jean-Pierre. And the horse changes into a prince; and it turns out that he's really the long-lost brother of the princess. So they're really *brothers*, too, like in the other story!

Following this delightful retelling many of the children said they were anxious to read this book. One girl, who had been unusually quiet throughout the session, shared something that had been puzzling her: "But it's so weird. I mean, how come a story from Canada can be so much like a story from Russia and a story from Ireland? And they're like Cinderella, too. I just don't get it! I mean who copied who?" Her questions opened the way for an exploration of the nature of the oral tradition and the transmission and evolution of folk literature across time and space from generation to generation and country to country.

Session Six

To highlight the significance of questions raised by their classmate the children were urged to take time to think about possible explanations in order to prepare for a discussion about traditional tales the following day. The dialogue continued as the children puzzled over these questions in informal conversations with peers and families during the intervening hours in and out of school. By the next group session they were ready for the challenge, and by the end of the session, after some impressive critical and creative thinking, they had formulated their explanations of the dynamics of the oral tradition, which were surprisingly similar to the conclusions drawn by professional folklorists who have studied the evolution of traditional tales.

Session Seven

After this study of traditional horse tales several sessions were devoted to modern stories about horses. *The Mare on the Hill* by Thomas Locker (1985) was held up at the beginning of the seventh session to invite comments and predictions. This gesture was all that was necessary to get the dialogue started.

- The picture on the cover looks like a photograph.
- I think it looks like one of those big paintings in the art gallery.
- So it's probably going to be a *real* story instead of a fantasy.
- It looks so peaceful [pointing to the landscape on the cover]. I wonder what the problem could be.

The teacher commented that this would be a good time to read the book and find out. Later, several children noted that the mare reminded them of *Black Beauty* because he had also been ill-treated. One child added, "But in *Black Beauty* the horse tells you what he feels and what he's thinking. In this book you just sort of have to figure out what the horse is thinking by what she *does*."

This comment led to a discussion of the story.

- You could tell she just didn't trust humans because she always ran away.
- *That* was the problem! Remember the grandfather said that her first owner was mean to her so now she's afraid of humans.
- That's what happened to Ginger in *Black Beauty*. But she would bite and get really fierce.
- The two boys in the story were so patient with the mare. It took her such a long time to figure out that they wouldn't harm her.
- My favorite part was when she came over to Aaron and ate a carrot out of his hand.
- That showed she finally learned to trust him.
- I loved the part when she had her baby—the little foal!
- That was such a neat picture with the sun just coming up, and it was so quiet!
- You don't know that! It's just a picture!
- But you can *imagine* what it's like. I mean if I could walk into it, I would go on tiptoe so I wouldn't frighten the mare.

This comment prompted the teacher to introduce the word *landscape* to describe the type of paintings used to illustrate the story. She gave them time to look carefully at each of the wonderful paintings and to discover the way the artist portrayed the cycle of seasons. In response to their interest she showed them other landscape paintings by Thomas Locker in his book, *Where the River Begins*.[2]

At the end of this group session the children were asked to read *The Silver Pony*, a wordless picture book (Ward, 1973). Holding up the book with its picture of a winged pony on the front cover the teacher asked them to make some predictions about the story.

- It's going to be a fantasy because there's a magical flying horse.
- Yes. It's probably going to be like the other stories about magical powers.
- Maybe it'll be a myth like Pegasus.

---

[2]Thomas Locker. *Where the River Begins*. Dial, 1984.

- I know that author. Didn't he write *The Biggest Bear?*[3]
- I remember that. But that was a *real* story.

The teacher suggested that they keep these comments in mind as they looked at this book independently. Before discussing the story at the next group session students were asked to retell the story in their own words on paper. By creating a text for this wordless book they could generate meanings by integrating the artist's picture clues and their prior knowledge—literary, experiential, and linguistic. Many of the children chose to work with a partner or in a small group.

Session Eight

The eighth session was devoted to a discussion of *The Silver Pony* (Ward, 1973). The teacher initiated a series of questions to guide an analysis of the narrative. Students were asked to support their responses with clues from the pictures and to share their reasoning.

1. Who were the main characters?
2. What words would you use to describe each?
3. What was the setting?
4. How was the setting important to the story?
5. What do you think the boy and father said to each other after the boy told him about the flying pony? Who would like to recreate this dialogue?
6. Why do you think the father spanked the boy?
7. In what way were the journeys of the boy and pony similar?
8. What do these journeys suggest about the theme of this story?
9. What do you think the doctor said to the parents? Who would like to dramatize this conversation?
10. How did the artist let you know how each of the characters was feeling or what he or she might be saying or thinking?
11. What do you think happened to the Silver Pony at the end of the story?
12. Why do you think the boy's father gave him a pony after he recovered from his illness? What did this tell you about the father? Who would like to dramatize this last scene?

These questions were designed to focus attention on the story sequence, the narrative components, the relationship between these components, and the logical connections between events in the story sequence. Question 10 encouraged students to make inferences about thoughts, feelings, and motives from the gestures, facial expressions, and body language of characters drawn by the artist. Several of these questions invited the children to dramatize scenes in the story by creating dialogue between the characters. By moving from reading to drama to generate meaning they gained a new perspective of their knowing.

Question 11 opened the way for a discussion of a more basic idea. Is this fantasy or realism? Because of the different interpretations generated by this group of students, a consensus regarding the question was never reached. Those children who saw this story as a fantasy said:

[3]Lynd Ward. *The Biggest Bear.* Boston: Houghton Mifflin, 1952.

- In the last journey, the Silver Pony got melted by the sun, like in that myth about Icarus.
- I think the Silver Pony got changed from a magic pony to a real one . . . the one the father gave the boy at the end of the story.
- The Silver Pony had a baby and it was the real pony the boy got at the end because the Silver Pony died.
- I don't think the Silver Pony died. I think she flew off to help more people like lonely children or someone in a flood.

Those who saw this as a realistic tale said:

- I think the boy just *imagined* the Silver Pony. So, it was never really there.
- Yeah. The Silver Pony was in his imagination, not in real life.
- Maybe the pony was like an imaginary friend. The boy needed a friend because he was lonely on that farm.
- And he imagined flying on the Silver Pony to other lonely children.
- Like in a daydream!
- When he got the *real* pony, he didn't *need* the Silver Pony anymore.
- It was a dream. Remember, he was sleeping when he first saw the Silver Pony. And then later he was in bed—in his pajamas—and that was a dream, too. He was sleepwalking and fell out the window. But he *dreamed* that he fell off the pony.

The dialogue generated by this question was especially interesting because the children concluded that there did not have to be just one correct way to interpret the story. As one child put it:

- I think Mr. Ward just wanted you to *think* about the story and to make up your own mind about what it means.

The last question, 12, was designed to encourage inferential thinking concerning the internal response of the father to events. The children revealed their grasp of the significance of his gift of the pony to the boy.

- The father remembered what the boy had said about the Silver Pony, and he realized—finally—that it was something the boy really wanted.
- Yeah—like you daydream about things you want to happen.
- The father realized that his son was lonely and needed a friend.
- The father didn't know it was the Silver Pony's baby, but the boy knew!
- The doctor might have told him that the boy was unhappy and that's why he was sleepwalking. That happened to my cousin. He kept walking in his sleep and had to go to a doctor.
- I think the father changed. He began to pay more attention to his son instead of just working and saying he was *lying* about the Silver Pony.
- I think he changed, too. He was trying to understand his son's problems.
- He gave him the pony because he realized he [his son] was lonely and he could ride to the other farms and play with kids his own age instead of just doing chores all day!

- I think that after this, the father will try to spend more time with the boy, and he'll try to find out what's bothering him and what he's really like.

    This dialogue reflected the children's flexibility and their willingness to accept two different interpretations of the story. In the context of these coexisting interpretations, they searched for deeper meanings and discovered themes of loneliness, isolation, interhuman communication, friendship, and love.

Session Nine

Since many of the children had by this time read independently other modern stories about horses, they were asked to give brief book talks about those books they would recommend to their classmates. At this group session the children were introduced to some of the "best modern horse stories": *Black Beauty* (Sewell, 1986); *The Black Stallion* (Farley, 1944); *Blaze and Thunderbolt* (Anderson, 1955); *King of the Wind* (Henry, 1948); *The Blind Colt* (Rounds, 1960); *Wild Appaloosa* (Rounds, 1983); *Dexter* (Bulla, 1973); and *Pecos Bill* (Kellogg, 1986) (*see* Bibliography).

    After each of the books was presented, its title was added to a chart which listed traditional and modern horse stories, as well as nonfiction about horses. Then the children were asked to consider the entire collection in order to generate some connecting links between the narratives recorded on the chart. The purpose of this exercise was to guide the children toward synthesis.

- A lot of the stories were about a friendship between a horse and a human.
- Like the Black Stallion [Farley, 1944] and Alec Ramsay and that girl and her horse in *Song of the Horse* [Kennedy, 1981].
- My favorite one was about that boy who couldn't speak and the blind horse he tamed.
- That was *Blind Outlaw* [Rounds, 1980].
- And the old stories had the same thing . . . like the story about Ivan and Greytail [*The Magic Horse*, (Reesink, 1974)] and the one about Jean-Pierre and the white horse ["Goldenhair" (Martin, 1986)]. They had these special friendships.
- And it's different than just having a pet. The horse and the human really take care of each other.
- And these special relationships have been going on for hundreds and hundreds of years! Even in those old old stories it's the same.
- And in a lot of different countries, too.
- And if you look at all the different pictures in the horse books—they're so beautiful! I mean, I think the horse is such a great animal. He always looks so proud and powerful.
- And the horse is really an intelligent animal.
- Before, the horse was more important. Like before cars were invented and when horses were used in the wars.
- But they're still really important . . . especially the race horses. Boy, they're worth a *lot* of money!
- I can see why there are so many good stories about horses. For example, horses have been

so helpful to people that the storytellers made up stories about horses who helped their owners with magical powers, like in the fairytales, or by being loyal and courageous like in the real stories.

• And I think those stories about flying horses were made up because when you ride really fast, it's almost like you're flying. Or maybe they got the idea from Pegasus.

• Anyway, the stories seem to make sense—even the magical ones—because they're really about the way we feel about horses. . . .

COMPOSING HORSE STORIES

Following this dialogue the children were asked to write horse stories. The ongoing, cumulative dialogue, which extended from one group session into the next, served as preparation for this writing assignment. Some students chose to draw from the folktale tradition in creating their stories; others preferred to use contemporary realism as their models. Several children who particularly liked to draw decided to create wordless picture books like *The Silver Pony*. In the process they discovered what a challenge this was. One child commented, "Now I really appreciate what Mr. Ward did!"

In the final sessions children were given an opportunity to share their original stories with the class. These stories were bound and illustrated and were presented with pride and received with respect. Indeed the dialogue which had started in response to the work of professional writers continued in these final sessions as the children discussed the stories composed by their classmates.

RESPONDING TO STUDENTS AND LITERARY RESPONSE

The idea for the horse tale Focus Unit originated in response to the expressed interests of students. Their input initiated as well as shaped the development of this Unit which, in turn, provided a context for meaningful and relevant literary and literacy experiences. These experiences reinforced the notion that reading and writing are meaning-generating processes, and served to extend and spread student interest in horse tales as well as other realistic animal stories. Long after the completion of this Unit the children continued to discover, read, recommend, and discuss informally with their classmates a wide range of traditional and modern, fiction and nonfiction books about animals. They wrote stories, poems, and informative booklets; and they moved easily between print, paints, and clay to make meaning and express their interests in the animal world. The personal histories, feelings, and interests which students brought to their transactions with literature shaped the nature of the meanings and insights generated in the course of these literary transactions and related meaning-making activities through which they extended their response to literature.

References

Goodman, Yetta. "Kid Watching: An Alternative to Teaching." Farr, B. P., and D. J. Strickler, eds. *Reading Comprehension: Resource Guide.* Bloomington, IN: Indiana University Reading Programs, 1980.

Harste, Jerome. "Cognitive Universals in Literacy and Literacy Learning: Toward a Practical Theory." Presented at the Spring Conference on Teaching English and the Language Arts, Columbus, OH. April 14, 1984.

Huck, Charlotte S., Susan Hepler, and Janet Hickman. *Children's Literature in the Elementary School.* N.Y.: Holt, Rinehart and Winston, 1987.

Sawyer, Wayne. "Literature and Literacy: A Review of Research." *Language Arts*, vol. 64, no. 1, January 1987, pp. 33–39.

Tunnell, Michael, and James Jacobs. "Using 'Real' Books: Research Findings on Literature Based Reading Instruction." *The Reading Teacher*, vol. 42, no. 7, March 1989, pp. 470–477.

Bibliography of Horse Stories

Traditional Stories

Alegria, Ricardo. *The Three Wishes: A Collection of Puerto Rican Folktales.* "The Castle of No Return," pp. 90–99. N.Y.: Harcourt, Brace and World, 1969.

Asbjornsen, Peter Christian, and Jorgen Moe. *The Squire's Bride: A Norwegian Folktale.* N.Y.: Atheneum, 1975.

Baruch, Dorothy. *Kappa's Tug-of-War with Big Brown Horse: The Story of a Japanese Water Imp.* Rutland: Charles E. Tuttle, 1962.

Belpré, Pura. *The Rainbow-Colored Horse—A Folktale from Puerto Rico.* N.Y.: Frederick Warne, 1978.

Bogdanovic, Toma. *The Fire Bird—A Russian Folk Tale.* N.Y.: Scroll, 1972.

Chang, Isabelle. *Chinese Fairy Tales.* "The Magic Stallion," pp. 12–19; "The First Horse-Head Fiddle," pp. 34–35. Barr, 1965.

Daniels, Guy, reteller. *The Tsar's Riddles or the Wise Little Girl.* Paul Galdone, illus. N.Y.: McGraw-Hill, 1967.

Demi, adaptor and illus. *The Hallowed House—A Folktale from India.* N.Y.: Dodd Mead, 1987.

Edmonds, I. G. *Ooka the Wise: Tales of Old Japan.* "Ooka and the Halved Horse," pp. 81–86. N.Y.: Bobbs-Merrill, 1961.

Galdone, Paul. *The Horse, the Fox and the Lion* (adapted from "The Fox and the Horse" by the Brothers Grimm). N.Y.: Seabury, 1968.

Goble, Paul. *The Girl Who Loved Wild Horses* (literary tale). Scarsdale, N.Y.: Bradbury, 1978.

Grimm, Brothers. *The Goose Girl.* Marguerite DeAngeli, reteller and illus. Garden City, N.Y.: Doubleday, 1964.

Hatch, Mary C., reteller. *More Danish Tales.* "The Little Horse," pp. 150–166. N.Y.: Harcourt and Brace, 1949.

Haviland, Virginia. *Favorite Fairy Tales Told in Norway.* "The Princess on the Glass Hill," pp. 3–29. Boston: Little, Brown, 1961.

Hodges, Margaret. *If You Had a Horse—Steeds of Myth and Legend.* N.Y.: Scribner's, 1984.

———, reteller. *The Little Humpbacked Horse—A Russian Tale.* N.Y.: Farrar, Straus & Giroux, 1980.

———. *Saint George and the Dragon.* Trina Schart Hyman, illus. Boston: Little, Brown, 1984.

Jagendorf, M. A., and C. H. Tillhagen. *The Gypsies' Fiddle and Other Gypsy Stories.* "Noodlehead and the Flying Horse," pp. 52–92. N.Y.: Vanguard, 1956.

Kellogg, Steven, reteller. *Pecos Bill—A Tall Tale.* N.Y.: Morrow, 1986.

Lexau, Joan M. *It All Began with a Drip, Drip, Drip . . .* N.Y.: McCall, 1970.

Manning-Sanders, Ruth. *A Book of Magic Horses.* London: Methuen, 1984.

Manton, Jo, and Robert Gittings. *The Flying Horses: Tales from China.* N.Y.: Holt, Rinehart and Winston, 1977.

Martin, Eva, reteller. *Tales of the Far North.* Laszlo Gal, illus. "Jean-Pierre and the Old Witch," pp. 61–

69; "Goldenhair," pp. 71–80; "Little Golden Sun and Little Golden Star," pp. 39–53. N.Y.: Dial, 1986.

Mayer, Marianna. *The Black Horse*. N.Y.: Dial, 1984.

Otsuka, Yuzo. *Suho and the White Horse*. Yasuko Hirawa, trans. N.Y.: Bobbs-Merrill, 1969.

Reesink, Marijke, reteller. *The Magic Horse*. N.Y.: McGraw-Hill, 1974.

Scott, Sally, reteller and illus. *The Magic Horse*. N.Y.: Greenwillow, 1985.

Turska, Krystyna. *Pegasus*. N.Y.: Franklin Watts, 1970.

Walker, Barbara. *How the Hare Told the Truth about His Horse*. N.Y.: Parents' Magazine Press, 1972.

Whitney, Thomas, trans. *The Story of Prince Ivan, The Firebird, and the Gray Wolf*. Nonny Hogrogian, illus. N.Y.: Scribner's, 1968.

Whitney, Thomas, trans. *Vasilisa the Beautiful*. Nonny Hogrogian, illus. N.Y.: Macmillan, 1970.

Modern Stories

Anderson, C. W. *Billy and Blaze*. N.Y.: Macmillan, 1936, 1964.

———. *Blaze Finds Forgotten Roads*. N.Y.: Macmillan, 1970.

———. *Blaze and the Forest Fire*. N.Y.: Macmillan, 1938, 1966.

———. *Blaze and Thunderbolt*. N.Y.: Macmillan, 1955.

Bauer, Marion. *Touch the Moon*. N.Y.: Clarion, 1987.

Bonzon, Paul Jacques. *The Runaway Flying Horse*. William Pene du Bois, illus. N.Y.: Parents' Magazine Press, 1976.

Brett, Jan. *Fritz and the Beautiful Horses*. Boston: Houghton Mifflin, 1981.

Bulla, Clyde. *Dexter*. N.Y.: Crowell, 1973.

Clark, Ann Nolan. *Blue Canyon Horse*. N.Y.: Viking, 1954.

Clymer, Eleanor. *The Horse in the Attic*. Scarsdale, N.Y.: Bradbury, 1983.

Cohen, Caron Lee. *The Mud Pony*. N.Y.: Scholastic, 1988.

Dragonwagon, Crescent. *Margaret Ziegler Is Horse-Crazy*. N.Y.: Macmillan, 1988.

Evans, Pauline, ed. *Best Book of Horse Stories*. Garden City, N.Y.: Doubleday, 1964.

Farley, Walter. *The Black Stallion*. N.Y.: Random House, 1944.

———. *The Black Stallion Legend* (20th in the series). N.Y.: Random House, 1983.

Henry, Marguerite. *Black Gold*. Chicago: Rand McNally, 1957.

———. *Justin Morgan Had a Horse*. Chicago: Rand McNally, 1954.

———. *King of the Wind*. Chicago: Rand McNally, 1948.

———. *Misty of Chincoteague*. Chicago: Rand McNally, 1947.

———. *Mustang, Wild Spirit of the West*. Chicago: Rand McNally, 1971.

———. *Stormy, Misty's Foal*. Chicago: Rand McNally, 1963.

Jeffers, Susan. *All the Pretty Horses*. N.Y.: Macmillan, 1974.

Kennedy, Richard. *Song of the Horse*. Marcia Sewell, illus. N.Y.: Dutton, 1981.

Locker, Thomas. *The Mare on the Hill*. N.Y.: Dial, 1985.

Rabinowitz, Sandy. *The Red Horse and the Bluebird*. N.Y.: Harper and Row, 1975.

Rounds, Glen. *The Blind Colt*. N.Y.: Holiday House, 1941, 1960.

———. *Blind Outlaw*. N.Y.: Holiday House, 1980.

———. *Stolen Pony*. N.Y.: Holiday House, 1948, 1969.

———. *Wild Appaloosa*. N.Y.: Holiday House, 1983.

Sewell, Anna. *Black Beauty*. New York: Macmillan, 1962 (1877).

———. *Black Beauty* (shortened adaptation of the classic). Robin McKinley, reteller; Susan Jeffers, illus. N.Y.: Random House, 1986.

Shub, Elizabeth. *The White Stallion* (beginning reader). N.Y.: Greenwillow, 1982.

Ward, Lynd. *The Silver Pony*. Boston: Houghton Mifflin. 1973.

ELEVEN

Cinderella Tales: A Multicultural Experience

MULTICULTURAL PERSPECTIVE

We live in a pluralistic society which is part of an increasingly interdependent and complex global society. The students in our classrooms are from widely divergent cultural and linguistic backgrounds. As educators we have the responsibility to promote understanding of these many cultures and ethnic groups and to help our students develop a world view which will prepare them to become citizens of the world community. Teachers can initiate global education at all grade levels by inviting students to bring their cultural histories and experiences into the classroom. Teachers can create an environment in which students make an effort to understand and respect the viewpoint of their peers and stand in the shoes of those whose background is different than their own. The dialogue (*see* Chapter 2) which plays a central role in the literary and literacy-learning experiences described in this book also plays a critical role in the social and cultural learning which is an integral part of the classroom community.

In a context of cultural interchange exposure to our literary heritage, our legacy from cultures around the world, can contribute significantly to the development of students' multicultural perspective and can enhance the self-image and self-esteem of minority children and especially those who are new to this country. Folklore reflects the culture in which it emerges and is sometimes called "the mirror of a people." Folklore provides a "way of looking at another culture from the inside out" (Yolen, 1981, p. 16).

This chapter presents a Focus Unit designed as a multicultural experience. It features variants of the Cinderella tale found in diverse cultures around the world. Global education can begin with cultural interchange and exposure to multicultural literature. Since the roots of all literature lie in folklore it seemed especially appropriate to use these old stories as the starting point for building a multicultural perspective.

THE CINDERELLA TALE

Cinderella is probably the best known of all folktales. Although most Americans are familiar with Walt Disney's version, which appeared in America in 1949 as a movie and then in mass-market picture books, or with Charles Perrault's "Cinderella, or The Little Glass Slipper," first printed in 1697, most are not aware of its early literary history and the variants which can be found in nearly every corner of the world. In 1893 an English folklorist, Marian Roalfe Cox, published a collection of 345 variants on the Cinderella theme. More than fifty years later a Swedish folklorist, Anna Birgitta Rooth, collected over 700 versions which she used as the basis for her *Cinderella Cycle* (1951).

One of the oldest written versions of Cinderella was found in a Chinese manuscript from the T'ang Dynasty (A.D. 618–907) about a girl named Yeh-hsien. The first European book to include a Cinderella tale was Giambattista Basile's *Pentamerone* of 1634 (Penzer, 1932). This is the story of Zezolla, the daughter of a widowed prince. Zezolla's nickname became *La gatta cennerentola*, or the cat among the cinders.

Stith Thompson notes the appearance of the Cinderella story around the world.

This story of Cinderella appears in no fewer than five hundred versions in Europe alone. It seems to be popular in India and Farther India and has been taken without change by Europeans to the Philippines and elsewhere in Indonesia. It is found among the North African Arabs, in the western Sudan, in Madagascar and on the island of Mauritius. It has also been well received in America. The French have brought it to Missouri and Canada, and the isle of Martinique. It has also been reported from Brazil to Chile. Especially interesting are the modifications of this story by the North American Indians, the Piegans of the Glacier Park area, the Ojibwa of the Great Lakes, and the Zuni of New Mexico. In the latter version an almost complete adaptation to the Zuni environment has been made (1977, p. 127).

Folktales have been handed down from generation to generation in writing or by word-of-mouth. They have been carried across continents and preserved through centuries. As each of these old stories traveled, it changed in relation to the geographical, linguistic, social, and historical contexts which defined its teller and audience. According to Jane Yolen (1976):

. . . the oldest stories were transmitted and transmuted, the kaleidoscope patterns of motifs changed by time and by the times, by the tellers and by the listeners, by the country in which they arose and the countries to which they were carried. The old oral tales were changed the way culture itself changes, the way traditions change, by an erosion/eruption as powerful in its way as any geological force.

Follow a story through its variants and you are following the trade routes, the slave routes, the route of a conquering army, or that of a restless people on the move (p. 23).

THE CINDERELLA FOCUS UNIT

The Focus Unit featuring variants of the Cinderella tale was introduced in a variety of school settings in the Rochester area, including elementary (grades 3–6) and secondary classes with both native and nonnative speakers of English. The nature of the Cinderella Focus Unit changed in accordance with the special needs and interests of the different age groups and the rich and diverse experiential and cultural backgrounds brought into each classroom by individual students. As each group of students became involved in exploring the Cinderella variants the Focus Unit evolved in accordance with their unique responses to this literary experience. Indeed the students actually created these Units. Teachers set the stage and invited them to become folklorists.

CINDERELLA AND LEP STUDENTS

Probably the most intriguing Cinderella Units were those which unfolded in classrooms for limited-English-proficient (LEP) children in the Rochester City School District. In 1986 the teachers in these classrooms participated in a collaborative research project with the author and another University of Rochester professor.[1] The purpose of the project was to discover if the Focus Unit model, originally designed for native speakers of English, could be adapted and used effectively with LEP students whose native languages included Spanish, Chinese, Vietnamese, Portuguese, Arabic, Khmer, and Haitian Creole, and who had been in an English-speaking environment for periods ranging from one month to three years.

The teachers participating in this project studied the current second-language reading research, as well as the research in literacy development of native speakers of English, and were encouraged to discover remarkably similar research findings in these areas. An extensive review of reading research by Stephen D. Krashen, a student of second language learning, suggests that reading competence "can be increased indirectly, through reading for genuine interest with a focus on meaning" (1985, p. 89). For LEP students, as well as for native speakers of English, Krashen stresses the importance of whole language rather than individually analyzed parts, the importance of "comprehensible input" rather than formal language analysis. In this context Krashen suggests that the LEP learners engage in "narrow reading," a process through which students concentrate on a topic or theme or on the works of a single author (1981). "The case for narrow reading is based on the idea that the acquisition of both structure and vocabulary comes from *many* exposures in a comprehensible context. . . . The more one reads in one area, the more one learns about the area, and the easier one finds subsequent reading in the area" (Krashen, p. 23). Narrow reading allows students to engage in deep reading and build up a knowledge base which can be brought to subsequent texts. The cumulative group and independent literary experiences in the Focus Unit provide a context for such narrow and deep reading. Students listen to or read each new story in light of all previous selections. In the process they learn effective strategies for activating relevant background to generate meaning.

A growing body of research suggests that LEP students do not have to wait until they are proficient in English before they can build meaning from text (Connor, 1984). "ESL learners are able to read English before they have complete oral control of the language. . . . Using their language and experiential background, readers predict their way through a text" (Hudelson 1984, p. 234).

With this theoretical support teachers were encouraged to develop a literature-based curriculum using the Focus Unit model. They chose to begin with a unit featuring "Cinderella"

---

[1]Professor Barbara Agor was an Assistant Professor at the University of Rochester in 1986. Currently, she is a teacher on special assignment to the Rochester Teacher Center.

because they thought that this tale or a variant would be familiar to most of the children. The LEP children would be invited to share their experiences with their classmates, make connections between their lives and one of the great stories of the world, and draw from their prior knowledge to interact with new texts.

The remainder of this chapter will be devoted to a discussion of the Cinderella Focus Unit as it emerged and took shape in these LEP classrooms and in classrooms of native speakers of English. The purpose of this discussion is to suggest ways to explore the remarkable transformations of this ancient tale as it traveled through the ages and across continents, and to share the responses of the many different children who became immersed in the study of Cinderella.

Session One

In order to introduce the notion of a cross-cultural study of the Cinderella story and its variants most of the teachers of native speakers of English opened the first group session with a survey of students' prior knowledge of this tale. Usually one student volunteered to present a brief outline of the Cinderella plot familiar to him or her. Then other students added details or challenged the validity of those presented by the first student. An informal debate emerged in almost every setting regardless of age, and set the stage for a discussion of the differences between the versions of this tale which students had drawn from their literary background. One question frequently raised by students was: "Which is the *real* Cinderella—the way Sam told it or the way Kerry said it was or the way I told it?" This question would switch the dialogue toward a focus on Cinderella as a traditional tale with a long and complex oral history before it was transcribed onto the page or reshaped as a modern literary tale. This examination of the traditional folktale as a literary genre called attention to the transformation of a tale as it is retold in different times and places by diverse storytellers and recreated in the form of the literary tale. The creators of literary tales "write about themselves. . . . The world of which they write is like a mirror that reflects the inside of their hearts, often more truly than they know" (Yolen, 1981, pp. 25–26). Some students were able to identify the source of the Cinderella story they had shared: Disney, Grimm, and Perrault were the names most frequently cited. Later, they would read the variants associated with each name and consider them as reflections of the men and their milieu.

The teachers of LEP students opened the first session by reading aloud one of the Cinderella tales and asking, "Have you ever heard a story like this before?" Although some of the students recognized this tale, many did not. Several noted Cinderella motifs in "Tom and Jerry," a television cartoon, but explained that they had not been read to at home in Rochester or in their native countries.

Though these students did not at first make use of a *literary* background, they did make connections with their *experiential* backgrounds as they listened to Cinderella variants. They recognized aspects of their own culture—words, rituals, food, household objects. For example, most were familiar with the mortar and pestle found in *Vasilisa the Beautiful* (Whitney, 1970), a Russian variant of Cinderella, or in the African story, *Nomi and the Magic Fish* (Phumla, 1972). One child reported that his uncle makes mortars and pestles out of wood even today. Another child commented that the fish in *Yeh-Shen* (Louie, 1982), the Chinese Cinderella, reminded him of the fish floating in the water of the temples of his homeland, Taiwan. Many of the children, uncomfortable with the rosy-cheeked blondes of popularized versions, happily pointed to the dark-haired heroines in the illustrations of Eastern variants of Cinderella. A Korean child was especially delighted with the illustrations in the Korean variant (Adams, 1982): "I have dresses just like those!"

Puerto Rican children, familiar with *las cenizas* (the ashes of Ash Wednesday), explained to their teacher that ashes were not dirty but rather a "sacred powder." They were eager to explain the religious significance of ashes. In a thoughtful discussion of "ashes" and "cinders" students analyzed Cinderella names such as "*Ashenputtel*" and "*Cenerentola*." Their teacher reported:

> The children were drawn out. It seemed to open them up—this connection with something so important to them. It was like a seminar. . . . The children's excitement continued after class. The discussion flowed into the hall and into the next day.

Some of the associations were very painful for the children and their teachers. In the Chinese and Vietnamese variants a step-relative eats the heroine's pet fish. This led a number of children to recall their own part in shocking and tragic experiences. A Vietnamese child, one of the boat people, told of his escape when he and his companions had eaten a dead child in order to survive. The same child went on to recall an earlier time of hunger when a neighbor invited his father to share in an evening meal. After the meal the father found out he had eaten the pet dog. He came home and was sick.

These LEP children were invited to bring their personal histories and prior knowledge into the classroom. The language they found in which to share their histories was far beyond what the writers of their carefully structured instructional texts presented to them or expected of them.

CINDERELLA VARIANTS: DEEP READING

The introductory session was followed by a series of discussions about Cinderella variants read aloud to the whole group or selected for independent reading. In each setting the direction of the Cinderella study was determined in large part by the interests and questions of the students. For example, in one class a student's question, "Do all Cinderella tales have a slipper?" led to a search for variants in which the slipper test was absent. In another setting the students decided to start with the oldest Cinderella tales such as *Yeh-Shen* (Louie, 1982), based on an ancient Chinese manuscript during the T'ang Dynasty and "The Cat Cinderella" (Penzer, 1932), an Italian tale identified as the earliest full telling of the tale in Europe. The second-language students were eager to hear variants from their homelands.

In every classroom students were invited to consider such questions as:

1. What elements in this story suggest that it is a Cinderella variant? Or How do you know this is a Cinderella story?
2. What elements in this story reflect its cultural origin? Or How do you know this story is from a particular country?
3. What elements in this story reflect universal human experience and qualities? Or In what

ways do these story characters feel and act like people in the real world? (The phrasing of any question will be determined by the age and literary experience of the students involved.)

A collection of diverse Cinderella variants (*see* Bibliography) was put on display to invite and facilitate exploration of this tale type. Students were invited to compare the variants from different cultures and to make connections between the story and their experience. They formed small dialogue groups; kept "Cinderella journals" in which they recorded personal responses, interpretations, and questions; and engaged in a variety of meaning-making activities such as creative writing, drama, art, and storytelling. They were invited to formulate questions which could be answered through special research projects. In every classroom students were invited to read each new text in light of previous ones, and to draw from their growing knowledge of Cinderella in particular and folklore and the language of literature in general.

THE POWER OF THREE

The majority of teachers who adapted the Cinderella Focus Unit to their classrooms discovered what became known as the "power of three." These teachers reported that by the time their students had heard and discussed three Cinderella tales, they demonstrated that they had acquired enough background to begin to take control of this literary study; to become active, questioning learners; and to feel empowered by their sense of competence and confidence as learners.

After students had encountered their fourth Cinderella variant comparisons and predictions came spontaneously.

- Oh, it's going to be like the Italian one . . .
- In the first one they met at a ball; in the second story they met at a festival; and in *this* one they meet at church!
- In this one the fairy godmother is a bird.

Almost every teacher noticed a growing excitement and enthusiasm by the third session.

- It started flowing out of them.
- They were tumbling over themselves to make comparisons.
- They got so excited about finding similarities and differences.
- My students started taking bets on the way a new variant would develop . . ."
- I noticed how they built on each other's responses.
- The joy of recognition was evident.

Teachers reported evidence that their students had begun to internalize and use the questions introduced in the initial sessions to suggest ways of interacting with these texts. For example, by the third session students spontaneously pointed out the elements of the story which identified it as a Cinderella variant. They initiated the search for "culture clues," a term introduced by a fourth-grade boy.

- You can tell that story [*Vasilisa the Beautiful* (Whitney, 1970)] is from Russia because it has Baba Yaga.

- In China a long time ago they used to bind a girl's feet so they would be tiny. That king in *Yeh-Shen* is so impressed by that tiny shoe because that was *beautiful* in those days—in China. So—it makes sense!
- In the Indian Cinderella, the main man is 'Strong Wind.' That sounds like the names in Indian legends. And he wears moccasins.
- Also—he's a friend of Glooskap. I read an Indian legend about him. And the way he pulls his sled with the Rainbow sounds like the way they talk in Indian legends.

By the fourth session students had begun to absorb a sense of the storytelling tradition. They no longer asked which was the "real" Cinderella. They were eager to find and explain the differences between variants. For example, those who read Italo Calvino's "Grattula-Beddàttula" (1980), an Italian tale, were surprised by the assertive and aggressive behavior of the Cinderella character, Ninetta. They noticed similar behavior in Basile's "Cat Cinderella" (Penzer, 1932). A Chinese student commented that none of the girls he knew were "*that* kind of girl." Another explained it this way:

> The difference is in how you're brought up. Like in China you learn to be respectful and polite. I'm sure Kongjee [the Korean Cinderella] and Yeh-Shen [the Chinese Cinderella] would *never* talk to their parents the way Ninetta and Zezolla did!"

Many of the older students were interested in investigating the difference between the Walt Disney version of Cinderella and the older traditional tales. Their investigations and conclusions will be discussed later in this chapter.

"The Indian Cinderella" (Cole, 1982) was frequently discussed in terms of its unique elements.

- Strong Wind wanted to marry the youngest daughter because she was honest. He wasn't interested in pretty clothes or a pretty face.
- It shows what's really important to the people who told that variant. They thought honesty was more important than shoe size or beauty.

In addition to their search for "culture clues," which reflected the differences between the cultural contexts of the variants, the students also looked for similarities which reflected universal human experience and emotions which cross cultural boundaries. All students could relate to Cinderella's feelings of being mistreated, unloved, and unappreciated. All of them could understand the emotional response to a mother's death and a father's remarriage. Many of the students had actually experienced the loss of a parent; many were, themselves, stepchildren. All students knew what it meant to dream of being special, admired, attractive. They could see that the Cinderella story is about these emotions and dreams.

Jane Yolen explains the universal appeal of the Cinderella story in a remarkable collection of eloquent and insightful essays about folklore.

> But beyond the cultural accoutrements, the detritus of centuries, Cinderella speaks to all of us in whatever skin we inhabit: the child mistreated, a princess or highborn lady in disguise bearing her trials with patience, fortitude, and determination. Cinderella makes intelligent decisions, for she knows that wishing solves nothing without the concomitant action. We have each of us been that child. (Even boys

and men share that dream, as evidenced by the many Ash-boy variants.) It is the longing of any youngster sent supperless to bed or given less than a full share at Christmas. And of course it is the adolescent dream (p. 37, 1981).

WRITING

Entries in the "Cinderella Journals" often served as catalysts for discussions which occurred in small dialogue groups. Entries frequently included questions which were of interest to the writer as well as members of the dialogue group.

The Magic Horse is a Russian tale [Reesink, 1974] about Ivan who sits on the stove. This is a *male* Cinderella. Is this the only one?

This question led to a search for other "male Cinderellas" and a comparative study of these variants. The children were impressed with the number of motifs *The Magic Horse* had in common with the Norwegian tale, "The Princess on the Glass Hill" (Haviland, 1961). They were also surprised by the differences between two Swedish variants: "Queen Crane" (Baker, 1960) and "The Princess and the Glass Mountain" (Baker, 1955). One student was excited to find an Irish variant, "Hookedy-Crookedy" (Wiggin, 1967), which had much in common with "Queen Crane," although Jack, the hero of the Irish tale, was the son of the King and Queen of Ireland and "Sheep-Peter" in "Queen Crane" started out as "a poor, poor boy."

Another student, who had read the Czechoslovakian variant, "The Shepherd's Nosegay" (Fillmore, 1958), commented that the hero in this tale was a prince disguised as a shepherd who received magic gifts in return for his kindness to a beggar. He added, "These things helped him win the Princess, so the beggar was like the fairy godmothers in the other stories."

This prompted a second look at the "male Cinderella" stories and the discovery that most of the heroes were given magical assistance as a reward for kindness. In the course of this search for the "kindness rewarded" motif, one student told about "Goldenhair," a Canadian variant which he had found in a beautifully illustrated collection, *Tales of the Far North* (Martin, 1984). He noted that after Jean-Pierre helped a white horse the horse helps Jean-Pierre become the mysterious knight who wins three battles for the king and appears at three tournaments arranged by the king to discover the identity of the knight. In the end the white horse helps the hero win the younger daughter of the king as his bride.

This study of "helper figures" in variants with masculine Cinderella characters led to another survey of those who helped the Cinderella heroines. Several questions in student journals about the nature of these helper figures served as the starting point for a comparative study by members of a small dialogue group. The research project which emerged will be described in a later section of this chapter.

In some of these small dialogue groups students enjoyed trading journals in order to respond to what someone else had written. Thus, the dialogue continued in written form as well as in face-to-face encounters. Often a student respondent would recommend a particular story for independent reading or provide an important insight. One child, in response to a complaint about the absence of pictures, explained, "You're supposed to dream about it." In this "community of learners" students shared literary experiences and taught each other about the world of story, about the reading process, and about themselves.

LANGUAGE DEVELOPMENT

The written and oral dialogue generated by exposure to the Cinderella literature was woven into the fabric of classroom experience. The oral dialogue often continued on the playground, as children argued a point or dramatized favorite scenes. Most of the teachers observed significant language development in these children. In addition to gaining confidence and competence as speakers and writers, the students were becoming better listeners and readers. Teachers also reported that their students were fascinated with the language of these traditional tales, and often incorporated interesting words and phrases into their writing and even in their daily conversation. One child commented about a recent purchase, "It cost me a dear price for this."

The LEP children especially found wonderful new words to absorb into their active vocabulary. Such words as *hearth, mermaid, gooseherd, gorgeous,* and *golden* were among the favorites. As they learned new words the students played with them. "Yeh-Shen," said one, "has a stepmother, stepsister, and stepfish." They also learned powerful words, such as *jealousy, dread, villain, evil, finery, wise,* and *orphan.*

Like Sylvia Ashton-Warner's "key vocabulary," which was developed as part of her organic teaching in a Maori school, these powerful words drawn from ancient tales held intense personal meaning for the children. They made each new word their own to serve as a resource for constructing "captions of inner vision . . . and the dynamic life itself" (1963, p. 29). Ancient storytellers created tales from their inner lives and from their understanding of universal human experiences. By entering into the world of folklore these children had gained access to the deeper meaning and challenges of human existence.

In addition to absorbing the rich language of literature children in every school setting began to develop language necessary to talk and write *about* literature. They used words like *main character, villain, setting, plot, conflict, theme,* and *viewpoint* to analyze a narrative. Terms such as *translated, retold, illustrated* came easily to the children, as they became serious students of literature.

CREATING NEW CINDERELLA VARIANTS

In preparation for composing their own Cinderella variants students reviewed the traditional variants they had heard or read and generated a list of the basic elements which could be used to identify a story as a Cinderella tale type. After a lively debate one group reached consensus about the list of distinguishing features.

1. The heroine (hero) usually is a princess (prince) or has a rich father.
2. The heroine (hero) is mistreated.
3. Her (his) real self is disguised with ashes, rags, animal skins, etc.
4. Someone helps her (him)—a fairy godmother, a fish, a horse, a bird, the mother's spirit, etc.
5. There's some kind of ball or festival or contest or church event where the heroine (hero) appears in an amazing costume.

6. The identity of the heroine (hero) is revealed by a token like a shoe or ring or golden apple.
7. The heroine (hero) is intelligent, independent, hard-working, practical, kind, and has a sense of humor.

Many of the students in this group commented on the difference between the elements on this list and those which they had previously associated with the Cinderella story.

- I used to think Cinderella was about mice and pumpkins and a magic wand. But we don't have *any* of those things on this list!

After a review of the basic elements of the Cinderella tale and some of the motifs found in different variants around the world most of the students in every setting were bursting with ideas and couldn't wait to get started on their stories. Many of these original narratives reflected the contemporary cultural context in which these children were immersed, as well as personal experiences and the inner life unique to each writer.

One fourth-grade girl wrote about a modern urban Cinderella who lives in a condo with her stepmother and two stepsisters. When an invitation to a ball arrived one day from Prince, "the stepsisters screamed, 'Oh my God! Mother!! Listen! Prince invited us to a ball!!' Cinderella asked, 'May I come, too?' 'Certainly not! You and your rags will embarrass us.' Cinderella ran out to the garden and sang 'Borderline' until she fell asleep." Later in the story a fairy godmother appears and uses her magic to get Cinderella to the ball where she meets Prince.

As she danced with him, she began to sing "Crazy for You." Prince said, "You have a great voice, sweetheart." Then he began to sing "Purple Rain." All of a sudden, the clock struck midnight and Cinderella remembered that she had to be home by midnight. So she ran down the stairs to her limousine, but she ran so fast she lost one of her shoes. . . . When Prince came out for a breath of air, he found the hot pink plastic shoe. So the next morning Prince went to every house in the city. When he got to the stepsister's condo, he heard someone singing "Crazy for You" in the garden. So he ran around the condo and found Cinderella sitting alone with only one shoe on. Prince said, "I love your singing, sweetheart. I'll call you Madonna." So they got married and moved to a nice little condo in the city. They had two children, a boy and a girl. They all sang happily ever after.

In a bilingual classroom many of the Hispanic children made Cinderella truly Puerto Rican, and in most cases chose not to include magical elements. "This is real life," explained one young writer who chose contemporary realism over fantasy for his story. One boy built a love story between Cyndi Lauper and the Karate Kid. His moral was: "You should fight for what belongs to you." Unfortunately the author was not able to present his story at the next group session; he had been suspended for fighting.

Many of the stories were clearly and painfully autobiographical. One writer was herself a stepdaughter. She named the characters in her solemn story after members of her own family.

A sixth-grade student from a poor rural community outside of Rochester experimented with the concept of "culture clues" as he composed his story, "Potato Peels." It begins:

Long, long ago there was a very kind and clever girl named Potato Peels. She lived in Ireland on a huge potato farm. She lived with her stepmother and three stepsisters.

The helper-figure who responds to the heroine's prayers is a leprechaun: ". . . short and chubby, with a red beard, pointed feet and ears, and a high pitched voice."

A classmate created a character named "Snow-in-the-Face" because his foster brother threw him into a snowbank if he "did not do something perfectly." Since his setting was China, this young writer introduced into his tale "a three-day Festival of Kites in honor of the Emperor's daughter's birthday."

Another student in this class placed her story in the future. It is the year 2010; the heroine is Spacia, the daughter of "the greatest space explorer in the whole galaxy."

The sixth-grade teacher was impressed with the quality of the stories produced by her students, and was especially interested to see evidence of their awareness of the cultural significance of motif variants and the rich language of folklore. These stories also reflected her students' vocabulary development and their willingness to experiment with language and literary ideas.

When students presented their stories in group sessions, the others responded with thoughtful comments and questions in much the same way they had responded to the work of professional writers. In anticipation of the types of questions raised in these group sharings many students began to reread and revise their stories before reading them to an audience. They were becoming critical readers of their own work as they grew more aware of their potential audiences.

STORYTELLING

The study of Cinderella provided a rich context for practicing the ancient art of storytelling. Students became storytellers for younger children, for their peers, and for their parents. As they prepared their stories they felt free to combine and embellish basic tale types and motifs. They had become part of the long tradition of storytellers who have engaged in this building-borrowing process for generations to produce and shape the oral tradition which is our literary heritage.

In a classroom of LEP students a popular local storyteller and author was a special visitor. Students joined together to prepare and present their favorite stories to him. The teacher overheard three of her students planning their presentations: "You can have Yeh-Shen, and I'll take the Magic Horse. That leave Brothers Grimm for you, OK?" Their guest, recognizing the quality of these presentations, responded with enthusiastic praise. Students treasured this positive feedback. Such rewards are rare for students whose English does not usually permit them the satisfactions available to native English-speakers.

Students experimented with visual aids to enhance their presentations or to clarify the content of their stories. They used finger puppets, flannelboards, chalkboards, pictures, and artifacts. A student who presented a Japanese variant of Cinderella wore a kimono. Another student, presenting the same tale in another classroom, used a Japanese fan very effectively.

They also used introductory and closing phrases associated with traditional storytellers in particular cultures. The usual opening phrase of a Japanese tale is *mukashi mukashi,* translated as "long long ago." Armenian tales often begin with "once there was and was not . . ." Diane Wolkstein, a well-known storyteller herself, describes Haitian storytellers who call out *Cric?* when they have a story to tell. The audience responds with *Crac!* if they want the storyteller to begin (1978).

The Scandinavian storyteller's conventional ending is:

Snip, snap, snout
This tale's told out.

Many of the LEP children brought a tradition of storytelling with them. They knew stories which their parents and grandparents had told them. Their teachers encouraged them to record these tales in order to preserve their literary heritage. These students, having already left their homelands behind, were eager to ensure that their stories would not be lost. They wrote at length, or dictated their stories. Their families became involved in this project. A tape recorder was passed around. Tapes were translated and transcribed. These remarkable tales were filled with rich language and images and brought into the classroom the personal histories and cultures of these children.

RESEARCH PROJECTS

The study of Cinderella variants from many cultures generated a wide range of special interest research projects. Individuals or small groups of students formulated questions about an area of special interest and then explored a variety of resources in search of some answers. Examples of such research projects suggest the variety of questions raised by students of different age levels and the variety of ways they represented and shared the results of their explorations.

Cultural Differences

The comparative study of Cinderella tales around the world stimulated questions about the clothing, food, architecture, geography, religion, and social customs which provide the rich texture of each variant. One small group of girls interested in costumes started with a careful survey of the types of clothing portrayed in illustrations or described in the texts. They then turned to other sources for information about and pictures of the clothing of these cultures and time periods. Eventually, they produced a book of detailed and carefully labelled drawings of the clothing worn by the heroines and heroes in the Cinderella variants.

One student's special interest in the distinctive architecture portrayed and described in the Russian tales prompted a survey of the huts and palaces found in Cinderella variants from other countries. This survey became the starting point for a more extensive study of architectural styles in different parts of the world.

An interest in the different "princess tests" or "bride tests" led one group to explore the cultural significance of the various criteria used in the choice of a bride or groom. After collecting relevant data and organizing a large chart to display the motif variants, these young researchers were able to make some very interesting interpretations about the values and social customs associated with particular cultures. The Chinese variant, "Yeh-Shen," reflects unusual appreciation of extremely small women's feet and the painful custom of "binding" which was fashionable by the tenth century and lasted until recent years. The term "golden lillies" was originated by an Emperor of the fifth century to connote women's small feet, a sign of beauty and gentility. In "Yeh-Shen" the king is entranced by the tiny slipper and is "determined . . .

to find the woman to whom the shoe belonged." These students concluded that the "shoe test" was used to estimate the beauty and nobility of a woman. They noted that in many of the European variants the shoe test was used to discover the identity of a mysterious woman. They decided that the "small shoe" motif was probably borrowed from the earlier Chinese variant.

The Russian variant, *Vasilisa the Beautiful* (Whitney, 1970), was used as another example of the "bride test." In this story, when the king is presented with evidence of Vasilisa's remarkable skill as a weaver and seamstress he is determined to find her. In "The Indian Cinderella" the "bride test" centers around truthfulness and intellectual honesty. In a Japanese variant, "Benizara and Kakezara" (Seki, 1963), Benizara or "Crimson Dish," an honest and gentle girl, is treated cruelly by her stepmother. When she is denied permission to attend a Kabuki drama her friends help her finish her chores, and a little box given to her by an old woman of the mountains provides her with a beautiful kimono so that she can go to the play. A nobleman sees her there and later sets up a test involving the extemporaneous composition of a classical song. Benizara's poem follows the 5-7-5-7-7 syllable arrangement of the Tanka poetic form. The nobleman chooses Benizara over her stepsister, whose poem observes none of the rules of meter required by traditional poetic styles.

In many of the variants with "male Cinderellas" the test is associated with physical skills and courage. In a Norwegian variant, "Princess on the Glass Hill" (Cole, 1982), the king's daughter is given to the man who can ride up over the hill of glass near the king's palace. In the Polish variant, "The Glass Mountain" (Lang, 1948), the test also requires scaling a glass mountain to reach the princess. After many bold knights and their splendid horses have tried and failed to reach the princess and have fallen to the bottom of the glass mountain, a youth decides to try his luck. This brave and shrewd lad manages to have an eagle carry him to the top of the mountain. In a Russian variant, *The Magic Horse* (Reesink, 1974), the Czar announces that his daughter will marry the man whose horse can jump as high as the third battlement of the royal palace.

Military skill determines the choice of a princess' husband in the Swedish "Queen Crane" (Baker, 1960), the Canadian "Goldenhair" (Martin, 1984), and the Irish "Hookedy-Crookedy" (O'Brien, 1986).

Students surveying "bride tests" were especially interested to discover the many cultural values reflected in these tales, since most of them had started with the notion that a pretty face and beautiful and fashionable clothes were what counted in selecting "a Cinderella" as the bride for a prince. As one student put it, "In the Disney Cinderella the prince didn't even *recognize* her until she put on her gorgeous ballgown!"

Students in this research group included story elements other than the "bride test" to provide evidence of values reflected in different variants. Many feature stepmothers and stepsisters who are jealous of the heroine's beauty, which is perceived as a threat to the stepsisters' marriage prospects. In contrast, a Jewish version of Cinderella from Eastern Europe, called "The Exiled Princess" (Schwartz, 1983), tells of a princess who is taught by her queen mother to be kind to the poor and to give generously to charity. When the queen dies, the king remarries. "[A]nd the stepmother disliked the princess, and especially did not like her generosity . . ." (p. 263). The stepmother convinces the king to expel the princess from the palace and to send her into exile in the forest. Fortunately the princess is able to find her way to a town where she becomes a servant in the rabbi's home. She eventually marries the rabbi's son and is reunited with her father.

Cinderella's Mother

Members of one research group focussed on helper figures in the Cinderella variants. They were especially interested in those story elements which related to the role of Cinderella's mother. They found a good deal of evidence to support the notion that supernatural help given to Cinderella is associated with the spirit of her dead mother. In *Vasilisa the Beautiful* (Whitney, 1970), the mother blesses her daughter on her deathbed and gives her a magical doll. The blessing and the doll provide the help Vasilisa needs, and seem to represent the essence of her nurturing mother figure. In the German variant, "Ashenputtel" (Cole, 1982), the mother tells her daughter that she will look down from Heaven and will be near her. When Ashenputtel plants a hazel twig on her mother's grave it becomes a fine tree and the home of a little white bird who grants the girl's wishes and provides for her needs. In "The Wonderful Birch" (Lang, 1966), a Russian variant, the mother is transformed into a black sheep and killed by a witch who takes her place as wife and mother. A birch tree grows from the place where the mother's bones are buried, and magically provides the daughter with clothes and a horse so that she can attend the festival and meet the king's son.

In "Rushen Coatie" (Jacobs, 1967), the queen tells her daughter that after her death a little red calf will come to her and will give her anything she needs. The stepmother orders the red calf to be killed, but the girl places its bones under a stone and the red calf returns to her when she is in need. She is given lovely clothes and glass slippers to wear to church at Yuletide. For three days she attends the church, and the prince sees her and falls in love with her more each day.

In some stories the dying mother gives the daughter something to hide her beauty in order to protect her against the evils which could befall a young single woman alone in the world. In a Japanese variant, "Sima Who Wore the Big Hat" (Marmur, 1960), the widow of a samurai, before her death, summons her beautiful and intelligent daughter and "placed a small box on the child's head and, above the box, a large hat shaped like a cup, so huge it covered her chin" (p. 26). For a long time the girl is unable to remove this strange headdress and has to endure ridicule and hardships because of it. However, when a nobleman's son falls in love with her and offers a prayer on her behalf, the hat falls off "uncovering Sima's radiant face in all its beauty" (p. 29). The box opens, revealing her inheritance of "gold and silver and diamonds and pearls."

Students in this research group concluded that early storytellers believed a loving mother, even after her death, could bless and help her child. A helpful animal could be a reincarnation of the dead mother. A fairy or a fairy godmother could represent the spirit of the dead mother even if no direct link between the girl and her dead mother was explicit in the story. They noted that in most cases the intervention of the mother was associated with magic or supernatural powers.

One interesting exception was "The Exiled Princess" (Schwartz, 1983). Here, the mother's legacy was her kindness and generosity and her bridal gown. With this legacy to sustain her, the exiled princess was able to make her way in the world and earn the respect and love of those she encountered. One student observed, "You have to read a *lot* of different variants to get the whole story. It's like we found pieces to a puzzle. . . . It helps you figure out a story that's missing something."

Cinderella and King Lear

Several high-school students read *Moss Gown* (Hooks, 1987), an old tale told in North Carolina where the first English colony was established in the sixteenth century. They were especially interested to discover that this tale blends elements of "Cap O' Rushes" (Haviland, 1959) and Shakespeare's *King Lear*, thus reflecting its English roots. In "Cap O' Rushes" a father asks his daughters how much they love him. The elder daughters give pleasing answers, but the youngest replies that she loves him as fresh meat loves salt. In anger, the father casts her off. At the conclusion of the story, after the girl marries, she is at last reunited with her father. By serving him unsalted meat she teaches him the meaning of her answer.

After reading *King Lear*, as well as other Cinderella variants with the "love like salt" element, students concluded that Shakespeare had probably borrowed from these variants of the Cinderella tale to create his *King Lear* play. The teacher followed up with a suggestion for further reading: an article by Alan Dundes in *Cinderella: A Casebook* (Dundes, 1983) entitled " 'To Love My Father All': A Psychoanalytic Study of the Folktale Source of *King Lear*" (pp. 229–244). Students were delighted to find such statements as:

> In the case of *King Lear*, it has long been recognized that the plot was borrowed in part from folklore. Specifically, the often discussed love-test of the opening scene has been recognized as tale type 923, Love Like Salt. . . . I hope to show that not only is the folktale in question a crucial source for *King Lear*, but that it is not possible to understand much of the inherent dramatic power of the play without knowledge of the underlying folktale and its essential psychological dimensions.

Dundes points out that in folklore most of the protagonists are sons or daughters, not parents. "It follows that Shakespeare's emphasis upon Lear . . . is a critical literary change from the folklore source" (p. 233). He also calls attention to the connection between *King Lear* and Cinderella variants such as Allerleirauh" (Brothers Grimm, 1972), in which the King wants to marry his own daughter because she most resembles his deceased wife. Dundes suggests ". . . that the 'love like salt' plot appears to be a weakened form of the folktale plot in which the 'mad' father tries to marry his own daughter . . ." The theme of incest is a powerful one and it would be no surprise to learn that it provides one of the most important undercurrents of *King Lear*" (p. 234).

Cinderella—A Profile

A number of groups studied the Cinderella variants to discover what kind of personality profiles emerged and what patterns could be found in a comparative study of the variants. Generally, this data was recorded on some sort of chart or on 5 × 8 cards which could be sorted and arranged on a table top. These research groups found a great deal of evidence to suggest that the heroines and heroes featured in these traditional tales were independent, intelligent, practical individuals whose kindness, humor, creativity, and hard work helped them to overcome the obstacles blocking their ways in the world. Students' surveys revealed that the Cinderella story is not one of rags to riches—most of the heroines and some of the heroes were of noble or royal birth. They were the offspring of kings, cave chiefs, Samurai, Indian chiefs, or wealthy merchants. But they maintained their integrity and self-respect in spite of the degrading and lowly position into which they were thrust. And through hard work, intelligence, kindness, and perseverance they earned the right to resume their proper places and regain their birthrights.

These students found two variants in which the Cinderella character was not portrayed as a strong and active individual. They were surprised to discover that the two variants most of them had known since their early years were actually exceptions to the rule. The profile of Cinderella presented in the Perrault (1988) and Disney versions differs significantly from that derived from heroines found in traditional tales throughout the world. These students discovered that the traditional Cinderella was *not* a "silly, helpless girl with a pretty face waiting for her Prince Charming to come along!" This discovery prompted a great many questions and a number of heated debates about gender stereotypes in literature and in reality.

Several older students enjoyed reading Jane Yolen's "America's Cinderella" in *Cinderella: A Casebook* (Dundes, 1983). Yolen discusses the nature of the change in the Cinderella tale as it moved from the oral tradition to a literary tale to the mass market version.

Perrault's "Cendrillon" demonstrated the well-bred seventeenth-century female traits of gentility, grace, and selflessness, even to the point of graciously forgiving her wicked stepsisters and finding them noble husbands.

The American "Cinderella" is partially Perrault's. The rest is a spun-sugar caricature of her hardier European and Oriental forbears, who made their own way in the world, tricking the stepsisters with double-talk, artfully disguising themselves, or figuring out a way to win the king's son. The final bit of icing on the American Cinderella was concocted by that master candy-maker, Walt Disney, in the 1950s. Since then, American's Cinderella has been a coy, helpless dreamer, a "nice" girl who awaits her rescue with patience and a song" (pp. 296–297).

To make Cinderella less than she is, then, is a heresy of the worst kind. It cheapens our most cherished dreams, and it makes a mockery of the true magic inside us all—the ability to change our own lives, the ability to control our own destinies" (p. 299).

The mass-market American "Cinderellas" have presented the majority of American children with the wrong dream. They offer the passive princess, the "insipid beauty waiting . . . for Prince Charming" . . . and thus acculturate millions of girls and boys. But it is the wrong Cinderella and the magic of the old tales has been falsified, the true meaning lost, perhaps forever" (p. 303).

One student responded with a defense of Perrault's heroine. "Even though she's not like the other ones, she's *much* better than Disney's Cinderella. At least she had a sense of humor . . . when she teased the stepsisters. And she used her brain . . . when she figured out how to get the coachman." Others searched for explanations for Disney's portrayal of Cinderella.

In one group discussions of sexist elements in the Perrault and Disney variants were enlivened by the input of several students who had discovered Jack Zipe's *Don't Bet on the Prince: Contemporary Feminist Fairy Tales in North America and England* (1986). One student in this small research group was especially eager to share a reference to Yolen's presentation of a "convincing demonstration of how an active and strong heroine was transformed into a docile and submissive girl in 'America's Cinderella'" (Zipes, 1986, p. 7). One of the feminist fairytales which Zipes includes in his collection is Yolen's "The Moon Ribbon" (1976, pp. 81–87), her own revision of "Cinderella." This story was shared with the group and thoughtfully analyzed in terms of the author's craft and intentions. Group members read other feminist fairytales recommended by Zipes and especially enjoyed the satirical interpretations of Cinderella: "Princess Dahli" (Lee, 1973) and "Gudgekin the Thistle Girl" (Gardner, 1976).

The research report which resulted from this extensive study of the transformation of Cinderella was well-received by the entire class. The report generated a good deal of interest in views of gender and power expressed in literature; and many students decided to explore this broader issue. New questions were raised, so new learning could emerge.

THE CINDERELLA FOCUS UNIT: A QUEST FOR MEANING

In each classroom setting the study of Cinderella variants provided a context for a multicultural experience. As students examined the variants they developed an appreciation of the cultural significance of motif variations. While the cultural content distinguishes one variant from another these tales share elements which reflect universal wishes, dreams, and problems of people. The study of Cinderella variants provided an opportunity to celebrate the rich diversity of our multicultural literary heritage as well as the bonds which draw us together and connect one variant to another across cultural boundaries.

In their study of traditional Cinderella tales found in world literature students discovered the nature of the oral tradition and the building-borrowing process which shaped and polished each tale as it was passed along by storytellers until it was written down and became literature. They discovered the changes caused by this movement from oral to written or literary form. Yolen's thoughtful analysis of the mass-market popularization of Cinderella (Yolen, 1983) ends with a warning:

> But it is the wrong Cinderella and the magic of the old tales has been falsified, the true meaning lost, perhaps forever (p. 303).

Fortunately for these children who became immersed in the study of Cinderella, the "true meaning" has *not* been lost. They found for themselves that "wishes [must be] accompanied by the proper action . . ." (Yolen, 1983, p. 303). They discovered that "[o]ne cannot receive without first giving" (Yolen, 1981, p. 70). They learned that the power of magic is limited. "It cannot change a heart or the state of the world, but only outward conditions. Cinderella's clothes and conditions are changed, not her personality or character" (Bosma, 1987, p. 3). They saw that in the traditional tales Cinderella's true character and beauty were recognized though she was dressed in rags and smudged with ashes. The hero or heroines in fairytales must *deserve* to live happily ever after.

References

Ashton-Warner, Sylvia. *Teacher*. N.Y.: Simon and Schuster, 1963.
Bosma, Bette. *Fairy Tales, Fables, Legends, and Myths: Using Folk Literature in Your Classroom*. N.Y.: Teachers College Press, 1987.
Carpenter, Humphrey, and Mari Prichard. *The Oxford Companion to Children's Literature*. N.Y.: Oxford University Press, 1984.
Cole, Joanna, selector. *Best-Loved Folktales of the World*. Garden City, N.Y.: Doubleday, 1982.
Connor, Ulla. "Recall of Text: Differences between First and Second Language Readers." *TESOL Quarterly*, 18, no. 2, 1984, pp. 239–256.
Cox, Marian Roalfe. *Cinderella: 345 Variants*. London: David Nutt, 1893.
Dundes, Alan, ed. *Cinderella: A Casebook*. N.Y.: Wildman, 1983.
Hudelson, Sarah. "Kan Yu Ret an Rayt en Ingles: Children Become Literate in English as a Second Language." *TESOL Quarterly*, 18, no. 2, 1984, pp. 221–238.
Krashen, Stephen D. "The Case for Narrow Reading." *TESOL Newsletter* 15, no. 6, 1981, p. 23.
———. *Inquiries and Insights*. Hayward, CA: Alemany, 1985.
Rooth, Anna Birgitta. *The Cinderella Cycle*. Lund: C.W.K. Gleerup, 1951.
Thompson, Stith. *The Folktale*. Berkeley: University of California Press, 1977.
Yolen, Jane. *Touch Magic: Fantasy, Faerie and Folklore in the Literature of Childhood*. N.Y.: Philomel, 1981.
———. "America's Cinderella." *Cinderella: A Casebook*. Alan Dundes, ed. N.Y.: Wildman, 1983, pp. 294–311.
Zipes, Jack. *Don't Bet on the Prince: Contemporary Feminist Fairy Tales in North America and England*. N.Y.: Methuen, 1986.

Bibliography of Cinderella Variants

Adams, Edward, ed. *Korean Cinderella*. Seoul International Tourist Publishing, 1982.
Baker, Augusta, ed. *The Golden Lynx and Other Tales*. "Kari Woodencoat," pp. 19–33; "Queen Crane," pp. 46–53. Philadelphia: Lippincott, 1960.
Baker, Augusta, selector. *The Talking Tree and Other Stories*. "Cinderella" (England), pp. 25–32; "The Princess and the Glass Mountain" (Sweden), pp. 88–103. N.Y.: Lippincott, 1955.
Bang, Garrett, trans. *Men from the Village Deep in the Mountain and Other Japanese Folktales*. "The Grateful Toad," pp. 27–31. N.Y.: Macmillan, 1973.
Belpré, Pura. *The Rainbow-Colored Horse*. N.Y.: Frederick Warne, 1978.
Berger, Terry, reteller. *Black Fairy Tales*. "The Moss-Green Princess" (Swazi), pp. 3–14. N.Y.: Atheneum, 1975.
Bowman, James, and Margery Bianco. *Tales from the Finnish Tupa*. Aili Kolehmainen, trans. "Liisa and the Prince," pp. 187–198. Chicago: Albert Whitman, 1936.
Briggs, Katherine, and Ruth Tongue, eds. *Folktales of England*. "Mossycoat," pp. 16–26. Chicago: University of Chicago Press, 1965.
Brown, Marcia, trans. *Cinderella* (French, Charles Perrault). N.Y.: Scribner's, 1954.
Calvino, Italo, trans. *Italian Folk Tales*. "Grattula-Beddàttula," pp. 523–529. N.Y.: Harcourt Brace Jovanovich, 1980.
Carpenter, Frances. *Wonder Tales of Dogs and Cats*. "The Enchanted Black Cat" (France), pp. 222–234. Garden City, N.Y.: Doubleday, 1955.
Chase, Richard, ed. *Grandfather Tales: American-English Folk Tales*. "Ashpet," pp. 115–123; "Catskins," pp. 106–114; "Like Meat Loves Salt," pp. 124–129. Boston: Houghton Mifflin, 1948.

Clarkson, Alelia, and Gilbert B. Cross. *World Folktales*. "The Indian Cinderella," pp. 43–48. N.Y.: Scribner's, 1980.

Climo, Shirley. *The Egyptian Cinderella*. N.Y.: Crowell, 1989. (First recorded by the Roman historian Strabo in the first century B.C.).

Cole, Joanna, ed. *Best-Loved Folktales of the World*. "Ashenputtel" (Germany), pp. 68–75; "Cinderella" (France), pp. 3–8; "Thousand Furs" (Germany), pp. 126–131; "Princess on the Glass Hill" (Norway), pp. 345–352; "The Indian Cinderella" (Canadian Indian), pp. 694–696. N.Y.: Doubleday, 1982.

Curtin, Jeremiah, collector. *Myths and Folktales of Ireland*. "Fair, Brown and Trembling," pp. 37–48. N.Y.: Dover, 1975.

Fillmore, Parker, reteller. *The Laughing Prince—Jugoslav Folk and Fairy Tales*. "The Girl in the Chest," pp. 203–217. N.Y.: Harcourt Brace and World, 1921.

Fillmore, Parker, ed. *The Shepherd's Nosegay: Stories from Finland and Czechoslovakia*. "The Shepherd's Nosegay," pp. 72–81. Eau Claire, Wis.: E.M. Hale, 1958 [1919].

Finlay, Winifred. *Tattercoats and Other Folktales*. N.Y.: Harvey House, 1976.

Galdone, Paul. *Cinderella*. N.Y.: McGraw-Hill, 1978.

Gardner, John. *Gudgekin the Thistle Girl and Other Tales*. "Gudgekin the Thistle Girl," pp. 3–20. N.Y.: Knopf, 1976.

Garner, Alan. *Alan Garner's Book of British Fairy Tales*. "Mossycoat," pp. 47–57. London: Collins, 1984.

Grimm, Brothers. *The Complete Grimm's Fairy Tales* (with a folkloristic commentary by Joseph Campbell). "Allerleirauh," pp. 326–331; "Iron Hans," pp. 612–620; "Cinderella," pp. 121–128. N.Y.: Pantheon, 1972 [1944].

Haviland, Virginia, ed. *Favorite Fairy Tales Told in England*. "Cap O' Rushes," pp. 76–88. Boston: Little, Brown, 1959.

———. *Favorite Fairy Tales Told in Italy*. "Cenerentola," pp. 3–18. Boston: Little, Brown, 1965.

———. *Favorite Fairy Tales Told in Norway*. "Princess on the Glass Hill," pp. 3–29. Boston: Little, Brown, 1961.

———. *North American Legends*. "Scarface" (North Pacific Indian), pp. 83–93; "Poor Turkey Girl" (Zuni), pp. 76–82; "The Indian Cinderella" (Canadian Indian), pp. 94–96. N.Y.: Collins, 1979.

Hooks, William, reteller. *Moss Gown*. N.Y.: Houghton Mifflin, 1987.

Jacobs, Joseph, collector. *Celtic Fairy Tales*. "Fair, Brown, and Trembling," pp. 169–181. N.Y.: Dover, 1968 [1892].

———, collector. *More English Fairy Tales*. "Tattercoats," pp. 61–65; "Rushen Coatie," pp. 150–155. N.Y.: Dover, 1967 [1894].

Jagendorf, M. *New England Bean-Pot: American Folk Stories to Read and to Tell*. "Cinderella of New Hampshire," pp. 37–45. N.Y.: Vanguard, 1948.

Karlin, Barbara, reteller. *Cinderella*. Boston: Little, Brown, 1989.

Kha, Dang Manh, told to Ann Nolan Clark. *In the Land of the Small Dragon* (Vietnamese variant). N.Y.: Viking, 1978.

Lang, Andrew, ed. *The Green Fairy Book*. "Allerleirauh, or the Many-Furred Creature" (Grimm), pp. 276–281. N.Y.: Dover, 1965 [1892].

———. *The Red Fairy Book*. "Kari Woodengown" (Scandinavian variant), pp. 192–207; "The Wonderful Birch" (Russian variant), pp. 114–127. N.Y.: Dover, 1966 [1890].

———. *The Rose Fairy Book*. "Donkey Skin," from *Cabinet des Fées*, pp. 1–14. N.Y.: David McKay, 1948.

Lang, Andrew, collector and ed. *Yellow Fairy Book*. "The Glass Mountain" (Poland), pp. 130–135. N.Y.: David McKay, 1948.

Lee, Tanith. *Princess Hynchatti and Some Other Surprises*. "Princess Dahli," pp. 95–111. N.Y.: Farrar, Straus & Giroux, 1973.

Louie, Ai-Ling, reteller. *Yeh-Shen: A Cinderella Story from China*. N.Y.: Philomel, 1982.

Manning-Sanders, Ruth. *A Book of Princes and Princesses*. "The She-Bear" (Italy), pp. 76–83. N.Y.: Dutton, 1969.

Marmur, Mildred, trans. *Japanese Fairy Tales*. "Sima Who Wore the Big Hat," pp. 25–30. N.Y.: Golden Press, 1960.

Martin, Eva, reteller. *Tales of the Far North*. "Goldenhair," pp. 71–80. N.Y.: Dial, 1984.

Mayo, Margaret, collector. *The Italian Fairy Book*. "Cenerentola and the Little Bird," pp. 105–113. London: Kaye and Ward, 1981.

Minard, Rosemary, ed. *Womenfolk and Fairy Tales*. "Cap O' Rushes," pp. 77–88. Boston: Houghton Mifflin, 1975.

Montresor, Beni. *Cinderella* (from the opera by Gioacchino Rossini). N.Y.: Pinwheel Knopf, 1973/1965.

Myers, Bernice. *Sidney Rella and The Glass Sneakers* (contemporary male Cinderella story for young readers). N.Y.: Macmillan, 1985.

O'Brien, Edna. *Tales for the Telling: Irish Folk and Fairy Tales*. "Hookedy-Crookedy," pp. 53–71. N.Y.: Atheneum, 1986.

Opie, Iona, and Peter Opie, eds. *The Classic Fairy Tales*. "Cinderella, or the Little Glass Slipper," pp. 123–127. N.Y.: Oxford University Press, 1974.

Penzer, N. M., ed. *The Pentamerone of Giambattista Basile*. London: John Lane, 1932, pp. 56–63. Reprinted in *Cinderella: A Casebook*. Alan Dundes, ed. N.Y.: Wildman, 1983, pp. 3–13.

Perrault, Charles. *Cinderella* (cassette with narration by Jessica Lange). Diane Goode, trans. and illus. N.Y.: Knopf, 1988.

———. *Cinderella*. Amy Ehrlich, reteller; Susan Jeffers, illus. N.Y.: Dial, 1985.

Phumla. *Nomi and the Magic Fish: A Story from Africa* (Zulu variant). N.Y.: Doubleday, 1972.

Pino-Saavedra, Yolanda, ed. *Folktales of Chile*. "Maria Cinderella," pp. 89–99; "The Little Stick Figure," pp. 99–103. Chicago: University of Chicago Press, 1967.

Reesink, Marijke. *The Magic Horse* (Russian variant). N.Y.: McGraw-Hill, 1974.

Schwartz, Howard, reteller. *Elijah's Violin and Other Jewish Fairy Tales*. "The Exiled Princess," pp. 263–269. N.Y.: Harper and Row, 1983.

Segal, Lore, trans. *The Juniper Tree and Other Tales from Grimm*, vol. II. "Bearskin," pp. 217–227; "Many-Fur," pp. 236–244. N.Y.: Farrar, Straus & Giroux, 1973.

Seki, Keigo, ed. *Folktales of Japan*. "Benizara and Kakezara," pp. 130–134. Chicago: University of Chicago Press, 1963.

Steel, Flora Annie, reteller. *Tattercoats: An Old English Tale*. Scarsdale, N.Y.: Bradbury, 1976.

Thorne-Thomsen, Gudrun, reteller. *East o' the Sun and West o' the Moon*. "The Princess on the Glass Hill" (Espen Cinderlad), pp. 101–111. N.Y.: Row Peterson, 1946.

Toor, Frances. *The Golden Carnation and Other Stories Told in Italy*. "Zezolla and the Date-Palm Tree," pp. 31–37. N.Y.: Lothrop, Lee & Shepard, 1960.

Voung, Lynette Dyer, adaptor. *The Brocaded Slipper and Other Vietnamese Tales*. Reading, MA: Addison-Wesley, 1982.

Whitney, Thomas, trans. *Vasilisa the Beautiful* (Russian variant). N.Y.: Macmillan, 1970.

Wiggin, Kate, and Nora Smith, eds. *The Fairy Ring*. "The Princess on the Glass Hill" (Scandinavia), pp. 69–79; "Tattercoats" (England), pp. 109–119; "Cap O' Rushes" (England), pp. 119–123; "Hookedy-Crookedy" (Ireland), pp. 125–145; "The Goose Girl" (Germany), pp. 236–243. Garden City, N.Y.: Doubleday, 1967 [1906].

Williams-Ellis, Anabel. *Tales from the Enchanted World*. "Cap O' Rushes" (England), pp. 8–16. Boston: Little, Brown, 1987.

Wolkstein, Diane, ed. *The Magic Orange Tree and Other Haitian Folktales*. "The Magic Orange Tree," pp. 13–21. N.Y.: Knopf, 1978.

Yolen, Jane. *The Moon Ribbon and Other Tales*. "The Moon Ribbon," pp. 1–15. N.Y.: Cromwell, 1976.

TWELVE

The Real Thief:
"Reading Like a Writer"

To become writers children must read like writers. To read like writers, they must see themselves as writers. Children will read stories, poems and letters differently when they see these texts as things they themselves could produce; they will write vicariously with the authors. But to see themselves as writers, they need collaboration from an interested practitioner (Smith, 1984, pp. 54–55).

For over twenty years Frank Smith has challenged practitioners to reflect on their beliefs and assumptions about the nature of literacy and literacy learning and the contexts which most effectively support literacy learning. He has encouraged practitioners to create supportive learning environments in which children see themselves as readers and writers, as "members of the literacy club."

It seemed appropriate and fitting that this final chapter highlight the close and complementary relationship between reading and writing, since this is such a critical component of the Focus Unit model in particular and literacy learning in general. Chapter 12 will concentrate on students engaged in the study of literature and in literacy learning who are learning to read like writers.

THE REAL THIEF

The study of a single text in the Focus Unit was used initially to demonstrate what it means to "read like a writer," and then as a springboard for a variety of reading and writing experiences. *The Real Thief* by William Steig (1973) was the single text selected as the core of this unit because it is worthy of careful and intensive study and highly recommended by students and teachers who have enjoyed reading it over the years. As the core of a Focus Unit it provided an excellent context for the study of narrative and an author's craft.

The Real Thief was introduced to students in fourth-, fifth-, and sixth-grade classrooms in a series of three consecutive sessions. In most classrooms students were given paperback copies of the book to allow them to follow the text as the teacher read it aloud. They could reread parts of it independently and in small groups for more extensive study. Before the story was read students tried to predict the nature of the story based on information gathered from the front cover: the title, the author, and the cartoon drawing of the uniformed goose standing at attention in front of a high stone wall. Many students predicted the story would be about "a character who really was a thief and another character who really was not." They all agreed that this would be categorized as animal fantasy because the goose on the cover is dressed as a human. In many classrooms the students had been introduced to William Steig, the author/ artist, and were familiar with his stories and cartoon drawings. Some predicted this story would be humorous because they recalled Steig's delightful picture books. Others thought it would "have a serious part, too, because Mr. Steig talks about serious things in his books like getting lost at sea or not being able to get people to understand you." Students drew from their prior knowledge and experience to make predictions about the story and to build a context for listening to *The Real Thief*. During the three read-aloud sessions students were encouraged to "live through" the story and to offer spontaneous comments, predictions, or personal responses at the end of each segment of this three-part tale. After students had a chance to share their thoughts and feelings they were invited to participate in an extensive study of the narrative as a reflection of the author's craft; in other words to "read like a writer" by focussing on what the author did to create this fine story.

THE STORY: A SUMMARY

The reader is first introduced to the central character, Gawain, a goose, who is the Chief Guard of the Royal Treasury for King Basil, a bear. Although Gawain is proud of this important position and is happy to serve his beloved king, he privately dreams of becoming a great architect. Gawain's world is shattered when he is accused, tried, and convicted of stealing from the Royal Treasury. The reader is allowed access into the mind and heart of Gawain as he struggles to grasp the reality of this nightmare.

In the second segment the reader next meets the real thief, Derek, a mouse, and learns about the events leading up to, during, and after the thefts as viewed through the eyes of this small creature. As Derek struggles with his guilt and his fear of punishment, the burden of his secret weighs heavily on him and makes him miserable.

In the third segment the focus returns to Gawain who has been in hiding, a fugitive and recluse ever since his escape through the courthouse window. Derek finds Gawain's hiding place, confesses his guilt, and asks Gawain's forgiveness. Together, they devise a plan to resolve the problem of appropriate punishment for the real thief, as well as for the townspeople and the King who had caused Gawain so much suffering. The story ends on a positive but somewhat bittersweet note. Gawain's dream of becoming an architect is realized, but he has been scarred by his experience.

STUDYING THE STORY

The narrative was studied in large and small groups, in story-journals, and through various independent reading and writing activities. Other communication systems—such as art, drama, and movement—extended and enriched the meaning-making process. Basic elements common to all imaginative literature—character, plot, setting, viewpoint, theme, and style—served as critical tools for literary analysis and for exploring the author's craft. Students' oral and written responses reflected their ways of making meaning, and generated the questions which guided the study. Students and teachers worked together to formulate key questions and to plan strategies for addressing these questions. Teachers negotiated with students about the nature of their participation in the study. This collaborative approach produced significant differences in the way *The Real Thief* was studied in different classroom settings.

Characters

In most classrooms the study of *The Real Thief* began with an analysis of the characters. For example, one class used a brainstorming session to generate a list of words to describe each character. Once they had pulled together what they knew about each character they were ready to work in small groups to create "word portraits." Students who had selected Gawain as their subject decided that two portraits would be needed: one to portray Gawain *before* the thefts and trial, and a second to portray him *after* these critical events. In the early portrait Gawain was described as "a proud, upright, trustworthy, loyal, responsible, and trusting individual who is loved and respected by the King and the townspeople, who serves the King faithfully out of love for him, and who privately dreams of becoming an architect." In the second portrait words such as "disillusioned," "bitter," "not as trusting," "not as idealistic," "wiser" were included to describe Gawain after the false accusation, the trial, and his escape to the forest. When these portraits were shared with the rest of the class students noticed that these "before and after" studies reflected the significant change in the central character. This observation prompted a second look at the other characters to determine what, if any, change could be detected in them. Most students felt that the King and townspeople had learned something about themselves as a result of the events following the thefts. Some believed that this self-knowledge changed them. All agreed that Adrian, the Prime Minister, did not change. Consensus about Derek was more difficult to reach.

- I bet he'd never want to go through *that* again. He *must* have learned that stealing doesn't pay.
- But he *did* get away without getting a real punishment. Maybe next time he'll figure he'd get lucky again!
- But he felt so *awful*!
- I think Derek is immature. He's like a little kid. He doesn't think about consequences when he does something. He just thinks of himself!
- I agree! And the author sort of *tells* you that Derek doesn't change. See on the last page . . . 'Derek secretly cemented the chink in the floor of the treasury. It wasn't really necessary,

but it made him feel better.' [p. 58] That shows that Derek doesn't really trust himself. He knows he could probably be tempted to steal *again* if that hole is still there. So—I think he *didn't* change.

The Author Reveals His Characters

Students were interested in the way the author provided readers with clues to help them build up a picture of each character and the relationships between characters. In response the teacher drew their attention to the author's craft by suggesting they look for techniques he used to reveal each character. After a careful examination of the text students listed the techniques they had identified. They found some information came from the private thoughts of a character, while other information came from the author's description of his physical appearance or from narrative comments. On the first page the author describes Gawain as he "stood on guard outside the new Royal Treasury . . . [He] held his head proudly on his long neck and his chest expanded in his red and gold uniform as they [the tourists] photographed him." On the next page the reader is given access to Gawain's thoughts: "Gawain found himself wishing for his old way of life—swimming in his pond, tilling his bed of herbs, raising prize cabbages and string beans, and drafting plans for strikingly original buildings" (p. 2). Further information is provided by the statements of other characters *about* Gawain. King Basil says, "He is an honorable goose, as everyone knows. I trust him as much as I do myself. The fact is, I love him as I would a son" (p. 10).

The thoughts of the townspeople provided additional information. "The town was aghast at the charges that had been laid against their beloved goose. . . . Gawain a thief? How utterly out of the question! However he had come to be accused of this dastardly crime, the luster of his name would surely be preserved" (p. 13).

Students found other examples of techniques used by the author to develop a character: how he behaved in a given situation; how other characters behaved toward him; and the language used by the character. They found Adrian's speech to the King especially revealing.

- The *way* he talks shows you how conceited he is. I know people just like that.
- Adrian uses such big words. He even uses Latin to show how great he is. You can just *picture* him—from the way he talks and the way he bowed to the King.
- Yuck! I knew right away I didn't like him.
- And *also* the author tells you that he's jealous of Gawain, so you know that's why he wants to get him in trouble. See, it says here—on page 10, "said Adrian with visible envy."

It is interesting to note that this list of literary techniques generated by students as they explored the author's craft is remarkably similar to what can be found in textbooks on literary analysis.

To expand this discussion of the author's craft and character development the teacher asked students to give a possible rationale behind Steig's choice of animal for particular characters. They came up with some logical reasons for each choice:

- Well Gawain is supposed to be proud and stand tall—so a goose with a long neck is perfect. He *looks* proud.

- And he has to be an animal that can fly because that's how he escapes.
- Basil is sort of gruff but loveable and not too bright—like a big furry bear! It's just right!
- And Derek has to be real small to get into that little hole in the treasury.
- He was so small—it made him feel inferior because the other animals were so big. I know how he feels.
- I know. I think he just needed something to make him feel more special.
- A mouse is timid. You feel sorry for him. But I think if Mr. Steig had made Derek a *rat*, it would be different. Then you wouldn't feel so sorry for him because rats are sly and sneaky . . . like in *Charlotte's Web* (E. B. White, 1952) . . . remember Templeton?
- Adrian was the sly and cunning one—like a cat! Cats are independent and act superior and not friendly. Adrian thinks he's better than everyone.
- I liked the way Basil smelled of honey. It reminds you he's a *bear*!

As students discussed Steig's choice of specific animals they began to understand how he used unique animal characteristics to define and develop each character more fully. They noticed that he developed his characters with believable human qualities and then at certain points reminded readers of specific animal qualities:

- I was so surprised when Gawain *flew* out the window. I *forgot* he was really a goose. Everything in the trial seemed so *human*—until he flew out of the courtroom!

After searching in the text for techniques used to develop each character students began looking for textual evidence of character change and the impact of events on the character. Because the entire story is told in only fifty-eight pages it was not difficult for these students—working independently, with partners, or in small groups—to locate such evidence in the text. They found, for example, a significant change in the townspeople in the course of the trial scene. Several students were able to pinpoint the exact moment of the change in their attitude toward Gawain and about the theft.

"Are you aware," said the King, "that the Kalikak diamond alone is worth millions, and that because of this thieving we will not be able to build the opera house we had planned, and that, furthermore, taxes will have to be raised?"
Everyone was attentive. They hadn't considered the consequences of the thefts (p. 16).

One student explained it this way: "As soon as the people began to worry about *taxes* they started to *believe* the evidence against Gawain and that he *was* the real thief." A second student responded, "It's just like my mom and dad are always worried about taxes so they always vote for the one [the presidential candidate] who's not going to raise taxes!" A third student read a passage which revealed to Gawain and to the reader that the townspeople had changed.

"I am an honest goose," said Gawain, and he turned to his friends for confirmation. They failed to meet his eye. They looked embarrassed. He was horrified at what he read on their faces. It was clear they had stopped believing in him . . . (p. 18).

Another passage two pages later reveals the change in Gawain:

"I am an honorable goose. How you could judge me otherwise, I do not know. Perhaps our Maker knows. Certainly He knows how much I once loved you. But now I HATE each and every living one of you, and with all my heart, for seeing evil in me that is not there. Shame on the lot of you!" (p. 20).

Students found evidence of a change in Derek after the initial theft. In the beginning he had entered the small opening into the Royal Treasury out of curiosity. When he saw the immense glittering treasure and thought of "his own digs, his home among the writhing roots of an old oak—he was slowly overcome with sickening envy" (p. 25). The moment "he decided he had to have a bright red ruby" was the moment he started to change. After this he initiated a series of thefts which involved items of increasing size and value. Each theft seemed to intensify his desire for more treasures.

No longer satisfied with the less than modest existence of an unimportant mouse, he went back for still more rubies, and then for more (p. 27).

Several students compared this second segment of *The Real Thief* with folktales such as the Brothers Grimm "The Fisherman and His Wife." One student observed that "both Derek and the wife got greedier and greedier until it seemed *nothing* could satisfy them!"

The impact of events on Derek's mood was examined by one group of students who charted his mood swings in relation to specific events. At a high point Derek is very pleased with the glorious effect of the treasures on his little place, and with the secret he carries as he "sauntered along the boulevard with his cane under his arm and his paws in his pockets, knowing he knew something no one else did" (p. 30). The peak is reached when Derek brings the Kalikak diamond to his place and turns it into a palace. The downswing begins when he learns that the robberies have been discovered and a trial is to take place. It is at this point that he begins to feel uncomfortable and his treasures begin to lose some of their luster.

In the three days before the trial, Derek came to realize that he was a thief. And not just a little thief, but a thief on a grand scale (p. 35).

He thinks of the possible punishments and decides not to confess unless Gawain is found guilty. He reassures himself that this would never happen. But when the unthinkable does occur, Derek slides into a state of depression, weighed down by thoughts of his own misery. "He wished he could go back in time to the turning point, the moment inside the treasury when he was smitten with envy of the King's wealth" (p. 37). But when he finally thinks of Gawain and how this poor soul must be feeling, Derek takes action to clear Gawain's name and restore his reputation. This was associated with a slight upward swing on the mood chart. When he returns the treasure the line on the chart moves slightly upward again. But on a relative scale Derek is still an unhappy mouse, knowing he is the sole cause of Gawain's misery and the "pall of gloom that hung over the whole kingdom . . ." (p. 41).

Character Types

The students who had created a word portrait of Adrian, the Prime Minister, identified him as the villain in the story. This identification of character type prompted a lively debate when the portrait was shared with the rest of the class.

- No. *Derek* is the villain because *he's* the real thief and starts the whole problem.
- But he's not anything like a regular villain. I mean—I felt sorry for him—and you never feel sorry for a villain!
- Derek's not the villain because he didn't *mean* to get Gawain in trouble. But Adrian was jealous and he really *wanted* to get him in trouble.
- Mr. Steig doesn't tell us very much about Adrian. But he's sort of the typical evil Prime Minister that's always making problems. It's like the story of Esther and Haman.
- I remember one of Dr. Seuss' stories that had a wicked prime minister, and he was jealous of this boy that the king liked!
- Oh, I know . . . it's *The King's Stilts*! [1939].
- Those characters are always trying to get the *good* people out of the way!
- See? Adrian *must* be the villain. He gets the King to change his mind about Gawain and to be suspicious of him. It says here on page 10 . . . "He trusted the operations of Adrian's mind more than he did his own instinct. . . . Having listened to an opinion he didn't really believe but was forced to respect, he grew confused and fell into muddled ponderings . . . he became convinced that his beloved Gawain, no matter his bright, innocent eyes, and despite his untarnished record, was a thief, and trusting him had been a doltish error" (pp. 10, 11).

The teacher now asked students to consider how the story might have been different if Adrian had *not* been included as a character. This question was introduced to help them define the role of the villain or antagonist in a narrative.

- I think the King wouldn't have changed his mind and would have tried to find the real thief in other ways. Like putting a twenty-four-hour guard *in* the treasury instead of just by the doors.
- Or they could've rigged up some kind of burglar alarm inside the treasury to catch anyone who *touched* the jewels.
- But Adrian convinced him that Gawain was guilty so he went and had the trial but he already had decided that Gawain would be convicted.
- So he made the people stop trusting Gawain, too. So then *everyone* was against him!
- *Without* Adrian Gawain wouldn't have had such an awful time.
- But then there wouldn't be any excitement or suspense. It wouldn't be much of a story!
- The villain starts the trouble—so the story can be interesting and you want to see how it turns out.
- The villain makes things go wrong and the other characters try to make them right again. Like if a giant is about to destroy a town—the *story* is about how they get rid of the giant and save the town.
- Or like this story I'm reading about a bully, and the boy who's the victim has to *do* something about getting beat up all the time. It's really a good book. It's called A *Bundle of Sticks* [Rhoads-Mauser, 1983]. The bully is the villain.
- So a villain is important for the *story* even though you *wish* he weren't *in* the story. I read that story about the bully. But in the end, the boy got a lot stronger and more self-confident. So the villain sort of forced him to change and not be so scared and nervous all the time.

Viewpoint

In one classroom the study of character development generated a discussion of "viewpoint" as a literary technique. Students noted that the author focussed on Gawain in the first segment and then shifted his attention to Derek in the second. One student observed, "The first part told the way Gawain sees things, and the next part tells it the way Derek sees things." The teacher introduced the term *viewpoint* for the literary technique they had discovered in the process of exploring the author's craft and reading like writers. They saw that by shifting the viewpoint the author was able to explore the impact of a single event, the discovery of the thefts, on two different characters. He was able to reveal the internal response of each character to this event.

When the teacher had read the story aloud to this class she had stopped at the end of the first segment and asked, "Do you think Gawain is innocent or guilty?" The unanimous opinion was that Gawain was *not* the real thief. During the subsequent discussion of viewpoint the teacher asked them to reread that first segment and to look for a possible explanation for their confidence in Gawain's innocence in spite of the fact that he has been convicted of stealing the treasure and sentenced to imprisonment in the castle dungeon. Students discovered that the reason they knew Gawain was innocent was that they had been told what was in Gawain's thoughts. As readers they had received privileged information. Only they had access to the privacy of Gawain's mind. The reader knew what other characters could *not* know. One student concluded with excitement: "Oh, so that's how Mr. Steig gets you to be on Gawain's side when everyone *else* turns against him. And that's why you feel so awful about the trial . . . and so angry at those people—I mean animals. I was so glad when he flew away!"

Responding to this insightful observation the teacher suggested that students begin to look for other examples of techniques authors use to elicit emotional responses from readers.

Plot

Another narrative element which received special attention was plot. Students who had previous experience diagramming narratives using a "story schema" (*see* Chapter 6) decided to use the language of story schema to analyze the plot of *The Real Thief*. First they identified the "initiating event" that set the plot into motion as the discovery of the disappearance of twenty-nine rubies from the Royal Treasury. Then they looked at the "internal response category" and noted that each of the characters responded in different ways, and that these internal responses changed as circumstances changed. They also found that the "goals," "attempts," "obstacles," and "consequences" differed with each character.

- Adrian's goal was to get the King to distrust Gawain because he was jealous. So—he gave that speech to convince Basil that Gawain is guilty. So that's what he *attempted* and it worked. So the *consequence* was just what he wanted.
- And Gawain's goal was to clear his name and clear up the mistake. At first he tried to find out the thief and to talk to the King. That was the *attempt*. And Adrian was the *obstacle*. He steps in, and poor Gawain ends up in jail.

- The townspeople at first want to clear up the mistake, too. So they go to the trial to back him up. But then the King says "taxes" and they can only think about money instead of their friend. So the *King's* speech is an obstacle this time . . . and it made the people change their goal.
- I think Derek's goal was his own comfort. When Gawain was accused, Derek seemed to be more concerned about himself than Gawain. I think he only decided to help Gawain because he wanted to get rid of his own guilty feelings. And in the last part when he confesses and gets forgiven, and then he sees he won't get punished . . . well, he feels great.

When these students focussed on the temporal sequence they noticed that the events were not introduced in chronological order, that the discovery of the thefts preceded the period in which the thefts occurred. When the teacher asked them to speculate on Steig's rationale for this arrangement of events one student exclaimed, "Oh, *here's* a technique that he uses to get us to feel a certain way. He makes us so curious, and we can't wait to find out who the *thief* is! It's suspenseful! If he put the second part about Derek first because it happened first it would spoil it. This way he really gets you interested!"

When they focussed on the "ending" category they agreed that the "solution" was clear.

- They realize Gawain is innocent, and he gets his good reputation back again. So the main problem is solved, and things are peaceful again between Gawain and the town.

They also agreed that major questions were resolved, loose ends tied, and the ending was satisfactory and reassuring. However, some students were uncomfortable about the way the punishment was handled.

- I don't think Derek should have gotten away with it. He should have been *punished* for stealing.
- But he *suffered* and *that* was his punishment.
- But that didn't seem right. That's not a *real* punishment.
- I know. I agree. But I guess it was up to Gawain. It was like if someone decides not to press charges against someone else.
- The King and the townspeople were punished for what *they* did to Gawain. They're *never* going to find out who the *real* thief is. That seemed okay.

The "punishment issue" was the topic of debate in every classroom in which the book was read aloud. Students freely expressed their personal opinions and listened to those of classmates. They held firmly to their notions of "crime and punishment," and rarely did students change their positions on this issue. Some chose to write an alternative ending for the story, revising Steig's resolution according to their ideas about the punishment question.

Setting

The study of the literary element "setting" was initiated in one group by a search for clues to determine the time and place of the story. The halberd was their first clue. When they looked up this new word in Webster's dictionary they found that a halberd is "a weapon used especially in the fifteenth and sixteenth centuries that consists typically of a battle-ax and pike mounted on a handle about six feet long." They also noticed that the next entry "halberdier" described Gawain: ". . . a guard who carries a halberd as a symbol of his duty." They were just about to identify the time of the story as "hundreds of years ago" when they noticed the cameras and modern clothing in the illustrations. So they concluded that Steig did not intend to create a specific time and place but "a sort of generic kingdom that could be long ago or even today!"

Then one student observed, "But Gawain is the name of one of King Arthur's knights. . . . So, maybe Mr. Steig wants you to think *this* could be the setting . . . sort of a Camelot but in more modern times." When this observation was shared with the class the teacher asked them what they knew about King Arthur. Quite a few of the students had some prior knowledge of Arthur and his knights.

- King Arthur was a king in England a long time ago.
- All the knights did brave deeds and they were great warriors and had a lot of adventures.
- The Knights of the Round Table were all loyal to King Arthur and served him. They were honest and noble and brave.
- They were always fighting against evil so Camelot would be a good place.

The teacher decided to read aloud *Sir Gawain and the Green Knight* (Hieatt, 1967), and asked students to think about possible connections between Gawain the goose and Sir Gawain the Knight.

- Well, Gawain was honest and noble like a knight.
- And he was loyal to King Basil and served him *faithfully* even though he really *wanted* to do something else.
- But he wasn't a warrior, just a guard. He didn't fight evil!
- He sort of did. He fought against injustice!
- He fought with words. . . . Against greed because of the taxes. . . . Against the betrayal of friends. But nobody would listen.
- And he was like Sir Gawain because in the end he was different. Sir Gawain discovers he's not perfect. And Gawain the goose discovers it's not a perfect world! And he isn't innocent or trusting anymore.

After this exploration of *The Real Thief* and the legends of King Arthur and his valiant knights the teacher decided to introduce another literary term. *Allusion* is an indirect reference to something or someone outside the text but within the knowledge background of the reader who recognizes the reference. The teacher explained that an author chooses his or her words very carefully and that each word can add to the meaning of the story. Then she asked them to consider Steig's choice of a name for the goose and how the name "Gawain" added to the meaning of the story.

- Well, if you *know* about Sir Gawain, then you *think* about the knights and King Arthur and Camelot and everything when you read *The Real Thief.*
- And it sort of connects the story to those old legends of knights fighting for the right, for justice!

- I think Mr. Steig *wanted* us to think about these things—like justice and honor. It's sort of the message—how you act toward other people.
- And even though it's just cartoon animals—you take it seriously because the author is talking about serious things like justice and trust.
- When I first heard *The Real Thief* I didn't know that other story about Gawain. But now it seems like even a better story for me. It's like I missed something before. I think we should have heard the *other* Gawain story first.

Theme

The discussion of the author's choice of a name for the central character led naturally into a consideration of the themes—the central meanings or significant truths inherent in the story. Students explored what the story says about justice, betrayal, friendship, human weakness, guilt, pride, trust, loyalty, greed, and reputation. Students discussed the connection between understanding these concepts and understanding human relationships. They spoke of innocence and experience and Gawain's loss of innocence as he encountered some of the harsh realities of human interaction. At the conclusion of the discussion of theme the teacher asked students to take a second look at the title and to consider meanings it might suggest beyond the obvious one.

- Derek is the *real* thief because he stole the treasures and not Gawain. But he's not *like* a real thief because he's not really bad.
- And *he* doesn't think he's a criminal.
- But he also stole Gawain's reputation. People didn't trust Gawain . . .”
- He also stole the *peace* in the town. At first everything was like Camelot, and then everyone was miserable—because of Derek!
- He stole Gawain's innocence! He'll never be the same again. He won't *trust* people as much.
- And the King and everyone will *always* feel sort of guilty about what they did.
- Derek stole jewels and also feelings.

Style

Some students were especially interested in the language of *The Real Thief*, the way Steig expressed his ideas through his choice and arrangement of words. A student familiar with other books by Steig commented, “He likes to use really interesting words.” Working with partners these students searched for interesting words, phrases, statements, or dialogue, and discussed what was so special about these “language samples” and how they enhanced the meaning of the story or helped to develop a character. When Gawain dreams about his plans for a new palace he thinks, “. . . it would be oviform—that is, it would have the ideal shape of the egg” (p. 2). The student who selected this language sample commented “It reminds us that Gawain is a *goose* but is very smart, and it shows Mr. Steig has a good sense of humor!” Another student collected words from Adrian's speech: “access or egress . . . culprit . . . begging your lofty forgiveness . . . despoil . . . unthinkable . . .” (p. 10). He explained that such words showed Adrian is the kind who is “always showing off and using big words and acting superior!”

One student found lines which meant a great deal to her personally. When Gawain was brought to the courthouse from the dungeon, the author notes: "The familiar town looked the same as always . . . but to Gawain . . . it was strange that it should look the same" (p. 13). This student explained that these few words expressed exactly how she had felt when she was going to her grandmother's funeral and ". . . I was feeling so sad and I looked around and the sun was out and the kids were playing and laughing—and it didn't seem right somehow. I know *just* how Gawain felt."

Other lines were selected which illustrated Steig's ability to capture universal human emotions and to convey a wealth of meaning with an economy of words. As Derek surveys the "glorious effect" of the treasures in his home the author expresses the mouse's thoughts: "If he could only share it with someone" (p. 29). This line generated a great many comments about one's need for a confidante to share one's thoughts and feelings and to impress others.

- If you get a brand new watch and you couldn't show it to anybody, it's not much fun. Or if you win first place at the swim finals—it would be awful hard to have to keep it a secret!
- It's nice to have a friend to talk to . . . and tell things . . . you feel better.

Another student had selected a line which follows Derek's response to Gawain's flight from the courtroom. Derek was certain that he would have confessed if Gawain had not escaped. Steig adds: "He had to think that" (p. 37). This student recognized the contribution of these few words to the growing picture of Derek as weak and self-centered.

- Steig tells you that Derek never really faces reality—especially about himself. Like when he says he's not a *real* criminal or when he says he *would* have confessed. He just says it to himself so he'll feel better—but you know it's not true. . . . Like yesterday my brother mowed the lawn and I said I *would* have done it if he didn't. But I think I probably would've tried to get out of it.

His classmates shared their experiences with self-deception, recognizing that Derek's strategies for easing his guilt feelings were like their own. They also understood the meaning of the line: "He wished he could go back to the turning point, the moment inside the treasury when he was smitten with envy of the King's wealth" (p. 37). Almost all students were able to think of times when they wished they had not done something and could turn back the clock.

Their collection of language samples also included such phrases as "a fugitive and a recluse" (p. 46), "pall of gloom" (p. 41), "thieving without malicious intent" (p. 51). They felt that the line which followed the return of Gawain—"The whole town slept well that night" (p. 57)—said a great deal about the emotional impact of this event on everyone involved.

LITERARY CONNECTIONS

After their study of the basic literary elements of *The Real Thief* students were invited to look for connections between this story and other fantasy or realistic novels. In one classroom the teacher suggested two books for independent reading, *Danny the Champion of the World* (Dahl, 1975) and *Fantastic Mr. Fox* (Dahl, 1970). Students discovered that in all three books the thief is a central character who is not viewed as a villain. One student observed, "In these three stories good and evil aren't as clear as in fairytales. It's not black and white. It sort of depends on the situation and the reasons . . . and *who* you steal from."

A comparative study of these stories—two animal fantasies and one realistic novel—generated some interesting responses in journals and dialogue groups. Students were particularly intrigued by the way the author of each book shaped the reader's emotional response to the text.

- Mr. Dahl makes you really admire Danny's father. He loves his son, he knows all about nature, he's a great mechanic, he tells *great* stories. Everyone seems to really like him. He just seems like the ideal dad. I wish *my* dad was like that!
- Danny was upset when he first found out that his dad was a poacher . . . he stole pheasants for sport. So was I . . . it didn't seem right.
- But the guy who owned them—Mr. Hazell—he's so mean and he's always trying to get Danny's dad off his land. And he's so nasty. He deserved it!
- So Mr. Dahl makes you *like* the thief and *hate* the victim. It's just like *Fantastic Mr. Fox*. He makes the farmers so disgusting and gross that *they* seem like the villains. And Mr. Fox— who steals from them—is a hero! He's a good husband and father. And everyone likes him.
- And even Danny becomes a poacher. But I wanted him to win—even though it's wrong. But that Mr. Hazell is so awful. I was glad they ruined his pheasant hunt.
- Did you see that movie about Butch Cassidy? He's an outlaw, but he's the hero. Everybody wants him to win.
- It's sort of like Robin Hood. They're outlaws, too. But they only rob from rich people and give the money to poor people.
- I was glad that the pheasants got away in the end and nobody *ate* them.
- It's a lot different in *The Real Thief*. Even though you like Derek and feel sorry for him, you *also* like Gawain and King Basil. The villain is sort of in the background . . . You don't see much of Adrian. Maybe the *real* villain is the *injustice* that happens. I don't know . . . this is a harder book. Mr. Steig makes you think and think and think!

The oral and written responses of these students demonstrated their ability "to read like writers." By comparing the literary techniques of two different authors they were able to reach new insights and take significant leaps in their understanding.

To set the stage for the discovery of additional literary connections one teacher arranged a display of books related in terms of theme or techniques. Those interested in continuing this inquiry were invited to select from this collection for independent reading. Another teacher set up a chart in his room and asked students to record the title and author of any book, discovered through independent choice, which they thought was connected in some way to *The Real Thief*. They could explain these literary connections in their journals, conferences with their teacher, or in dialogue groups. Frequently another student would choose a book from the list on this chart and try to figure out what connection was identified by the classmate who had read it first. Thus *Ash Road* (Southall, 1965), *Pigman* (Zindel, 1968), *One-Eyed Cat* (Fox, 1984), *A Taste of Blackberries* (Smith, 1973), and *Good-Bye, Chicken Little* (Byars, 1979) were put on the list because all dealt with guilt and responsibility. The Southall and Fox books explored in depth the burden of secret guilt. *The Witch of Blackbird Pond* (Speare, 1958) was selected because of the witch trial. *My Brother Sam Is Dead* (Collier, 1974) was selected because of the false accusation against Sam. *The Cold and Hot Winter* (Hurwitz, 1988) is about a fifth-grade boy who accuses his best friend of dishonesty and theft and later discovers that this friend was not responsible for the series of thefts which prompted the accusation.

These young readers discovered themes that related to significant truths of human experience, and that interpersonal relationships could be found in animal fantasy, contemporary realistic fiction, and historical fiction. As they read these different genres and discussed the stories with friends, in their journals, or with the teacher their responses revealed that they were, indeed, developing the habit of "reading like writers."

CONNECTIONS BETWEEN THE STORY WORLD AND STUDENT'S WORLD

Throughout discussions of *The Real Thief* students had found interesting connections between the story world and their own lives. They understood how a particular character might feel because they, too, had been through a similar experience. Or they recognized a type of character because they knew someone who behaved in a similar manner. They discussed actions and reactions of characters in terms of what *they* might have done in similar circumstances. They made connections between the significance of taxes in Basil's kingdom and the significance of the tax question in a recent presidential election.

In one classroom students were invited to write in their journals about specific connections between this story and their personal experiences. A number of students wrote about their own experiences as victims of false accusations by a parent, teacher, sibling, or friend. Some wrote about the betrayal of a trusted friend. Others revealed deeds which had caused *them* to feel guilty and miserable. One student concluded such an entry with: ". . . so *I* know just how Derek was feeling, and I really felt sorry for him!!" A few students shared experiences with false accusations in which they had accused a friend of a deed which they later discovered was the fault of another. Many children enjoyed this exercise and continued to engage in this "bridge-building" process as they added new entries in their journals about other books which held personal meaning for them.

EXTENDING THE LITERARY EXPERIENCE ACROSS THE CURRICULUM

Social Studies

A sixth-grade teacher used *The Real Thief* as a starting point for a study of the system of courts in the United States. The arrest and court scenes in this book generated a number of interesting questions and comments about the procedures used to apprehend Gawain, the suspect, and the nature of the trial itself. One student noted, "If Gawain lived in the United States the police would have to show him a warrant for his arrest and read him his rights!" Another student added, "And I don't think you have to stay in jail before your trial unless you murdered someone. Gawain should have gotten out on bail. That's what they do on T.V." Others raised questions about the trial.

- Shouldn't they have a jury?
- What about a lawyer? Gawain should have a lawyer.
- Don't you need more evidence than that? Isn't that called circumstantial evidence?

   Gradually a list of comments and questions was generated and used to introduce the study of the court system in the United States. After reading about the workings of an American court and the different types of courts at state and federal levels; and after becoming familiar with such terms as plaintiff, defendant, verdict, indictment, subpoena, summons, petition, appeal, and public defender students were ready for a trip to the courthouse to observe a jury trial. At the conclusion of this study one student commented, "In *The Real Thief*, King Basil sat in the judge's seat under those big brass scales that are supposed to stand for justice. But they sure didn't know much about justice in *that* story!" Several students decided to rewrite the arrest and trial scenes using "America today" as the setting and their new knowledge of the way our system of justice works. They soon discovered that this change in the setting and the rules of justice operating within this setting produced significant changes in the story as a whole. It actually became a different story. This writing project not only served to reinforce these students' understanding of the system of justice in the United States, it also highlighted the close relationship between setting and plot in the development of a narrative.

Drama

In many classrooms students dramatized various scenes of special interest. They particularly enjoyed reconstructing the arrest and court scenes. Several students enacted Adrian's speech to the King; others recreated the reunion of Gawain and Derek. One student mimed Derek's emotional journey, beginning with the initial discovery of the treasure through the series of thefts and ending with Gawain's trial and escape. Two students constructed an additional scene in which Gawain is lying on a couch talking to his psychiatrist about his experience and its impact on him.

Composition

In the course of studying *The Real Thief* the teachers and students came up with various ideas for exploring narrative through writing activities other than journals. One group produced a "character study" of Derek. First they wrote a detailed report of the events and his response to them. They examined his behavior and his thoughts. Second they presented an analysis of his personality based on their own interpretation of this data. Finally they attempted to reconstruct his "history" to explain why he was all alone, what had happened to his family, and why he had behaved as described in the story.

   In a fourth-grade classroom students wrote diaries from Gawain's viewpoint. They produced first-person accounts of the events as seen through the eyes of Gawain as they imagined his internal responses. One boy wrote:

Dear Diary,
   Some of the royal treasure was gone today and I got blamed for it. But I think I know who did it. But I don't know how the person got in. I stand there all day with my halberd and nobody gets in.

In his next entry he wrote:

Dear Diary,
   Now for *sure* I know who did it. It's that cat Adrian. That dumb cat. But I still don't see how he gets in. He's gone too far now.

Several students wrote up accounts of the trial and subsequent events as if they were newspaper reporters following a front-page story. Others chose to retell the story from the perspectives of different characters. They found that in order to tell the story through the eyes of Basil or Adrian they had to imagine new events and inner responses to account for the time between Gawain's flight and his return. One student especially enjoyed writing Adrian's story. He portrayed Adrian's wicked delight with the turn of events. How happy he was to see his plan had worked and Gawain was finally out of the way! This student showed Adrian's attempts to become the King's confidante and his bitter disappointment at Gawain's triumphant return and the joyful and loving reception given him by the King and the town.

Those who were dissatisfied with the way Steig had concluded his narrative chose to construct an alternative ending. One student developed a sequence of events which followed Derek's public confession of the truth, but which led eventually to a satisfying resolution.

New stories were created around the themes of injustice and betrayal. Some of these were realistic stories based on personal experience. Others were fantasies.

In all, a great deal of writing was generated from the study of *The Real Thief*. Much of this reflected students' growing awareness of the "author's craft." These young authors had begun to read like writers and to use in their own writing some of the knowledge they had acquired from reading and discussing literature.

Art

In many classrooms a special interest in cartoon art emerged as students explored Steig's book illustrations and his *New Yorker* cartoons. Some studied the work of other cartoon artists in children's literature, such as Dr. Seuss, Steven Kellogg, José Aruego, and James Marshall. A number of young cartoonists blossomed in these classrooms. Some recreated the events of popular fables using humorous cartoon characters and "balloon dialogue." Others created new stories using cartoonlike illustrations.

In one classroom in which "cartoon fever" had reached its peak, a student discovered Betsy Byars' *The Cartoonist* (1978). This novel by a Newbery Award-winning author soon became one of the "top choices" for independent reading. Another student shared his discovery of *My Life as a Cartoonist* (Kurtzman, 1988), an autobiography of the creator of MAD magazine.

A dialogue group in another classroom was especially intrigued with Gawain's vision of an oviform palace. They decided to design original buildings, taking the perspective of architects who would have different notions about the nature of the "ideal shape." One designed a beehive-shaped palace to represent King Basil's perspective. A second palace, shaped like a large golden wedge of cheese, represented a mouse-architect's vision.

Independent Reading and Research Projects

In most classrooms students studied Steig as an author and artist. They read his picture books and novels; they found examples of his *New Yorker* cartoons; they read about him as an individual. A student engaged in such a study of the man and his work, commented: "When you read about his characters and see his cartoons, you really feel like you know the way he *thinks* about life. He seems to be so happy. And he really understands how people feel."

Several groups decided to focus on Roald Dahl. Most were familiar with *Charlie and the Chocolate Factory* (Dahl, 1973) and *James and the Giant Peach* (Dahl, 1961), and were delighted to discover other books by the author of these "top choices." After reading *Danny the Champion of the World* (Dahl, 1975), *The BFG* (1982), *Fantastic Mr. Fox* (1970), and *The Witches* (1983), they compared his stories and put together a list of recurring themes and literary techniques. One student was especially excited to discover that the story Danny's father told him at night was an abbreviated version of *The BFG* published seven years later. Those who had previously studied Steig's animal fantasies, compared and contrasted these two writers in terms of style, characters, and view of life as revealed in their writing. One student who had particularly enjoyed *Abel's Island* (Steig, 1976) and *Dominic* (Steig, 1972), and had been somewhat disturbed by *Danny the Champion of the World*, shared this thoughtful appraisal: "It seems to me that Mr. Steig likes people and sees the good in them. He doesn't even have any really bad villains. But Mr. Dahl seems to focus on the bad side of people. He has *so* many awful characters who are mean or gross."

Knights and castles emerged as another topic of interest for special study in a group whose members shared a common enthusiasm for the game of "Dungeons and Dragons." They read legends of King Arthur and the brave deeds of his Knights, such as *The Sword in the Stone* (White, 1939), *Sword of King Arthur* (Williams, 1968), *Stories of King Arthur and His Knights* (Picard, 1955), *The Sword and the Circle* (Sutcliff, 1981), *Sir Gawain and the Loathly Lady* (Hastings, 1985), and *Tales of King Arthur* (Riordan, 1982). They discovered other medieval heroes, such as Robin Hood and Saint George, and especially enjoyed Ann McGovern's *Robin Hood of Sherwood Forest* (1970) and Margaret Hodges' *Saint George and the Dragon* (1984). When the librarian introduced them to David Macaulay's *Castle* (1977), the result was a number of detailed and carefully labelled castle drawings.

One student found *Merry Ever After* (Lasker, 1976) and added this to the growing collection of "medieval books." As they discovered other books that fit into the general topic of knights and castles, they also found new connections among the books and increased their knowledge of medieval life and legend.

Weeks after this particular study, in the course of their independent reading experiences, several members of this group came across modern fantasies which are rooted in Arthurian legend. They discovered Susan Cooper's *The Grey King* (1975), the fourth in a series of five books known as *The Dark Is Rising*; Jane Yolen's *The Acorn Quest* (1981), a parody of Arthur's Knights of the Round Table and their pursuit of the Holy Grail; and James Berry's *Magicians of Erianne* (1988), a fantasy-adventure about Ronan who is fighting for peace in King Arthur's kingdom. They discovered Katherine Paterson's *Park's Quest* (1988), a contemporary realistic tale about a boy whose daydreams of King Arthur and the age of chivalry provide a backdrop for his own quest. One student who had read this sensitive novel commented, "The author *assumes* you've already read about King Arthur and Sir Gawain. I was glad I did . . . because it helped you figure out what was going on."

These students recorded their discoveries in an appendix to their "knights and castles" report. The annotated bibliography in this appendix brought these titles to the attention of classmates who, in turn, selected these books for their independent reading.

When attention was focussed on literary connections between *The Real Thief* and other stories with related themes, students were introduced to many new titles and authors, and new possibilities for independent reading were opened to them. Because this independent reading occurred in a social context, favorite books were regularly shared with other members of the "literacy club." Ideas for "reading projects" frequently evolved out of the sharing.

Two sixth-grade students decided to collaborate on a comparative study of two novels which had impressed them deeply: *Ash Road* (Southall, 1965) and *One-Eyed Cat* (Fox, 1984). They used the class study of *The Real Thief* as preparation and a guide for a thoughtful analysis of these two haunting novels of terrible secrets and guilt.

"THE LITERACY CLUB"

"The Literacy Club" is Frank Smith's metaphor for the social nature of literacy learning. The ongoing dialogue in the classroom provides a social context for reading and writing as meaning-making and communicative processes. Children can learn about reading and writing by interacting with their teachers, with each other, with the authors of books they read or hear, and with the implied readers of their own writing. Children learn to read and write by becoming readers and writers. Children can learn to read like writers and acquire the knowledge writers need if they perceive themselves as members of the literacy club.

The study of *The Real Thief* generated a wide range of group and individual reading, writing, research, and creative activities which reflected students' ability to read like writers and to use literary knowledge they acquired in the course of cumulative literature-learning experiences. The quality of involvement observed in these classrooms suggests that most of the students did, indeed, perceive themselves as readers and writers, as active members of the literacy club. Ongoing dialogues, formal and informal, about the literature they had heard or read, suggested that these students also perceived themselves as members of the "literary club." They shared literary experiences in a social context and collaborated as readers and writers in a literary environment.

When *The Real Thief* unit or any other Focus Unit was introduced to students at the beginning of the school year it set the stage for subsequent literature-based, reading-writing experiences. Students continued to respond to literature in their journals, in dialogue groups, in conferences, and in informal interactions. They read new texts in light of previous ones and made connections between the texts. They constructed bridges between the story world and their own world. They learned to read like writers to become writers. They experimented with diverse communication systems to express ideas and feelings, construct meanings, and extend literary experiences. And as they learned about literature and what it says about human experience and universal truths, they also learned about the language of literature as readers and writers in a community of learners.

References

Smith, Frank. "Reading Like a Writer." *Composing and Comprehending*. Julie Jensen, ed. Urbana, IL: ERIC and NCRE, 1984, pp. 47–56.

Bibliography for the Real Thief Focus Unit

Berry, James R. *Magicians of Erianne*. N.Y.: Harper and Row, 1988.
Byars, Betsy. *The Cartoonist*. N.Y.: Viking, 1978.
————. *Good-bye Chicken Little*. N.Y.: Harper and Row, 1979.
Collier, James Lincoln, and Christopher Collier. *My Brother Sam Is Dead*. N.Y.: Four Winds, 1974.
Cooper, Susan. *The Dark Is Rising*. N.Y.: Atheneum, 1973.
————. *The Grey King*. N.Y.: Atheneum, 1975.
Dahl, Roald. *The BFG*. N.Y.: Farrar, Straus & Giroux, 1982.
————. *Charlie and the Chocolate Factory*. N.Y.: Knopf, 1973 (1964).
————. *Charlie and the Great Glass Elevator*. N.Y.: Knopf, 1972.
————. *Danny the Champion of the World*. N.Y.: Knopf, 1975.
————. *Fantastic Mr. Fox*. N.Y.: Knopf, 1970.
————. *James and the Giant Peach*. N.Y.: Knopf, 1961.
————. *The Witches*. N.Y.: Farrar, Straus & Giroux, 1983.
Fox, Paula. *One-Eyed Cat*. N.Y.: Bradbury, 1984.
Hastings, Selina. *Sir Gawain and the Loathly Lady*. N.Y.: Lothrop, Lee & Shepard, 1985.
Hieatt, Constance, reteller. *Sir Gawain and the Green Knight*. N.Y.: Crowell, 1967.
Hodges, Margaret. *Saint George and the Dragon*. Trina Schart Hyman, illus. Boston: Little, Brown, 1984.
Hurwitz, Johanna. *The Cold and Hot Winter*. N.Y.: Morrow, 1988.
Kurtzman, Harvey. *My Life as a Cartoonist*. N.Y.: Minstrel/Pocket, 1988.
Lasker, Joe. *Merry Ever After: The Story of Two Medieval Weddings*. N.Y.: Viking, 1976.
Macauley, David. *Castle*. Boston: Houghton Mifflin, 1977.
McGovern, Ann. *Robin Hood of Sherwood Forest*. N.Y.: Scholastic, 1970.
Paterson, Katherine. *Park's Quest*. N.Y.: Lodestar/Dutton, 1988.
Picard, Barbara. *Stories of King Arthur and His Knights*. N.Y.: Henry Z. Walek, 1955.
Rhoads-Mauser, Pat. *A Bundle of Sticks*. N.Y.: Atheneum, 1983.
Riordan, James. *Tales of King Arthur*. Victor Ambrus, illus. N.Y.: Rand McNally, 1982.
Seuss, Dr. *The King's Stilts*. N.Y.: Random House, 1939.
Smith, Doris Buchanan. *A Taste of Blackberries*. N.Y.: Crowell, 1973.
Steig, William. *Abel's Island*. N.Y.: Farrar, Straus & Giroux, 1976.
————. *Dominic*. N.Y.: Farrar, Straus & Giroux, 1972.
————. *The Real Thief*. N.Y.: Farrar, Straus & Giroux, 1973.
Southall, Ivan. *Ash Road*. N.Y.: St. Martins, 1965.
Speare, Elizabeth. *The Witch of Blackbird Pond*. Boston: Houghton Mifflin, 1958.
Sutcliff, Rosemary. *The Sword and the Circle*. N.Y.: Dutton, 1981.

White, E. B. *Charlotte's Web*. N.Y.: Harper and Row, 1952.
White, T. H. *The Sword in the Stone*. N.Y.: Putnam, 1939.
Williams, Jay. *Sword of King Arthur*. N.Y.: Crowell, 1968.
Yolen, Jane. *The Acorn Quest*. N.Y.: Crowell, 1981.
Zindel, Paul. *Pigman*. N.Y.: Harper and Row, 1968.

APPENDIX A

Focus on Literature: Resources

I. About Children's Literature

Bader, Barbara. *American Picturebooks from Noah's Ark to the Beast Within*. N.Y.: Macmillan, 1976.

Bauer, Caroline. *This Way to Books*. N.Y.: Wilson, 1983.

Butler, Francelia. *Sharing Literature with Children: A Thematic Anthology*. N.Y.: David McKay, 1977.

Butler, Francelia, and Richard Rotert, eds. *Triumphs of the Spirit in Children's Literature*. Hamden, CT: Library Professional Publications, 1986.

Carpenter, Humphrey, and Mari Prichard. *The Oxford Companion to Children's Literature*. N.Y.: Oxford University Press, 1984.

Chambers, Dewey. *Children's Literature in the Curriculum*. Chicago: Rand McNally, 1971.

Cianciolo, Patricia. *Illustrations in Children's Books*. Dubuque, IA: William C. Brown, 1976.

———. *Picture Books for Children*. Chicago: American Library Association, 1981.

Cullinan, Bernice E., ed. *Children's Literature in the Reading Program*. Newark, DE: IRA, 1987.

Cullinan, Bernice, and Carolyn Carmichael. *Literature and Young Children*. Urbana, IL: National Council of Teachers of English, 1977.

Cullinan, Bernice E., Mary K. Karrer, and Arlene M. Pillar. *Literature and the Child*. N.Y.: Harcourt Brace Jovanovich, 1981.

Egoff, Sheila. *Thursday's Child: Trends and Patterns in Contemporary Children's Literature*. Chicago: American Library Association, 1981.

Harrison, Barbara, and Gregory Maguire, eds. *Innocence and Experience: Essays and Conversations on Children's Literature*. N.Y.: Lothrop, Lee & Shepard, 1987.

Hearne, Betsy. *Choosing Books for Children: A Commonsense Guide*. N.Y.: Delacorte, 1981.

Hearne, Betsy, and Marilyn Kaye, eds. *Celebrating Children's Books: Essays on Children's Literature in Honor of Zena Sutherland*. N.Y.: Lothrop, Lee & Shepard, 1981.

Hickman, Janet, and Bernice E. Cullinan, eds. *Children's Literature in the Classroom: "Weaving Charlotte's Web."* Needham Hgts., MA: Christopher-Gordon, 1989.

Hopkins, Lee Bennet. *The Best of Book Bonanza*. N.Y.: Holt, Rinehart and Winston, 1980.

Huck, Charlotte, Susan Hepler, and Janet Hickman. *Children's Literature in the Elementary School.* N.Y.: Holt, Rinehart and Winston, 1987.

Lamme, Linda Leonard. *Raising Readers: A Guide to Sharing Literature with Young Children.* N.Y.: Walker, 1980.

Lanes, Selma G. *Down the Rabbit Hole: Adventures and Misadventures in the Realm of Children's Literature.* N.Y.: Atheneum, 1971.

LeGuin, Ursula K. *The Language of the Night: Essays on Fantasy and Science Fiction.* N.Y.: Putnam, 1979.

Lukens, Rebecca J. *A Critical Handbook of Children's Literature.* Glenview, IL: Scott, Foresman, 1986.

Meek, Margaret, Aidan Warlow, and Griselda Barton. *The Cool Web: The Pattern of Children's Reading.* N.Y.: Atheneum, 1978.

Meeker, Alice. *Enjoying Literature with Children.* N.Y.: Odyssey, 1969.

Moss, Joy F. "The Fable and Critical Thinking," *Language Arts,* 57, January 1980, pp. 21–29.

———. *Focus Units in Literature: A Handbook for Elementary School Teachers.* Urbana, IL: NCTE, 1984.

———. "Reading and Discussing Fairy Tales—Old and New." *The Reading Teacher,* vol. 35, no. 6, March 1982, pp. 656–660.

Moss, Joy F., and Sherri Oden. "Children's Story Comprehension and Social Learning." *The Reading Teacher,* vol. 36, no. 8, April 1983, pp. 784–790.

Nelms, Ben F., ed. *Literature in the Classroom: Readers, Texts, and Contexts.* Urbana, IL: NCTE, 1988.

Nodelman, Perry. *Words about Pictures: The Narrative Art of Children's Picture Books.* University of Georgia Press, 1989.

Norton, Donna E. *Through the Eyes of a Child: An Introduction to Children's Literature.* Columbus, OH: Merrill, 1987.

Paterson, Katherine. *Gates of Excellence: On Reading and Writing Books for Children.* N.Y.: Elsevier/ Nelson, 1981.

———. *The Spying Heart: More Thoughts on Reading and Writing Books for Children.* N.Y.: Dutton/ Lodestar, 1988.

Purves, Alan C., and Dianne L. Monson. *Experiencing Children's Literature.* Glenview, IL: Scott, Foresman, 1984.

Roser, Nancy, and Margaret Frith, eds. *Children's Choices: Teaching with Books Children Like.* Newark, DE: IRA, 1983.

Rudman, Masha Kabakow. *Children's Literature: An Issues Approach.* N.Y.: Longman, 1984.

Sadker, Myra Pollock, and David Miller. *Now Upon a Time: A Contemporary View of Children's Literature.* N.Y.: Harper and Row, 1977.

Sale, Roger. *Fairy Tales and After: From Snow White to E. B. White.* Cambridge, MA: Harvard University Press, 1978.

Sebesta, Sam L., and William Iverson. *Literature for Thursday's Child.* Palo Alto, CA: Science Research Associates, 1975.

Sendak, Maurice. *Caldecott & Co.: Notes on Books and Pictures.* N.Y.: Farrar, Straus & Giroux, 1989.

Sims, Rudine. *Shadow & Substance: Afro-American Experience in Contemporary Children's Fiction.* Urbana, IL: NCTE, 1983.

Sloan, Glenna Davis. *The Child as Critic: Teaching Literature in Elementary and Middle Schools.* N.Y.: Teachers College Press, 1984.

Smith, Lillian. *The Unreluctant Years.* N.Y.: Viking, 1967.

Stewig, John Warren. *Children and Literature.* Boston: Houghton Mifflin, 1988.

Stewig, John Warren, and Sam L. Sebesta, eds. *Using Literature in the Elementary Classroom.* Urbana, IL: NCTE, 1978.

Sutherland, Zena, and May Hill Arbuthnot. *Children and Books.* Glenview, IL: Scott, Foresman, 1986.

Trelease, Jim. *The Read-Aloud Handbook.* N.Y.: Penguin, 1985.

White, Mary Lou. *Children's Literature: Criticism and Response.* Columbus, OH: Merrill, 1976.

II. Periodicals

The Booklist. American Library Association. Chicago, IL.

The Bulletin of the Center for Children's Books. Graduate Library School, University of Chicago Press, Chicago, IL.

Children's Literature in Education. Agathon Press, N.Y.

Cricket Magazine. Open Court, LaSalle, IL.

The Horn Book. Boston, MA.

Interracial Books for Children Bulletin. Council on Interracial Books for Children, N.Y.

Language Arts. National Council of Teachers of English (NCTE), Urbana, IL.

The Lion and the Unicorn. Johns Hopkins University Press, Baltimore, MD.

The New Advocate. Christopher-Gordon, Boston, MA.

Phaedrus: An International Annual of Children's Literature Research, James Fraser, ed. Fairleigh Dickinson University, Madison, N.J.

School Library Journal. R. R. Bowker, Philadelphia, PA.

Top of the News. Association for Library Services to Children and the Young Adult Services Division of the American Library Association. Chicago, IL.

The WEB: Wonderfully Exciting Books. Ohio State University, The Reading Center, Columbus, OH.

Wilson Library Bulletin. H. W. Wilson, Bronx, N.Y.

III. Focus on Folk Literature

Aardema, Verna. *Tales from the Story Hat.* N.Y.: Coward, McCann and Geoghegan, 1960.

————. *More Tales from the Story Hat.* N.Y.: Coward, McCann and Geoghegan, 1966.

Ackhurst, Joyce Cooper. *The Adventures of Spider, West African Folk Tales.* Boston: Little, Brown, 1964.

Aesop. *Aesop's Fables.* Louis Untermeyer, selector and adaptor. N.Y.: Golden Press, 1966.

Afanas'ev, Aleksandr, collector. *Russian Fairy Tales.* N.Y.: Pantheon, 1945/1973.

Andersen, Hans Christian. *The Complete Fairy Tales and Stories* (Danish). Erik Christian Haugaard, trans. Garden City, N.Y.: Doubleday, 1974.

Asbjornsen, Peter Christian, and Jorgen E. Moe. *East of the Sun and West of the Moon and Other Tales.* N.Y.: Macmillan, 1963.

————. *Norwegian Folk Tales.* Pat Shaw Iversen and Carl Norman, trans. N.Y.: Viking, 1961.

Barbeau, Marius. *The Golden Phoenix and Other Fairy Tales from Quebec.* Michael Hornyansky, reteller. Toronto: Oxford University Press, 1980 (1958).

Barber, Richard. *A Companion to World Mythology.* N.Y. Delacorte, 1979.

Bettelheim, Bruno. *The Uses of Enchantment: Meaning and Importance of Fairy Tales.* N.Y.: Knopf, 1976.

Bond, Ruskin, reteller. *Tales and Legends from India.* Sally Scott, illus. N.Y.: Franklin Watts, 1982.

Booss, Claire, ed. *Scandinavian Folk and Fairy Tales: Tales from Norway, Sweden, Denmark, Finland, Iceland.* N.Y.: Avenel, 1984.

Bosma, Bette. *Fairy Tales, Fables, Legends, and Myths: Using Folk Literature in Your Classroom.* N.Y.: Teachers College Press, 1987.

Briggs, Katherine. ed. *A Dictionary of British Folk-Tales in the English Language.* Bloomington: Indiana University Press, 1970.

————. *An Encyclopedia of Fairies: Hobgoblins, Brownies, Bogies, and other Supernatural Creatures.* N.Y.: Pantheon, 1976.

Bulfinch, Thomas. *Age of Fable: Or, Stories of Gods and Heroes.* Glendale, CA: Heritage, 1958.

Calvino, Italo, selector and reteller. *Italian Folktales*. N.Y.: Harcourt Brace Jovanovich, 1980.

Campbell, Joseph. *The Hero with a Thousand Faces*. Princeton, N.J.: Princeton University Press, 1968 (c1949).

Carlson, Atelia, and Gilbert B. Croff. *World Folktales: A Scribner Resource Collection*. N.Y.: Scribner's, 1980.

Carlson, Ruth, compiler and ed. *Folklore and Folktales around the World*. Newark, DE: IRA, 1972.

Carpenter, Frances. *The Elephant's Bathtub: Wonder Tales from the Far East*. N.Y.: Doubleday, 1962.

Chase, Richard. *The Jack Tales* (Appalachian American Tales). Boston: Houghton Mifflin, 1943.

Cole, Joanna. *Best-Loved Folktales of the World*. Garden City, N.Y.: Doubleday, 1982.

Colum, Padraic, ed. *A Treasury of Irish Folklore*. N.Y.: Crown, 1954.

Colwell, Eileen. *Round about and Long Ago: Tales from the English Counties*. Boston: Houghton Mifflin, 1974.

Cook, Elizabeth. *The Ordinary and the Fabulous: An Introduction to Myths, Legends, and Fairy Tales for Teachers and Storytellers*. N.Y.: Cambridge University Press, 1969.

Courlander, Harold. *The King's Drum and Other African Tales*. San Diego, CA: Harcourt Brace Jovanovich, 1962.

D'Aulaire, Ingri, and Edgar Parin. *Book of Greek Myths*. N.Y.: Doubleday, 1962.

————. *Norse Gods and Giants*. N.Y.: Doubleday, 1967.

DeRoin, Nancy. *Jataka Tales: Fables from the Buddha* (India). Boston: Houghton Mifflin, 1975.

Dorson, Richard M., ed. *Folktales Told Around the World*. Chicago: University of Chicago Press, 1975.

Downing, Charles. *Tales of the Hodja* (Turkey). N.Y.: Henry Z. Walck, 1965.

Erdoes, Richard, ed. *The Sound of Flutes and Other Indian Legends*. Paul Goble, illus. N.Y.: Pantheon, 1976.

Evslin, Bernard. *Signs and Wonders: Tales from the Old Testament*. Charles Mikolaycak, illus. N.Y.: Four Winds, 1981.

Favat, Andre. *Child and Tale: The Origins of Interest*. Urbana, IL: NCTE, 1977.

Fillmore, Parker. *Shepherd's Nosegay* (Finland and Czechoslovakia). Katherine Love, ed. N.Y.: Harcourt Brace Jovanovich, 1958.

Frye, Northrop. *The Educated Imagination*. Bloomington: Indiana University Press, 1964.

Grimm, Brothers. *The Complete Grimm's Fairy Tales*. Padraic Colum, introducer; Joseph Campbell, commentator. N.Y.: Pantheon, 1944, 1972.

Hamilton, Virginia, reteller. *In the Beginning: Creation Stories from around the World*. N.Y.: Harcourt Brace Jovanovich, 1988.

Hamilton, Virginia. *The People Could Fly* (Black American Folktales). N.Y.: Knopf, 1985.

Haviland, Virginia. *Favorite Fairy Tales Told in Italy* (series). Boston: Little, Brown, 1965.

————, adaptor. *Favorite Fairy Tales Told in Spain* (series). Boston: Little, Brown, 1963.

————. *Favorite Fairy Tales Told around the World*. Boston: Little, Brown, 1985.

He Liyi, trans. *The Spring of Butterflies and Other Chinese Folk Tales*. Neil Philip, ed. London: William Collins, 1985.

Jacobs, Joseph, ed. *Celtic Fairy Tales*. N.Y.: Putnam, n.d.

————, ed. *English Fairy Tales*. N.Y.: Putnam, n.d.

————, ed. *Indian Fairy Tales*. N.Y.: Putnam, n.d.

————. *More English Fairy Tales*. N.Y.: Putnam, n.d.

Jagendorf, Mortiz. *New England Bean Pot: American Folk Stories to Read and Tell* (series). N.Y.: Vanguard, 1948.

Lang, Andrew, reteller. *The Arabian Nights*. David McKay, 1951 (1946).

Leach, Maria, and Jerome Fried, eds. *Funk and Wagnall's Standard Dictionary of Folklore, Mythology and Legend*, vols. I and II. N.Y.: Funk and Wagnall's, 1949.

Lester, Julius. *The Tales of Uncle Remus: The Adventures of Brer Rabbit*. N.Y.: Dial, 1987.

Luthi, Max. *Once Upon a Time: On the Nature of Fairy Tales.* Bloomington: Indiana University Press, 1976.

Martin, Eva, reteller. *Tales of the Far North* (Canadian). Laszlo Gal, illus. N.Y.: Dial, 1984.

Manning-Sanders, Ruth. *A Book of Dragons* (subject collection). N.Y.: Dutton, 1965.

McCarty, Toni, collector. *The Skull in the Snow and Other Folktales.* N.Y.: Delacorte, 1981.

McHargue, Georgess. *The Impossible People: A History Natural and Unnatural of Beings Terrible and Wonderful.* N.Y.: Holt, Rinehart and Winston, 1972.

Minard, Rosemary, ed. *Womenfolk and Fairy Tales.* Boston: Houghton Mifflin, 1975.

Muller-Guggenbuhl, Fritz. *Swiss-Alpine Folk-Tales.* Katharine Potts, trans. N.Y.: Henry Z. Walck, 1958.

Olenius, Elsa, selector. *Great Swedish Fairy Tales.* John Bauer, illus.; Holger Lundbergh, trans. N.Y.: Delacorte/Seymour Lawrence, 1973.

Opie, Iona, and Peter Opie, illus. *The Classic Fairy Tales.* N.Y.: Oxford University Press, 1974.

Ozaki, Yei Theodora, compiler. *The Japanese Fairy Book.* Rutland, VT: Charles E. Tuttle, 1970.

Perrault, Charles. *Perrault's Complete Fairy Tales.* N.Y.: Dodd, 1961.

Phelps, Ethel Johnston, ed. *The Maid of the North: Feminist Folk Tales from around the World.* N.Y.: Holt, Rinehart and Winston, 1981.

Propp, Vladimir. *Morphology of the Folktale.* Austin: University of Texas Press, 1968.

Ransome, Arthur. *Old Peter's Russian Tales.* Nashville: Thomas Nelson, 1917, 1976.

Riordan, James, reteller. *Tales from the Arabian Nights.* Victor G. Ambrus, illus. N.Y.: Hamlyn, 1983.

Sadler, Catherine Edwards, adaptor. *Treasure Mountain: Folktales from Southern China.* N.Y.: Atheneum, 1982.

Sakade, Florence, ed. *Japanese Children's Favorite Stories.* Rutland, VT: Charles E. Tuttle, 1958.

Sawyer, Ruth. *The Way of the Storyteller.* N.Y.: Viking, 1942, 1962.

Schwartz, Howard, reteller. *Elijah's Violin and Other Jewish Fairy Tales.* N.Y.: Harper and Row, 1983.

———. *Miriam's Tambourine: Jewish Folktales around the World.* N.Y.: Seth, 1986.

Seki, Keigo. *Folktales of the World* (series). Chicago: University of Chicago Press, 1963.

Stoutenberg, Adrien. *American Tall Tales.* N.Y.: Viking, 1966.

Tashjian, Virginia, ed. *Once There Was and Was Not* (Armenian). Boston: Little, Brown, 1966.

Thompson, Stith. *The Folktale.* Berkeley: University of California Press, 1977.

———. *Motif Index of Folk-Literature* (six volumes). Bloomington: Indiana University Press, 1955–1958.

Travers, Pamela L. *About the Sleeping Beauty.* N.Y.: McGraw-Hill, 1975.

Turner, Philip. *Brian Wildsmith's Illustrated Bible Stories.* N.Y.: Franklin Watts, 1969.

Tyler, Royall, trans. and ed. *Japanese Tales.* N.Y.: Pantheon, 1987.

Uchida, Yoshiko. *The Dancing Kettle and Other Japanese Folk Tales.* N.Y.: Harcourt Brace Jovanovich, 1949.

———. *The Magic Listening Cap: More Folk Tales from Japan.* N.Y.: Harcourt Brace Jovanovich, 1955.

———. *The Sea of Gold and Other Tales from Japan.* N.Y.: Scribner's, 1965.

Vo-dinh, adaptor. *The Toad Is the Emperor's Uncle: Animal Folktales from Vietnam.* N.Y.: Doubleday, 1970.

Vuong, Lynette Dyer. *The Brocaded Slipper and Other Vietnamese Tales.* Reading, MA: Addison-Wesley, 1982.

Walker, Barbara. *A Treasury of Turkish Folktales for Children.* Hamden, CT: Linnet Books/Shoestring, 1988.

White, Anne Terry. *The Golden Treasury of Myths and Legends.* N.Y.: Golden Press, 1959.

Wilson, Barbara Ker. *Scottish Folk Tales and Legends.* N.Y.: Henry Z. Walck, 1954.

Wolkstein, Diane, compiler. *The Magic Orange Tree and Other Haitian Folktales.* N.Y.: Knopf, 1978.

Yolen, Jane, ed. *Favorite Folktales from around the World.* N.Y.: Pantheon, 1986.

Yolen, Jane. *Touch Magic: Fantasy, Faerie and Folklore in the Literature of Childhood*. N.Y.: Philomel, 1981.

Zajdler, Zoe, compiler. *Polish Fairy Tales*. Chicago: Follett, 1968.

Zipes, Jack. *Fairy Tales and the Art of Subversion*. London: Heinemann, 1983.

IV. About Authors and Artists

Aldis, Dorothy. *Nothing Is Impossible: The Story of Beatrix Potter*. N.Y.: Atheneum, 1969.

Blair, Gwenda. *Laura Ingalls Wilder*. N.Y.: Putnam, 1981.

Blegvad, Eric. *Self-Portrait: Erik Blegvad*. Reading, MA: Addison-Wesley, 1979.

Blishen, Edward, ed. *The Thorny Paradise: Writers on Writing for Children*. N.Y.: Penguin, 1975.

Block, Irving. *The Lives of Pearl Buck: A Tale of China and America*. N.Y.: Crowell, 1973.

Bredsdorff, Elias. *Hans Christian Andersen: The Story of His Life and Work*. N.Y.: Scribner's, 1975.

Brown, Marcia. *Lotus Seeds: Children, Pictures, and Books*. N.Y.: Scribner's, 1986.

Bulla, Clyde Robert. *A Grain of Wheat: A Writer Begins*. Boston: Godine, 1985.

Commire, Anne. *Something about the Author: Facts and Pictures about Contemporary Authors and Illustrators of Books for Young People*. Detroit: Gale Research Service, 1971 to present.

Cott, Jonathan. *Pipers at the Gates of Dawn: The Wisdom of Children's Literature*. N.Y.: Random House, 1983.

Dahl, Roald. *Boy: Tales of a Childhood*. N.Y.: Farrar, Straus & Giroux, 1984.

DeMontreville, Doris, and Elizabeth Crawford, eds. *Fourth Book of Junior Authors and Illustrators*. N.Y.: H. W. Wilson, 1978.

DeMontreville, Doris, and Donna Hill. *Third Book of Junior Authors*. N.Y.: H. W. Wilson, 1972.

Doyle, Brian. *The Who's Who of Children's Literature*. N.Y.: Schocken, 1969.

Duncan, Lois. *Chapters: My Growth as a Writer*. Boston: Little, Brown, 1982.

Fritz, Jean. *Homesick: My Own Story*. N.Y.: Putnam, 1982.

Fuller, Muriel, ed. *More Junior Authors* (companion volume to *The Junior Book of Authors*, 1951). N.Y.: H. W. Wilson, 1963.

Giff, Patricia Reilly. *Laura Ingalls Wilder: Growing Up in the Little House*. N.Y.: Viking, 1987.

Godden, Rumer. *Hans Christian Andersen: A Great Life in Brief*. N.Y.: Knopf, 1955.

Hautzig, Esther. *The Endless Steppe: Growing Up in Siberia*. N.Y.: Crowell, 1968.

Hoffman, Miriam, and Eva Samuels, eds. *Authors and Illustrators of Children's Books: Writings on Their Lives and Works*. N.Y.: R. R. Bowker, 1972.

Hopkins, Lee Bennett. *Books Are by People*. N.Y.: Citation, 1969.

————. *More Books by More People*. N.Y.: Citation, 1974.

Hyman, Trina Schart. *Self-Portrait: Trina Schart Hyman*. Reading, MA: Addison-Wesley, 1981.

Jones, Helen, ed. *Robert Lawson, Illustrator*. Boston: Little, Brown, 1972.

Karl, Jean. *From Childhood to Childhood: Children's Books and Their Creators*. N.Y.: John Day, 1970.

Kelen, Emery. *Mr. Nonsense: A Life of Edward Lear*. N.Y.: Norton, 1973.

Kingman, Lee, ed. *The Illustrator's Notebook*. Boston: Horn Book, 1978.

————. *Newbery and Caldecott Medal Books: 1956–1965*. Boston: Horn Book, 1965.

————. *Newbery and Caldecott Medal Books: 1966–1975*. Boston: Horn Book, 1975.

————. *Newbery and Caldecott Medal Books, vol. 5, 1976–1985*. Boston: Horn Book, 1987.

Kingman, Lee, Grace Hogarth, and Harriet Quimby. *Illustrators of Children's Books, 1967–1976* (series). Boston: Horn Book, 1978.

Kirkpatrick, Daniel, ed. *Twentieth-Century Children's Writers*, 2nd ed. N.Y.: St. Martin, 1983.

Kunitz, Stanley, and Howard Haycroft. *The Junior Book of Authors*. N.Y.: H. W. Wilson, 1951.

Lane, Margaret. *The Magic Years of Beatrix Potter*. N.Y.: Frederick Warne, 1978.

————. *The Tale of Beatrix Potter: A Biography*. N.Y.: Frederick Warne, 1946, 1968.

Lanes, Selma G. *The Art of Maurice Sendak*. N.Y.: Abrams, 1980.

Larkin, David, ed. *The Art of Nancy Ekholm Burkert*. N.Y.: Harper and Row, 1977.

Lee, Betsy. *Judy Blume's Story*. Minneapolis: Dillon, 1981.

Lenski, Lois. *Journey into Childhood: The Autobiography of Lois Lenski*. Philadelphia: Lippincott, 1972.

Little, Jean. *Little by Little: A Writer's Education*. N.Y.: Viking, 1987.

Mahony, Bertha E., and Elinor Whitney, compilers. *Contemporary Illustrators of Children's Books*. Detroit: Gale Research Service, 1978.

Meyer, Susan E. *A Treasury of the Great Children's Book Illustrators*. N.Y.: Abrams, 1982.

Milne, Christopher. *The Enchanted Places*. N.Y.: Penguin, 1974.

Naylor, Phyllis. *How I Came to Be a Writer*. N.Y.: Atheneum, 1978.

Preiss, Byron, ed. *The Art of Leo and Diane Dillon*. N.Y.: Ballantine, 1981.

Richter, Hans Peter. *I Was There*. N.Y.: Holt, Rinehart and Winston, 1972.

Schwarcz, Joseph H. *Ways of the Illustrator: Communication in Children's Literature*. Chicago: American Library Association, 1982.

Senick, Gerard, ed. *Children's Literature Review* (series). Detroit, MI: Gale Research Service, 1976–1983.

Singer, Isaac Bashevis. *A Day of Pleasure: Stories of a Boy Growing Up in Warsaw*. N.Y.: Farrar, Straus & Giroux, 1969.

Townsend, John Rowe. *A Sense of Story: Essays on Contemporary Writers for Children*. Boston: Horn Book, 1973.

———. *A Sounding of Storytellers: New and Revised Essays on Contemporary Writers for Children*. N.Y.: Lippincott, 1979.

Ward, Martha E., and Dorothy A. Marquardt. *Authors of Books for Young People*. Metuchen, N.J.: Scarecrow, 1971 (supplement, 1979).

———. *Illustrators of Books for Young People*. Metuchen, N.J.: Scarecrow, 1975.

Weiss, Jerry, ed. *From Writers to Students: The Pleasures and Pains of Writing*. Newark, DE: IRA, 1979.

Wilder, Laura Ingalls. *West from Home: Letters of Laura Ingalls Wilder, San Francisco, 1915*. Roger MacBride, ed. N.Y.: Harper and Row, 1974.

Wintle, Justin, and Emma Fisher. *The Pied Pipers*. N.Y.: Two Continents, 1975.

Wood, James. *The Lantern Bearer: A Life of Robert Louis Stevenson*. N.Y.: Pantheon, 1965.

Zemach, Margot. *Self-portrait: Margot Zemach*. Reading, MA: Addison-Wesley, 1978.

V. Book Selection Aids

Arbuthnot, May Hill, Margaret Mary Clark, Harriet G. Long, and Ruth M. Hadlow, compilers. *Children's Books Too Good to Miss*. Cleveland: Case Western Reserve University Press, 1980.

Baskin, Barbara, and Karen Harris. *Books for the Gifted Child*. N.Y.: R. R. Bowker, 1980.

———. *More Notes from a Different Drummer: A Guide to Juvenile Fiction Portraying the Disabled*. N.Y.: R. R. Bowker, 1984.

———, compilers. *Notes from a Different Drummer: A Guide to Juvenile Fiction Portraying the Handicapped*. N.Y.: Bowker, 1977.

Beyond Fact: Nonfiction for Children and Young People. Chicago: American Library Association, 1982.

Brewton, John, G. Meredith Blackburn, and Lorraine Blackburn, compilers. *Index to Poetry for Children and Young People* (1976–1981). N.Y.: H. W. Wilson, 1984.

Cathon, Laura, Marion Haushalter, and Virginia Russell, eds. *Stories to Tell to Children*. Pittsburgh: University of Pittsburgh Press, for the Carnegie Library of Pittsburgh Children's Services, 1974.

Davis, Enid. *A Comprehensive Guide to Children's Literature with a Jewish Theme*. N.Y.: Schocken, 1981.

Dreyer, Sharon, ed. *The Bookfinder: A Guide to Children's Literature about the Needs and Problems of Youth Aged 2–15.* Circle Pines, MI: American Guidance Service, 1977.

Eastman, Mary Huse. *Index to Fairy Tales, Myths and Legends.* Westwood, MA: Faxon, 1926, 1937, 1952.

Elleman, Barbara, ed. *Children's Books of International Interest.* Chicago: American Library Association, 1985.

Fassler, Joan. *Helping Children Cope: Mastering Stress through Books and Stories.* N.Y.: Free Press, 1978.

Fisher, Margery. *Who's Who in Children's Books: A Treasury of the Familiar Characters of Childhood.* N.Y.: Holt, Rinehart and Winston, 1975.

Flemming, Carolyn, and Donna Schatt. *Choices: A Core Collection for Young Reluctant Readers.* Evanston, IL: John Gordon Burke, 1983.

Gillespie, John. *More Junior Plots.* N.Y.: Bowker, 1977.

Gillespie, John, and Diane Lembo. *Introducing Books: A Guide for the Middle Grades.* N.Y.: R. R. Bowker, 1970.

————. *Juniorplots: A Book Talk Manual for Teachers and Librarians.* N.Y.: R. R. Bowker, 1967.

Haviland, Virginia. *The Best of Children's Books, 1964–1978.* Library of Congress. N.Y.: University Press Books, 1981.

————. *Children's Literature: A Guide to Reference Sources.* Washington, D.C.: Library of Congress, 1966, 1972, 1977.

Haviland, Virginia, and William Jay Smith, compilers. *Children and Poetry: A Selective Annotated Bibliography.* Washington, D.C.: Library of Congress, 1979.

Hearne, Betsy. *Choosing Books for Children: A Commonsense Guide.* N.Y.: Delacorte, 1981.

Ireland, Norma. *Index to Fairy Tales, 1949–1972* (supplement to Eastman indexes). Westwood, MA: Faxon, 1973.

————. *Index to Fairy Tales, 1973–1977.* Westwood, MA: Faxon, 1979.

Kimmel, Margaret Mary, and Elizabeth Segal. *For Reading Out Loud! A Guide to Sharing Books with Chidren.* N.Y.: Delacorte, 1983.

Larrick, Nancy. *A Teacher's Guide to Children's Books.* Columbus, OH: Merrill, 1960.

Lass-Woodfin, Mary Jo, ed. *Books on American Indians and Eskimos: A Selective Guide for Children and Young Adults.* Chicago: American Library Association, 1977.

Lima, Carolyn. *A to Zoo: Subject Access to Children's Picture Books.* N.Y.: R. R. Bowker, 1985.

Lynn, Ruth N. *Fantasy for Children: An Annotated Checklist and Reference Guide.* N.Y.: R. R. Bowker, 1983.

MacDonald, Margaret. *The Storyteller's Sourcebook: A Subject, Title and Motif Index to Folklore Collections for Children.* Detroit: Gale Research/Neal-Schuman, 1982.

Monson, Dianne, ed. *Adventuring with Books: A Booklist for Pre-K to Grade 6.* Urbana, IL: NCTE, 1985.

Nicholson, Margaret. *People in Books: A Selective Guide to Biographical Literature Arranged by Vocations and Other Fields of Reader Interest.* N.Y.: H. W. Wilson, 1969.

Pelowski, Anne, compiler. *The World of Children's Literature.* N.Y.: R. R. Bowker, 1968.

Pflieger, Pat, and Helen Hill, eds. *A Reference Guide to Modern Fantasy for Children.* Westport, CT: Greenwood, 1984.

Quimby, Harriet, and Margaret Mary Kimmel. *Building a Children's Literature Collection.* Middletown, CT: Choice, 1983.

Schoen, Isabel. *A Hispanic Heritage: A Guide to Juvenile Books about Hispanic People and Cultures.* Metuchen, N.J.: Scarecrow, 1980.

Sutherland, Zena, ed. *The Best in Children's Books: The University of Chicago Guide to Children's Literature 1973–1978.* Chicago: University of Chicago Press, 1980.

Tway, Eileen, ed. *Reading Ladders for Human Relations.* Urbana, IL: NCTE, 1981.

Ullom, Judith, compiler. *Folklore of the American Indians: An Annotated Bibliography*. Washington, D.C.: Library of Congress, 1969.

White, Mary Lou, ed. *Adventuring with Books—A Booklist for Pre-K to Grade 6*. Urbana, IL: NCTE, 1981.

Ziegler, Elsie. *Folklore: An Annotated Bibliography and Index to Single Editions*. Westwood, MA: Faxon, 1973.

APPENDIX B

Literacy Learning: Resources

Applebee, Arthur. *The Child's Concept of Story*. Chicago: University of Chicago Press, 1978.

Atwell, Nancie. *In the Middle: Writing, Reading, and Learning with Adolescents*. Portsmouth, N.H.: Boynton/Cook, 1986.

Bissex, Glenda. *Gnys at Work: A Child Learns to Read and Write*. Cambridge: Harvard University Press, 1980.

Butler, Andrea, and Jan Turbill. *Towards a Reading-Writing Classroom*. Portsmouth, N.H.: Heinemann (PETA), 1984.

Calkins, Lucy McCormick. *The Art of Teaching Writing*. Portsmouth, N.H.: Heinemann, 1986.

————. *Lessons from a Child*. Portsmouth, N.H.: Heinemann, 1983.

Cazden, Courtney. *Classroom Discourse: The Language of Teaching and Learning*. Portsmouth, N.H.: Heinemann, 1988.

Chukovsky, Kornei. *From Two to Five*. Miriam Morton, trans. and ed. Berkeley: University of California Press, 1968.

Clark, Margaret. *Young Fluent Readers*. Portsmouth, N.H.: Heinemann, 1976.

Clay, Marie M. *The Early Detection of Reading Difficulties*, 3rd ed. Portsmouth, N.H.: Heinemann, 1985.

Durkin, Dolores. *Children Who Read Early*. N.Y.: Teachers College Press, 1966.

Fulwiler, Toby, ed. *The Journal Book*. Portsmouth, N.H.: Boynton/Cook, 1987.

————. *Teaching with Writing*. Portsmouth, N.H.: Boynton/Cook, 1987.

Goelman, Hillel, Antoinette Oberg, and Frank Smith. *Awakening to Literacy*. Portsmouth, N.H.: Heinemann, 1984.

Goodman, Kenneth. "Reading: A Psycholinguistic Guessing Game." *Journal of the Reading Specialist*, 4, May 1967, pp. 126–135.

————. *What's Whole in Whole Language?* Portsmouth, N.H. Heinemann, 1986.

Graves, Donald. *Writing: Teachers and Children at Work*. Portsmouth, N.H.: Heinemann, 1983.

Hancock, Joelie, and Susan Hill, eds. *Literature-Based Reading Programs at Work*. Portsmouth, N.H.: Heinemann, 1988.

Hansen, Jane. *When Writers Read.* Portsmouth, N.H.: Heinemann, 1987.

Hansen, Jane, Thomas Newkirk, and Donald Graves, eds. *Breaking Ground—Teachers Relate Reading and Writing in the Elementary School.* Portsmouth, N.H.: Heinemann, 1985.

Harste, Jerome, Kathy Short, and Carolyn Burke. *Creating Classrooms for Authors: The Reading-Writing Connection.* Portsmouth, N.H.: Heinemann, 1988.

Harste, Jerome, Virginia Woodward, and Carolyn Burke. *Language Stories and Literacy Lessons.* Portsmouth, N.H.: Heinemann, 1984.

Holdaway, Don. *The Foundations of Literacy.* Portsmouth, N.H.: Heinemann, 1979.

———. *Independence in Reading.* Portsmouth, N.H.: Heinemann, 1980.

Hornsby, David, Deborah Sukarna with Jo-Ann Parry. *Read On: A Conference Approach to Reading.* Portsmouth, N.H.: Heinemann, 1988.

Jagger, Angela, and M. Trika Smith-Burke, eds. *Observing the Language Learner.* Newark, DE: IRA and Urbana, IL: NCTE, 1985.

Jensen, Julie M., ed. *Composing and Comprehending.* Urbana, IL: NCTE, 1984.

———. *Stories to Grow On: Demonstrations of Language Learning in K–8 Classrooms.* Portsmouth, N.H.: Heinemann, 1988.

Johnson, Terry D., and Daphne R. Louis. *Literacy through Literature.* Portsmouth, N.H.: Heinemann, 1987.

Langer, Judith A., and M. Trika Smith-Burke, eds. *Reader Meets Author/Bridging the Gap—A Psycholinguistic and Sociolinguistic Perspective.* Newark, DE: IRA, 1982.

McCracken, Robert A., and Marlene J. McCracken. *Stories, Songs, and Poetry for Teaching Reading and Writing: Literacy through Literature.* N.Y.: Teachers College Press, 1986.

Meek, Margaret. *Learning to Read.* Portsmouth, N.H.: Heinemann, 1986.

Murray, Donald M. *Expecting the Unexpected: Teaching Myself—and Others—to Read and Write.* Portsmouth, N.H.: Boynton/Cook, 1989.

———. *Learning by Teaching: Selected Articles on Writing and Teaching.* Portsmouth, N.H.: Boynton/Cook, 1982.

———. *A Writer Teaches Writing,* 2nd ed. Boston: Houghton Mifflin, 1985.

Newkirk, Thomas, and Nancie Atwell, eds. *Understanding Writing: Ways of Observing, Learning, and Teaching.* Portsmouth, N.H.: Heinemann, 1988.

Newman, Judith, ed. *Whole Language—Theory in Use.* Portsmouth, N.H.: Heinemann, 1985.

Parry, Jo-Ann, and David Hornsby. *Write On: A Conference Approach to Writing.* Portsmouth, N.H.: Heinemann, 1988.

Rosenblatt, Louise. *The Reader, the Text, the Poem.* Carbondale, IL: Southern Illinois University Press, 1978.

Routman, Regie. *Transitions: From Literature to Literacy.* Portsmouth, N.H.: Heinemann, 1988.

Smith, Frank. *Essays into Literacy.* Portsmouth, N.H.: Heinemann, 1983.

———. *Joining the Literacy Club: Further Essays into Education.* Portsmouth, N.H.: Heinemann, 1988.

———. "Reading Like a Writer." *Composing and Comprehending.* Julie Jensen, ed. Urbana, IL: Eric, NCRE, 1984, pp. 47–56.

———. *Reading Without Nonsense,* 2nd ed. N.Y.: Teachers College Press, 1985.

———. *Understanding Reading: A Psycholinguistic Analysis of Reading and Learning to Read.* Hillsdale, N.J.: Lawrence Erlbaum, 1988.

———. *Writing and the Writer.* N.Y.: Holt, Rinehart and Winston, 1982.

Stewig, John Warren. *Read to Write: Using Children's Literature as a Springboard to the Teaching of Writing,* 3rd ed. N.Y.: Richard C. Owen, Publishers, 1990.

Teale, William. "Positive Environments for Learning to Read: What Studies of Early Readers Tell Us." *Language Arts,* vol. 55, no. 8, November/December 1978, pp. 922–932.

———. "Toward a Theory of How Children Learn to Read and Write Naturally." *Language Arts,* vol. 59, no. 6, September 1982, pp. 555–570.

Teale, William, and Elizabeth Sulzby, eds. *Emergent Literacy: Writing and Reading*. Norwood, N.J.: Ablex, 1986.

Temple, Charles, Ruth Nathan, Nancy Burris, and Frances Temple. *The Beginning of Writing*. Needham Heights, MA: Allyn and Bacon, 1988.

Wells, Gordon. *The Meaning Makers: Children Learning Language and Using Language to Learn*. Portsmouth, N.H.: Heinemann, 1986.

Index of Concepts Associated with Focus Units

About the Author

Joy Moss's goal as an educator is to bring literature into the lives of children. She has been actively involved in sharing and exploring whole language philosophy with teachers and administrators, and in encouraging parents to read to their children.

As a teacher at the Harley School in Rochester, New York, Moss designed a literature program which has become an integral part of the school curriculum and which has been the basis of her professional writing for two decades.

She is an Adjunct Associate Professor at the University of Rochester Graduate School of Education, is a consultant to schools in her area, and has lectured at many conferences on literature and literacy learning.

Professor Moss is the author of *Focus Units in Literature* and of a number of journal articles.